The Dartmoor Reaves

Cirencester College, GL7 1XA
Telephone: 01285 640994

cirencester
college

Andrew Fleming

The Dartmoor Reaves

Investigating Prehistoric Land Divisions

B.T.Batsford Ltd London

for Nicholas
and Matthew

Typeset by Tek-Art Ltd, Kent
and printed in Great Britain by
The Bath Press, Bath
for the publishers B.T. Batsford Ltd
4 Fitzhardinge Street, London W1H 0AH

ISBN 0 7134 5665 5 (cased)
ISBN 0 7134 5666 3 (limp)

Contents

The illustrations

Preface

This book is about some remarkable prehistoric land boundaries, the reaves of Dartmoor, the largest stretch of open wilderness in southern England, and the story of how they were investigated in the years between 1972 and the present day. It describes how the reaves were recognised as prehistoric land boundaries in the 1820s, and how this knowledge was lost until recent times. The Dartmoor Reave Project, formed to study the reaves, undertook landscape archaeology, as I tried to reconstruct the pattern these boundaries made in the landscape; survey work as my team mapped one of the largest reave systems, 3000 hectares (7500 acres) in area and over six kilometres (four miles) from end to end; and excavation of settlement sites in a tiny part of this reave system. The book also explains how the reaves fit into the prehistory of Dartmoor, as it is known at present. The study of these major field systems and land boundaries has implications for other parts of the British Isles and the way we think about the later prehistoric communities of north-west Europe, a theme which I consider in the final chapter.

This book is intended for people with a general interest in prehistory, in Dartmoor, and in what it is like to carry out an archaeological investigation. I have mostly tried to write it as a story, although space limitations have curtailed some of the more expansive (as well as the more self-indulgent!) narrative in my first draft. I would like to have been able to produce the excavation report and my analysis of the Dartmeet parallel reave system at the same time as this book — if not earlier — and thus complete the academic documentation of the research project. In the end it seemed more important to communicate quickly with a wider audience; I must apologise, however, to fellow archaeologists for certain gaps in subject matter and documentation. Still, I hope some of them may enjoy this book. Some of the subject-matter, especially the history of reave study, the landscape pattern, and general matters of interpretation, has been dealt with in more detail in various books and journals (see the section of further reading at the back of the book). Also at the back of the book are some suggestions about sites worth visiting. I have tried to provide enough maps for readers to follow most of the text, but I have not been able to indicate the precise whereabouts of every place-name; readers who have the 1:25000 Ordnance Survey Outdoor Leisure map of Dartmoor may find it useful.

The Dartmoor Reave Project could not have operated without the support and help of many individuals and institutions, and the publication of this book is the best way I know of thanking them. For financial support I am grateful to the British Academy, the Society of Antiquaries of London, the Leverhulme Trust, Dartmoor National Park Authority, the Devonshire Association, the University of Sheffield and several individual donors. For permission to work in various places I am grateful to Dartmoor National Park Authority, the Holne Commoners, the South West Water Authority, the Spitchwick Commoners, the Duchy of Cornwall and several other landowners and tenants. I owe thanks to Ian Mercer, Tom Greeves, Debbie Griffiths, Nick Atkinson and Eric Blachford from Dartmoor National Park for their help and support; Nic Ralph, David Maguire, Martin Jones, Kris Williams and Ian Linn for environmental work and advice; Chris Grimbley (survey) Trevor Corns, Wayne Sheedy and Mireille (developing and printing photographs); Tom Greeves, John Collis, Elizabeth Gawne, John Somers Cocks, Chris Chapman, Collin Bowen, Peter and Dot Hills, the late Hermon French, the late Algy May, Norman Perryman, Joe Turner, Rosemary Robinson, Iris Woods, the late Miss R. Cave-Penney, Admiral Sir James Eberle, Mr David Powell, Frances Lynch, Tom Williamson, Emma Plunkett Dillon and Freda Wilkinson, for various kinds of practical help and advice; I hope those inadvertently omitted from this list will forgive me. I am grateful to many local people for all kinds of things, ranging from hot baths to good conversation, from oiled wheelbarrows to slaked thirst; above all, perhaps, for giving me some understanding of what it is like to live and farm on the edge of the Moor, a sense of place which was missing after my Herefordshire boyhood. I hope this book gives something back.

My greatest thanks, however, must be reserved for

the volunteers who helped with excavation and survey work. They endured driving rain, drizzle, sleet, fog, cold, heat, dust, flies, sheep-ticks, sunburn, monotony, alcohol poisoning, predatory dogs, and some terrible jokes, usually with irrepressible humour and fortitude. For many of them, I hope, Dartmoor's beauty and character made some of the privations worthwhile. I am grateful to all who helped on the Project, and especially to the following: Martyn Barron, Alison Betts, Steve and Sue Clews, Tony Comer, Sarah Connolly, Sarah Curtis, Tom Gledhill, Frances Griffith, Phillipa Harrap, Peter Herring, Jo Higson, Dave and Jenny Hooley, Brenda James, Jim McNeill, Topher Martyn, Ros Nichol, Sue O'Neill, the late Steve Payne, Isabelle Ruben, Alan and Gill Turner, Julie Turner, Di Warmington, Martin Weiler, Kris Williams, and Simon Woodiwiss.

Sheffield, February 1988

1: Discovery

Dartmoor is the most extensive tract of wild upland in the south of England. Most people imagine it as it was portrayed by Sir Arthur Conan Doyle in *The Hound of the Baskervilles* – a bleak and sinister place, of swirling mists and melancholy. For Conan Doyle, whose first acquaintance with Dartmoor was in the summer of 1882, when he was a general practitioner in Plymouth, it was also a place abounding in the relics of the remote past. And this was how it struck the dutiful Dr Watson, sent down to Baskerville Hall to make some initial investigations. This was his report:[1]

MY DEAR HOLMES:
My previous letters and telegrams have kept you pretty well up to date as to all that has occurred in this most God-forsaken corner of the world. The longer one stays here the more does the spirit of the moor sink into one's soul, its vastness, and also its grim charm. When you are out upon its bosom you have left all traces of modern England behind you, but, on the other hand, you are conscious everywhere of the homes and the work of the prehistoric people. On all sides of you as you walk are the houses of these forgotten folk, with their graves and the huge monoliths which are supposed to have marked their temples. As you look at their gray stone huts against the scarred hillsides you leave your own age behind you, and if you were to see a skin-clad, hairy man crawl out from the low door, fitting a flint-tipped arrow on to the string of his bow, you would feel that his presence there was more natural than your own. The strange thing is that they should have lived so thickly on what must always have been most unfruitful soil. I am no antiquarian, but I could imagine that they were some unwarlike and harried race who were forced to accept that which none other would occupy.

Before writing *The Hound of the Baskervilles*, which was published in 1901, Conan Doyle visited Dartmoor with a friend, who recounted a local legend about a phantom hound; the visit and the legend must have been the writer's main sources of inspiration. I like to think also that he was able to draw on two recently-published books – Sabine Baring-Gould's *Book of Devon*, published in August 1899, and his *Book of Dartmoor*, published in July 1900.[2] The Rev. Baring-Gould was a keen archaeologist, a member of the Dartmoor Exploration Committee, whose reports on their excavations of prehistoric settlement-sites

started appearing in the *Transactions of the Devonshire Association* in 1894. These excavations were primitive by modern standards, and the eleven reports which the Committee published between 1894 and 1906 are very thin, especially considering that they apparently dug over 200 hut-circles. Nevertheless, the Dartmoor campaign was one of the earliest attempts in Britain to investigate ancient settlement sites, and to break away from that compulsive habit of nineteenth-century archaeologists, digging burial mounds. And the finds included pottery, flint tools, querns and cooking-holes, providing some concrete details for Baring-Gould and Sir Arthur Conan Doyle when they described the way of life of the inhabitants of the hut-circles. Above all, the Committee's work had demonstrated that the latter were prehistoric in date.

The youngest member of the Dartmoor Exploration Committee was Richard Hansford Worth, who was just twenty-five when the excavations started in 1893. Worth became the committee's secretary. Much later, towards the end of his life, he wrote a number of articles which established his position as the leading authority on Dartmoor; these were brought together after his death, as *Worth's Dartmoor*.[3] After 1906 little further excavation of settlement sites took place, and Worth's syntheses relied a great deal on the Committee's earlier work.

The Dartmoor Exploration Committee was disbanded in 1950, the year of Worth's death. Shortly afterwards its sole survivor, C.A. Ralegh Radford, attempted a re-assessment of Dartmoor's prehistory, based partly on an analysis of potsherds recovered from the early excavations.[4] At about the same time Lady Aileen Fox also provided a synthesis, as well as conducting her own excavations on two important sites – an enclosure on Dean Moor, in the Avon valley (fig. 67) and a settlement at Kestor (fig. 11), on north-east Dartmoor.[5] Fox and Ralegh Radford established that most of the pottery found in the early excavations dated from the Bronze Age, around 2000–1500BC. They were interested in the diversity of the settlement remains on the Moor. There were hut-circles within enclosures (also known as 'pounds') and groups of free-standing hut-circles,

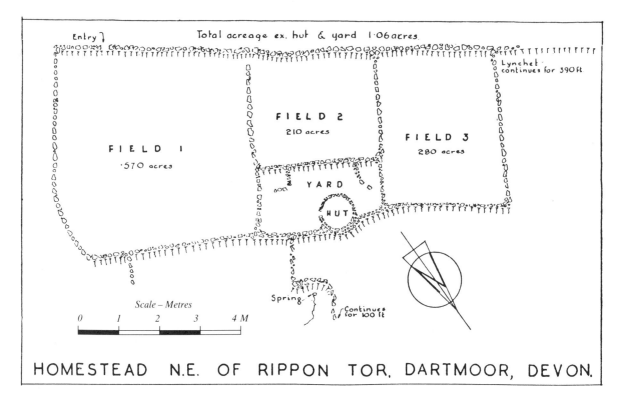

Entry

Total acreage ex. hut & yard 1·06 acres.

FIELD 1
·570 acres

FIELD 2
·210 acres

FIELD 3
·280 acres

Lynchet
continues for 390 ft

YARD

HUT

Scale – Metres

| 0 | 1 | 2 | 3 | 4 M |

Spring

Continues
for 100 ft

HOMESTEAD N.E. OF RIPPON TOR, DARTMOOR, DEVON.

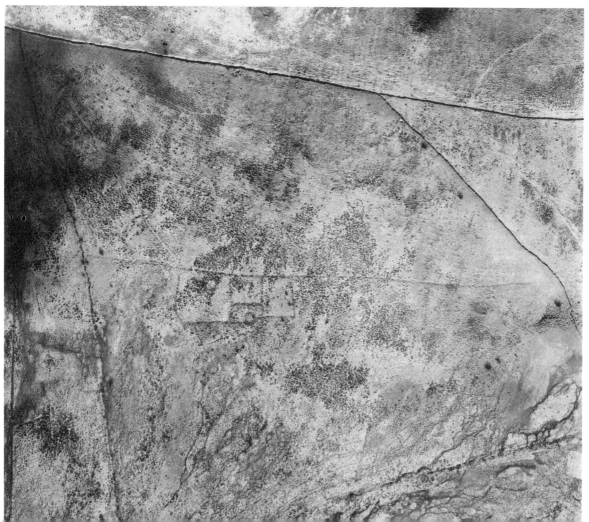

1 (above) Fox's plan of a 'homestead' near Rippon Tor, published in 1954, with its tiny 'fields' and detailed area measurements, gave an impression of small-scale agriculture which did not take into account the scale of the associated land boundary system (below). *Plan after Fox, photo: National Monument Record*

making up settlements of varying size and character; and, as E.C. Curwen, an interloper from Sussex, had suggested in 1927,[6] there were also groups of small, rectangular walled fields. In some places it was apparently possible to pick out individual homesteads; Lady Fox provided a good example from Rippon Tor, on the eastern side of Dartmoor (fig. 1). Here was a hut-circle beside a spring, with its own little yard and three little walled plots totalling 0.4 hectares (1.06 acres); Lady Fox calculated that cultivation must have been supplemented by stock-raising.

Most of the fields were to be found on the eastern side of Dartmoor; the greatest concentration of 'pounds' occurred to the south and west, especially in the valleys of the Avon, the Erme and the Plym (though Grimspound, the one best known to visitors, is on the eastern side of the Moor). This distributional pattern (fig. 2) seemed to have an obvious geographical explanation. As Fox pointed out:[7] 'under present conditions the eastern fringe is noticeably drier than the western or centre part of the Moor, the difference amounting to more than ten inches of rain in a year. Consequently this area is better suited to arable cultivation . . . .' Thus, it was argued, fields and pounds were contemporary with one another, because their distributions were complementary. While pastoralists grazed their flocks and herds in the exposed south-western valleys, people more dependent on cereals tilled their little plots on Dartmoor's sheltered eastern flank.

It was this wealth of visible Bronze Age remains which first aroused my interest in Dartmoor. As an archaeology student in the mid-sixties I always wondered why such an apparently rich area had not been more fully exploited by archaeologists, especially considering how difficult it appeared to be to find Bronze Age settlement sites in other parts of Britain. So in 1970, while devising a field course programme for archaeology students at the University of Sheffield, I decided to take the opportunity to see the Dartmoor remains at first hand. Our first trip was essentially archaeological tourism; I was learning as I went along, and the already elderly coach driver aged visibly as we negotiated the narrow Devon lanes. The archaeology was wonderful, but I rapidly realised the educational limitations of simply showing the students the sites; for the 1972 course the students were equipped with pencils and note-books and were en-

couraged to discover and interpret the archaeological sites for themselves. I invited John Collis, an old friend from student days who had just joined the staff at Sheffield, to accompany us.

So it came about that one day in May 1972 John and I were eating our sandwiches in a large walled enclosure on Lee Moor, on the south-western edge of Dartmoor. It was very peaceful (after all, we had managed to get away from the students for a couple of hours). In front of us were the glistening white heaps of waste from the Whitehill Yeo china clay pit, a patchwork of hedged fields, and in the distance the South Devon coast.

The enclosure (fig. 3) was a large one, almost square in plan, with thick walls of chunky granite blocks; it was visible from a long way off, having been built right in the middle of a broad, slightly dished hillside. Inside the enclosure were fifteen or sixteen small hut-circles, most of them in pairs, joined together or side by side. The main entrance led through the top wall, up towards the higher ground, like the one at Grimspound. Indeed there were other points of comparison with Grimspound – the large size, the thick walls, the small but numerous hut-circles. But there was one other feature of note. Joined onto one side of the enclosure was a tumbled wall (fig. 4), very similar in appearance to the enclosure wall itself. It was disappearing into the distance, along the side of the hill. And when we looked at the other side of the enclosure, there was another wall, running off into the distance as if to continue the line of the first; the enclosure, it seemed, was simply incorporated into the line. Maybe it was medieval, and thus of no great interest to prehistorians like us; after all, it did seem to have been constructed later than the enclosure. And there was certainly nothing about long boundary-walls in any of the general accounts of Dartmoor's prehistory. Best to ignore it, perhaps, and move off to a less problematic site.

However, we were curious about this ancient-looking wall, so we decided to follow it, setting off in a south-easterly direction (fig. 5). After a while the wall began to look even more ancient, as a stretch of exposed granite blocks gave way to a section shrouded in grass and whortleberry bushes; at one point the wall had impeded the local drainage, and peat had built up behind it. We followed the wall around the hillside, for the best part of one kilometre (2/3 mile). Then it stopped; it had run up to another old-looking wall, making a T-junction. This one ran straight up and down the hillside. We followed it downhill; it thinned out a bit and had been robbed in some places. But there was no doubt about where it was heading – straight for a modern wall corner, where a nineteenth-century drystone wall, having climbed the slope,

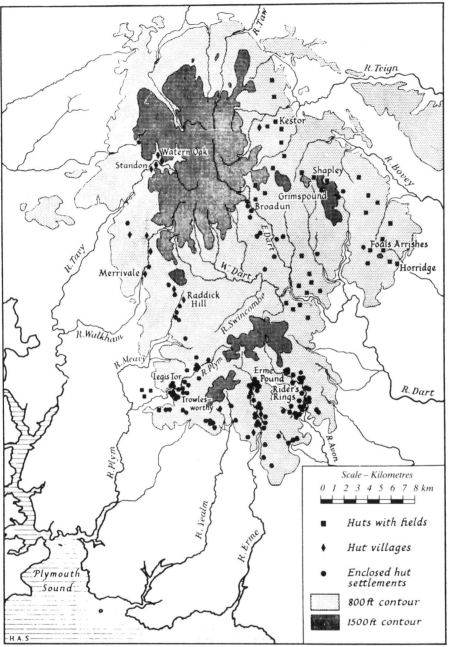

2 Fox's map of Dartmoor, published in 1964, shows a striking contrast between south and south-west Dartmoor, with its 'pastoral' enclosures, and eastern Dartmoor, with its 'huts with fields'. There is now more evidence for fields on the south and south-west fringes and at the NW corner of the Moor. The high density of enclosures and houses on the W and SW side of the Moor, compared with that of other areas, is still something of a mystery. *After Fox*

3 Air view of the Cholwichtown Main enclosure, Lee Moor, which is incorporated in the line of a reave. Observation of this relationship in May 1972 was the starting-point of the modern investigation of reaves. *Photo: A. Fleming*

turned sharply through ninety degrees to run along the contour, forming the top wall of a group of fields in current use. We could no longer follow our ancient wall; its line had been taken over by a much more recent successor.

We turned and retraced our steps, following the old wall back up the hill to the T-junction; it was apparently heading for the top of the hill, which is a spur of the broad ridge between the Plym and the Yealm. The map labelled it 'Penn Beacon' and

marked a prehistoric burial cairn there. It was rougher going now, with boulders and thick whortleberry bushes. Before we reached the top of the hill we stumbled across a small walled enclosure. It looked typically prehistoric; although it was shrouded in vegetation, it was possible to make out the low wall of a circular, free-standing building within it, and two or three smaller buildings apparently incorporated in the line of the wall. As we traced the plan of this enclosure among the dense vegetation, we realised that it was

4 The first reave to be followed, near Cholwichtown Main enclosure, which is in the background. *Photo: J. Collis*

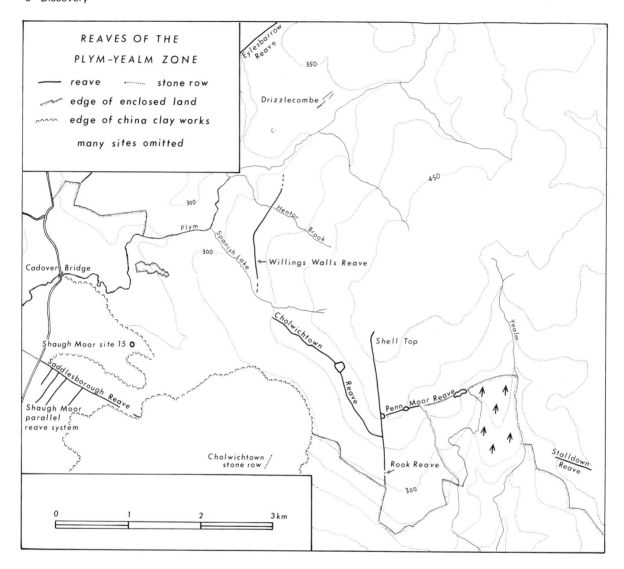

REAVES OF THE
PLYM-YEALM ZONE

—— reave ········· stone row

edge of enclosed land

edge of china clay works

many sites omitted

5 Map of the reaves in the Plym/Yealm area (south-west Dartmoor) traced by John Collis and the author in May 1972. Note the position of the critical D-shaped enclosure, where Penn Moor Reave meets Rook Reave. The map also shows the position of the nearest parallel reave system, on Shaugh Moor, and three excavated sites – the Cholwichtown stone row, with its important environmental evidence; the enclosure known as Shaugh Moor site 15 (both these sites are now obliterated by china clay workings) and Saddlesborough Reave, which overlay traces of a fence and bank. Further to the SE, Stalldown Reave is apparently an unfinished contour reave. To the NW, Eylesbarrow Reave is the next watershed reave.

D-shaped in plan, and in fact it was marked on the map as having one straight side. Why should this be? Looking up and down the line of the straight side, we observed that there was a very good reason; the enclosure was *attached* to the wall which we had been following. We couldn't actually see a butt-joint, but the situation was obvious from the plan anyway.

As John immediately pointed out, this could only mean one thing. If one made the conventional assumption that the enclosure was prehistoric, then the wall to which it was attached must be prehistoric too. It was a dramatic moment. Spurred on by the excitement of our discovery, we carried on up to the Bronze Age burial cairn on Penn Beacon. The wall stopped on the cairn but continued on the other side; in other words, the cairn had been included in the line. Of course, this didn't prove that the wall was of Bronze Age date; after all, a modern barbed-wire fence could also have been aligned on the cairn. But given that the wall was now known to be prehistoric, the relationship posed some interesting questions. When the wall was built, was the cairn just a convenient landmark to aim for, or was it already part of a system of boundary-markers? Was the person buried in the cairn known to the wall-builders, in life or in legend?

It was a bleaker world on the moor-top, with deeper peat and less varied patterns of vegetation. The wall continued for almost another kilometre (²/₃ mile), running just behind a granite tor called Shell Top, and swerving as if to run along the main water-shed, the broad ridge leading towards the heart of the South Moor. But then it stopped, as the peat deepened, and we began to notice the characteristic rectangular cuttings where peat had been cut for fuel in the not-too-distant past. Further along the ridge we hunted for our wall, hoping that the peat-cutters had spared it in some places. But it had gone. So we went back down, to the D-shaped enclosure. It was then that we realised that there was another wall, running in an easterly direction, leading away from the enclosure though not definitely attached to it. We seemed to have discovered a whole *system* of boundary-walls! This new one was also running round the contour; it led us to another enclosure, incorporated in the boundary-line just like the one where we had been having our lunch. But this enclosure was smaller, about 60–70m (200–230ft) across, with eight huts in it. Beyond the enclosure, the wall ran down to a stream; on the other side, its course around the hillside was continued by another recent drystone wall, running along the upper edge of an even more recent conifer plantation. There seemed little doubt that the nineteenth-century wall-builders had chosen to use the line of a much more ancient boundary.

It was time to return to our coach, and the students whom we were supposed to have been supervising. That evening, discussing our discoveries, we realised that one of our walls was actually marked on the 6-inch map; it was one which we had seen but did not have time to follow, running in a north-westerly direction from the square enclosure where we had started. The map showed it running from the enclosure round the contour for about 800m (900 yards), apparently ending on a burial cairn. Next we went directly to the burial cairn, and noticed immediately that the map-makers had been wrong to end the wall here; in reality it continued for about 200m (220 yards) *beyond* the cairn, to become engulfed in an extensive peat-bog to the south-east of Great Trowlesworthy Tor.

From this point to the place where we had abandoned our pursuit the previous afternoon, we knew that it was possible to follow these ancient boundary-walls continuously for a distance of over four kilometres (2½ miles). Evidently we had encountered an extensive system of prehistoric land boundaries, noticeable enough in one place to be marked on an Ordnance Survey map, but apparently unknown to archaeologists! Naturally enough, we spent as much as possible of the next couple of days looking for similar walls in the area. Further searches on the broad ridge between the Plym and the Yealm proved fruitless, but we were more fortunate on the eastern side of the Plym valley, where we discovered another wall over one kilometre (²/₃ mile) long. This one also started from the Great Trowlesworthy Tor peat-bog, but this time from its northern edge, where we could find it by thrusting a ranging-pole through the peaty mud; obviously the bog has increased its area since prehistoric times.

As we followed the wall northwards, there were some interesting observations to be made. Soon after we had crossed that most romantically named of Dartmoor streams, the Spanish Lake, we came to a place where the wall had been robbed out – and there in the gap were the ruins of a small medieval long-house, with a couple of out-houses and a ruined wall enclosing a small front garden or yard. The demolition of our wall to make room for a medieval long-house demonstrated that our wall was older than the later Middle Ages, when inhabited long-houses like this one could be found out here, in the upper Plym valley.

We followed the wall further north, past a place where it had been faced with stones up to one metre (3ft) tall, standing up like a row of jagged teeth. Then a little further north the wall changed course, turning through an angle of almost 40 degrees. This was at a point on a slight shoulder, the only place from which the wall-builders could have seen both ends of the boundary. From this point onwards the wall was no longer running along the contour; it was aiming in a more north-easterly direction, across the Hentor Brook and straight across the middle of a broad, flattish apron of land, where we could see that its course was adopted by a recent, but now ruined, drystone wall. But before we arrived at the brook, we noticed another significant relationship. Our wall was running through a little group of small cairns, and it had apparently incorporated two of them in its line. Now these small cairns are quite common on the fringe of Dartmoor; investigations by treasure-hunters and archaeologists have shown that they tend to be constructed around what the early antiquaries called *kistvaens* and are now more commonly simply called cists. These cists, small stone boxes made out of undressed slabs, were apparently used for burial in the earlier part of the Bronze Age, at a time when copper, rather than true tin-bronze, was in use. It has to be said, however, that few have been scientifically excavated, and that bone is destroyed by the acidity of the soil. Our little cemetery, in fact, contained a cist whose capstone had been unceremoniously pulled off (fig. 62). It was significant that our wall ran right through a small early Bronze Age cemetery without respecting it in any way. We had already noted two cases where our newfound walls incorporated large Bronze Age cairns. So it was beginning to look as if the walls were later than many of the burial monuments of the earlier part of the Bronze Age, and contemporary with the classic Dartmoor 'pounds' or enclosed settlements, since we had observed three cases where such enclosures were attached to, or incorporated in, the boundary-lines.

Further north, the wall was less interesting; after crossing Hentor Brook its line was continued by a more recent wall, which eventually diverged from the course of its ancient predecessor, lengths of which could be seen running downslope towards the river Plym.

We went back to Sheffield with plenty to talk about. We had discovered something like seven kilometres (4½ miles) of ancient walling, and had been able to show that the walls almost certainly dated from the later part of the Bronze Age. We decided to come back as soon as possible, with a small group of volunteers, and put these ancient boundaries on the map. But was it really possible that nobody had noticed these walls before? John wrote to Ann Hamlin, a former colleague of his at Exeter University, to ask about this.

Her reply was very useful. It turned out that Dartmoor people called these walls 'raves'; fortunately, this works out as 'reaves' when pronounced without the local accent! And two local amateur historians, Elizabeth Gawne and John Somers Cocks, had written an article entitled 'Parallel reaves on Dartmoor' which had been published only four years previously in the *Transactions of the Devonshire Association*.[8] We quickly got hold of a copy, and started to read it with mounting excitement. For Gawne and Somers Cocks had made some even more remarkable discoveries.

They had been studying medieval field patterns in the Widecombe area, on the eastern side of the Moor, and this had led them to investigate what they called 'the puzzling low banks, locally "reaves" which run nearly parallel to each other over large areas'. These showed up particularly well on air photographs. Intrigued, they extended their search over the whole of the Moor, concentrating particularly on the eastern part where the parallel reaves seemed to be most extensive and well-preserved. This is what they had to say:

It has been found that large areas of eastern Dartmoor, sometimes of several square miles, are striped with low reaves which are long, parallel and generally straight between one aiming point and the next. They are quite distinct from, and far larger in area than, the field-systems surrounding medieval farmsteads, which often obliterate them, though sometimes adapting them, and over wide areas cannot be accepted as field systems at all but rather are land divisions. Where there are cross-banks their distance apart is out of all proportion for medieval plough-strips, and they ignore physical features such as streams in their layout in a way that medieval fields never do. A number of Late Bronze/Early Iron Age settlements lie within them . . . . A distinct difference shows on air-photographs between the parallel reaves and the medieval banks, which is confirmed on the ground. It is concluded that they must be pre-Saxon and, because of their obvious relationship, contemporary with or even earlier than the Late Bronze/Early Iron Age settlements with 'Celtic' fields.

The word reave is derived from the Old English *raew* meaning a row – whether of houses, stones or anything else. On Dartmoor the word reave is given to any low bank or line of stones made for whatever purpose, and reaves are found almost anywhere save on the highest blanket-bog areas. Many of them occur singly and doubtless mark some sort of prehistoric or later land boundary.

Gawne and Somers Cocks provided sketch-plans of their two largest sets of 'parallel reaves'. The most remarkable of these was located near Dartmeet, the point where the East Dart and the West Dart converge to form one river. Apparently it had a long axis of at least six kilometres (four miles). As the two historians pointed out 'this one system, open moorland apart, has had a greater or lesser influence on the shape and lay-out of existing fields over an area of hardly less than 5000 acres'. In other words, medieval and more recent field boundaries had tended to follow the lines of parallel reaves, so that there were sizeable areas of predominantly long, rectangular fields conforming to one axis. What was more, the Dartmeet system went right up to the edge of the steep-sided valley of the river Dart, just below Dartmeet, and re-appeared on the same axis on the other side.

Naturally, Gawne and Somers Cocks consulted the most recent archaeological literature. Some of their parallel reaves apparently went right through the prehistoric settlement at Foale's Arrishes, a site lying beside the Ashburton-Widecombe road, not far from Rippon Tor. Here there was a group of about half a dozen hut-circles, associated with small, rectangular fields. Conventional wisdom held that the long reaves had nothing to do with the prehistoric fields. This was how C.A. Ralegh Radford had described the parallel reaves in 1952: 'the plan is dominated by a number of long straight banks of stone running down the slope. They start near the crest of the ridge and continue for between 500 and 600 yards . . . . Blackslade was a

Domesday holding and there is no reasonable doubt that the long banks of stone at Foale's Arrishes mark the medieval plough strips of this manor.' Fox, too, thought that the long reaves had resulted from what she called 're-modelling' in the Middle Ages.[9]

It is much to the credit of Gawne and Somers Cocks that they refused to deny the evidence of their own eyes – the archaeological evidence, in fact. They knew what medieval field-banks looked like; there were some good examples at Houndtor, Manaton, where a late medieval settlement had been recently excavated. Wherever reaves and medieval banks were found together in the same place, the reaves were always seen to be stratigraphically earlier. They did not fit in with known medieval administrative boundaries; it seemed that 'the very ruthlessness of their layout . . . does not accord with the medieval way of life'. It was also noted that 'in a few cases prehistoric burial mounds appear to have been used as markers'. So the reaves could be dated somewhere between the earlier part of the Bronze Age and the tenth century AD. Gawne and Somers Cocks went on to note the close links between parallel reaves and prehistoric fields and hut-circles in specific places like Foale's Arrishes and Kestor, and the fact that on eastern Dartmoor reaves and concentrations of hut-circles occurred in the same areas. It looked, then, as if the parallel reaves could be dated to the later Bronze Age or earlier Iron Age. Not having evidence like our D-shaped enclosure, Gawne and Somers Cocks could not be too insistent on this point.

But they had made a significant breakthrough, albeit one which was not immediately recognised by archaeologists. As John Somers Cocks was to explain to me later, 'the medievalists thought the reaves were prehistoric, and the prehistorians thought they were medieval!'

After reading this article, John Collis and I knew we could add to knowledge of reaves in two ways. One was to supply some more direct evidence, in the form of our D-shaped enclosure, that the reaves were almost certainly of the same date as most of the ancient fields, enclosures and hut-circles on Dartmoor. Secondly, we could present a system of single reaves, in a zone of upland pasture containing hut-circles and enclosures, to add to Gawne's and Somers Cocks' parallel reave systems.

Having recruited a small group of helpers, we went back in June to put the reaves on the map and produce a more detailed plan. We split into two groups, planning the reaves at a scale of 1:1000, laying out long base-lines along them by eye with ranging-poles, and taking offset measurements at intervals as necessary. It was not difficult to tie in the base-lines with existing maps of the area – many man-made

features, including some prehistoric enclosures and one stretch of reave, were already marked.

Then we returned to Sheffield, and wrote an article.[10] We gave the reaves names, which are much easier to remember and use than letters or numbers; who would want to refer to the stone circle Long Meg and her Daughters as Cumbria 14? The reaves which we had traced became, in order, Cholwichtown Reave, Rook Reave, Penn Moor Reave, and Willings Walls Reave (fig. 5). It was not hard to agree on the main implications of our discoveries – a date for the reaves in the later Bronze Age, and the fact that they represented a kind of land division which was different from the parallel reave systems of Gawne and Somers Cocks.

It also seemed virtually certain from their character that our reaves had been built in a fairly open landscape. The case of Willings Walls Reave, mentioned above, was instructive. Here it is impossible to see one end of the reave from the other, but the builders, utilising a place on a slight shoulder from which it *is* possible to see both ends, were able to lay out a fairly direct course with only one angle change, on the shoulder itself. Boundaries built through wooded terrain would surely have been more sinuous, and in any case they would probably have been built from locally available material – as wooden fences. The idea that Dartmoor must have been relatively treeless at this time was confirmed by the pollen analysis carried out in the 1960s by Ian Simmons.[11]

Another question had to be considered. Had we simply stumbled across a number of individual boundary-walls, or could the reaves be said to be interdependent, forming what could be termed a *system* of land boundaries? And did the relationship between the reaves and the terrain suggest how these boundaries might have operated? The answers to these questions seemed to be interrelated. Three of the reaves – from east to west, Penn Moor, Cholwichtown and Willings Walls – seemed to be following the contour in a more or less continuous line. It seemed hard to envisage one without the others; their relationship to the terrain suggested that they could be seen as components of a single *contour reave*. At right angles to the contour reave was Rook Reave, which was obviously part of the same system, since it was joined by the contour reaves. It too took account of the terrain, being laid out to run along the watershed between the Plym and the Yealm. So these boundaries did seem to be part of a system laid out with respect to the main features of the terrain.

From first principles, it seemed that the boundaries might have operated as territorial boundaries, separating the land of one human group from that of another. Or they might have functioned as land-use boundaries; for example, separating arable land from pasture, infield from outfield, or summer pasture from winter pasture. Since the quality of the land on either side of Rook Reave is much the same, it seemed likely that this reave was a territorial boundary rather than a division of land-use. But John and I could not agree about the function of the contour reaves. I saw them as land-use divisions, separating the exposed, peat-shrouded watershed from the drier, more sheltered slopes lower down. John insisted that there was no significant difference between the two zones, and he saw the whole area as undifferentiated rough grazing land. We had to agree to disagree.

But could it really be the case that Gawne and Somers Cocks were the first to notice the reaves? Apparently not. A quick survey of old guide books, topographical accounts and archaeological literature showed that most of the reaves which John and I had stumbled upon had been noted or mentioned in passing. For instance, William Crossing's celebrated *Guide to Dartmoor*, first published in 1909,[12] referred to the junction of reaves below Penn Beacon; when we looked up the word 'reave' in Crossing's glossary of local terms, there was a whole page of explanation! However, Crossing evidently thought that reaves were of relatively recent date.

But it turned out that they had been a subject of study in much earlier times, indeed the object of a correspondence in the pages of a now defunct newspaper, *Besley's Exeter News*, in 1825. At this time the word 'prehistory' had still to be invented, and the sub-division of the remote past into a Stone Age, a Bronze Age and an Iron Age had only just been devised, in Scandinavia. Yet at this early date there were local antiquaries who considered that the reaves were probably prehistoric (or 'British', in their terminology) and that they were analogous to the linear earthworks of Wessex. So what had happened between 1825 and the time of William Crossing to convince the experts that reaves were relatively recent, and hence of little interest? It seemed that there was a strange case of lost knowledge here, which would have to be investigated some day.

In writing our report, we had to assess the wider significance of our discovery. From a national perspective, the finding of new prehistoric land boundaries was not too surprising. Not far away, in Wiltshire, Hampshire and Dorset, boundaries formed by banks and ditches, known as linear earthworks, had been recognised by archaeologists for a long time. So had the so-called 'Celtic' field systems, patchworks of small rectangular fields which showed up because earthern banks known as lynchets had accumulated at their lower edges as a result of soil creep when the fields were in use. Work done mainly between the two World Wars had convinced archaeologists working in Wessex that many of these field systems and linear earthworks were of later Bronze Age or Iron Age date.[13]

Another region of England noted for its extensive networks of linear earthwork boundaries was East Yorkshire. On the chalk Wolds these had been noted and mapped by J.R. Mortimer at the beginning of this century;[14] they too sometimes incorporated Bronze Age burial mounds. Most of these earthworks, like their counterparts in Wessex, have now been ploughed down, and survive at best as soil-marks on freshly-ploughed land. Some of the linear earthworks on the Corallian Limestone of the Tabular hills, to the north of the Vale of Pickering, have survived better. The dating evidence for the Yorkshire boundaries is not particularly good, but one or two of them can be shown to date from the later part of the Bronze Age.

So there were already indications of a well-ordered countryside in other parts of England by the later Bronze Age; so in terms of the national picture, the Dartmoor discoveries were not unexpected. But in Wessex and Yorkshire most of the linear earthworks and ancient field systems had been swept away by the plough, and for the most part these prehistoric boundary patterns had to be painstakingly fitted together from soil-marks and crop-marks seen from the air and recorded by aerial photography. The same was true for settlement sites; it was not easy to establish relationships between settlement sites and the land boundaries which might have accompanied them. So by comparison with other parts of England, Dartmoor looked a magnificent prospect. There were reaves standing up to half a metre above the ground surface, walled field systems sometimes covering several hundred hectares, and a pasture zone with so many enclosures and house remains that a near-complete settlement-pattern must surely be available for study.

This seemed important at the time. It was widely recognised that prehistorians studying the agriculturally-based peoples of prehistoric Europe would have to develop some kind of model of relationships between human communities and the land upon which they depended for food and other necessities. Theories about the organisation of people in relation to land involved questions of territoriality and land ownership, the size of the settlements in which people lived, the distribution and density of population, how access to different resources was secured, and so on. Archaeologists of the early seventies turned out to be compulsive magpies, borrowing theories from anthropology, economic history, systems theory, and locational geography.

It seemed that locational geography might provide some kind of initial theoretical approach to the question of prehistoric territoriality. Thus David Clarke imposed a hexagonal lattice on a distribution map of hillforts in Kent; Stan Stanford drew circles around his Herefordshire hillforts; Colin Renfrew fitted Thiessen polygons to maps of long barrows in Wiltshire, chamber tombs on the Isle of Arran, and stone temples in Malta.[15] It seemed to me, however, that such recourse to this rather abstract approach was somewhat hasty. What if one could use the survival of settlement sites, field systems and land boundaries to pick up territorial pattern directly?

So it is not surprising that we were excited by our Dartmoor discoveries. Here the settlement sites were not only well-preserved and relatively well dated; they were also apparently accompanied by contemporary land boundaries and well-preserved field systems, the parallel reaves of Gawne and Somers Cocks. No need, then, for Thiessen polygons or any other sort of polygons; the boundaries were marked out on the ground. Moreover, Dartmoor is quite a large area of moorland, so it ought to be possible to work on a regional scale. At last, it seemed, here was an opportunity to tackle some of the problems concerning the relationship between communities and their land, using a really good data set. As John and I pointed out in our article, published in 1973, 'work on the social and economic significance of linear boundaries in Britain is in its infancy'. Dartmoor, however, seemed to offer a way forward; future prospects looked bright.

2: A curious case of lost knowledge

The next two or three years were a time of discovery, of looking for new reaves and finding them. The story of a how a few lines pencilled on maps emerged as a meaningful pattern of ancient land boundaries will be told in the next two chapters. But there was one intriguing question which led me into the library rather than into the field. How did it come about that reaves were correctly interpreted in 1825, in the infancy of archaeology, and then virtually ignored by serious archaeologists for 150 years? How could miles of ancient land boundaries, clearly visible on the ground and located in a landscape well-known for its archaeological wealth, come to be overlooked for such a long time?

Whenever I had the opportunity, I put in a day's work at the University Library in Cambridge, or the Bodleian at Oxford, trying to find out more about the history of Dartmoor archaeology, and what the early antiquaries had thought about reaves. I was helped by the kindness of other researchers like Leslie Grinsell and Tom Greeves, who drew my attention to manuscript material which they had come across in their work on Dartmoor burial mounds and tin-mining. So gradually I was able to piece together the story of how reaves were originally discovered, and how archaeologists came to lose interest in them.

It all started in the 1820s – a critical decade in the history of Devon archaeology. Kent's Cavern is now a tourist attraction on the outskirts of Torquay, advertised on local buses as if it were some sort of night-club. Not many of its visitors realise that Kent's Cavern once played a crucial role in helping us to understand our own history.[1] The finding of flint implements and the bones of extinct animals sealed by a layer of stalagmite convinced Father MacEnery, who started work here in 1825, that humanity must have originated long before 4004 BC, the date then accepted for the Creation. Although MacEnery's ideas were not well received at the time, his work did stimulate further investigations, notably by William Pengelly, whose work here and later at Windmill Hill Cave, Brixham, vindicated MacEnery's conclusions. But the man who started the ball rolling was not MacEnery; that honour goes to another Devon antiquary, Thomas Northmore, who excavated at Kent's Cavern in 1824.[2] One of his objectives was to recover organic remains, and in this he was richly rewarded, picking up the bones of animals long extinct in England, like the cave bear and the hyena.

Northmore,[3] who was then fifty-six, lived at Cleve House, a fine residence overlooking Exeter, for which city he stood for Parliament in 1818 in the Radical interest. He was a dynamic, independent-minded man, in some respects ahead of his time. He was one of the first advocates of Parliamentary reform; he pressed for the establishment of a museum in Torquay (a town which he described as 'delightful, but now too crowded'). But Northmore received little recognition for his work. He failed to get elected to Parliament. His pioneer work at Kent's Cavern was overshadowed by that of his successors. He seems to have been somewhat bitter because scientists like Davy and Faraday had taken the credit for discovering the condensation of gases; he claimed to have been first in the field. Although Northmore lived just outside Exeter, his work, like mine later on, was helped by recent road improvements, and he evidently visited Dartmoor regularly to see its archaeological remains. One of his antiquarian friends on Dartmoor was the Rev. James Holman Mason, rector of the parish of Widecombe (fig. 6). Mason's duties took him regularly to Postbridge and Princetown, and he is said to have been responsible for the construction of the bridge at Bellever, to take him and other travellers across the East Dart. Northmore used his good offices as a Justice of the Peace to save the lovely old clapper bridge, the predecessor of Mason's new bridge, from being pulled down. Mason also showed Northmore the impressive prehistoric walled enclosure known as Grimspound, and together they seem to have done a little restoration work there. In 1829 Mason engaged a surveyor called Shillabeer, and got him to make a proper plan of the site, arguably the first adequate plan of a prehistoric settlement site to be drawn in Britain (fig. 7).[4]

If you leave Grimspound by its original entrance, on the southern side, you can scramble up the hill on to the dark, broad-backed ridge of Hameldown, with its impressive Bronze Age burial cairns. There are two reaves running across the ridge, dividing it into three roughly equal parts (fig. 10). Hameldown Reave North runs through a slight saddle, between the heads of two streams; further south, Hameldown Reave South runs downhill in an easterly direction from Two Barrows. Both of these reaves are near the north-west corner of the Widecombe parish boundary. Did Mason first come across them when he was taking part in the perambulation of the boundaries? At any rate it was Mason who showed one or both of these reaves to Northmore, probably in the summer of 1825; on 22 August in that year he wrote him a letter on the subject. Two days later, another cleric wrote to Northmore about reaves. This was the Rev. John Pike Jones, curate of North Bovey, a parish which has Grimspound on its boundary. Jones was

6 James Holman Mason, rector of the parish of Widecombe, one of the original discoverers of reaves. He was one of a group of Devon antiquaries whose fieldwork in the 1820s and 1830s initiated the study of Dartmoor archaeology. His work and his property interests often took him into the Upper Dart basin. *Photo: S. Woods*

also a keen antiquary; he had published a book about the Moretonhampstead area in 1823, and was evidently writing another on the antiquities of Devon. Some of this has survived in manuscript form in the Bodleian Library. Jones apparently sent Thomas Northmore a copy of this manuscript.

The following December, Northmore published two short pieces on reaves and other matters in *Besley's Exeter News*, making use of the comments he had received in the letters from Jones and Mason.[5] From these articles, and from Jones's manuscript, which Northmore did not cite in full, it is possible to gain a good idea of the discussions which had taken place about reaves, and the attitudes of the three men. Apparently it was Mason who had drawn attention to the reaves, but Jones who did most of the fieldwork. It was he who provided the most workmanlike description, and came out most strongly in favour of a prehistoric date:[6]

Ancient Dykes have been traced through the uncultivated parts of this parish over Hamilton (Hameldown) and from thence across Dartmoor. They generally run in a straight direction, are formed of loose stones, and are from four to seven feet in breadth. They are raised above the level of the ground, and are frequently lost in the bogs; in the inclosed grounds they cannot be traced, the stones having been removed. These roads were most probably formed by the Britons at an early period, and they are accompanied in their course with erect stones, circles and monuments which have generally been attributed to the British period. The Romans appear to have avoided Dartmoor altogether . . . .

But it also emerges that Jones was confused about the function of these antiquities, referring to them also as roads. What is more, he changed his mind at some stage, because the second word in the above paragraph had originally been 'Trackways', before Jones crossed it out and substituted the word Dykes, as he did a little further on in the same manuscript. His conclusion was that 'the above mentioned Dykes were most probably thrown up as lines of division, at an early period, in connection with the limits of Dartmore and its borders . . . .' This time the word 'Dykes' was not a later emendation.

Perhaps these changes were made under Thomas Northmore's influence. At any rate, Northmore was in no doubt about the function of reaves. Not only did he entitle his articles 'Of the ancient Dykes, or Division-lines on Dartmoor', he also stated at the outset: 'I deemed them to be . . . Dykes for the separation or division of lands; and have therefore not hesitated to so denominate them, instead of Trackways; for they bear no resemblance to roads, being carried over tors and through swamps, and being in structure more like walls than roads'.

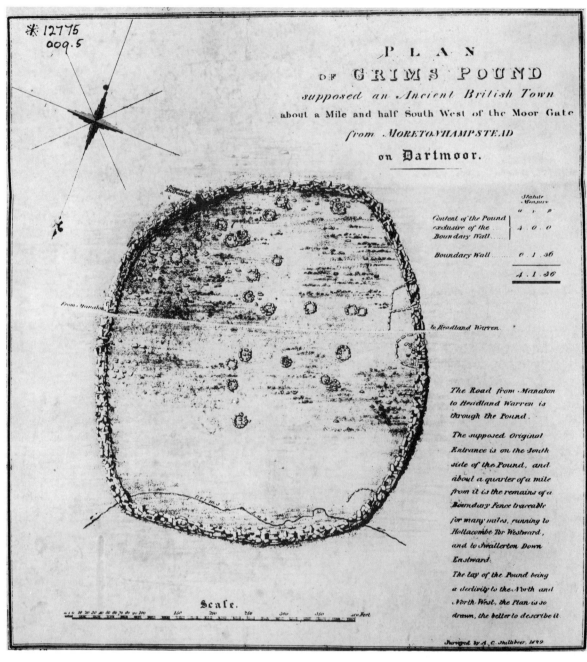

PLAN
OF GRIMS POUND
supposed an Ancient British Town
about a Mile and half South West of the Moor Gate
from MORETONHAMPSTEAD
on Dartmoor.

	Statute Measure		
	a	*r*	*p*
Content of the Pound exclusive of the Boundary Wall	4	0	0
Boundary Wall	0	1	36
	4	1	36

The Road from Manaton to Headland Warren is through the Pound.

The supposed Original Entrance is on the South side of the Pound, and about a quarter of a mile from it is the remains of a Boundary Fence traceable for many miles, running to Hollacombe Tor Westward, and to Swallerton Down Eastward.

The lay of the Pound being a declivity to the North and North West, the Plan is so drawn, the better to describe it

Scale.

Surveyed by A. C. Shillabeer, 1829.

7 Perhaps the earliest good quality plan of a prehistoric settlement site in Britain was that of Grimspound. This major prehistoric enclosure was surveyed in 1829 by A. C. Shillabeer, a professional surveyor whose work included the tramway (eventually the railway) to the recently-founded settlement at Princetown. *Photo courtesy West Country Studies Library, Exeter*

Northmore was unhappy about the absence of dating evidence, and admitted to wondering sometimes whether the reaves might relate to the later Middle Ages, when Dartmoor was a Royal Forest, in other words a game reserve. Perhaps this was why he did not quote Jones' opinion concerning their date.

Northmore was immensely excited by Dartmoor's archaeological riches; 'this vast table-land', he wrote, 'is one abundant storehouse of Celtic remains.' Long before Sites and Monuments Records came into being, he called for a complete record of Dartmoor's antiquities, in the form of a large-scale map: 'every barrow, every carnedd, every Druidical circle, stone, pillar or idol – and in short every remnant of antiquity, and particularly the Division Dykes, should be justly, and truly delineated . . . and why, my countrymen, is not such a work put in hand forthwith – while there are heads to direct, and hands to execute? Money surely cannot be wanting: let only three or four men of wealth set, by their subscriptions, the work agoing – and it is half done!'[7]

So Mason discovered the reaves, and Jones and Northmore between them reached the correct conclusion about their function and dating. But where did the idea about trackways come from? Here we come to a very strange part of the story. It seems that it was the discussions between these three men which led to the rise of that remarkable creature of the nineteenth-century imagination – the so-called 'great central trackway'.

It is not altogether certain how the concept originated. The evidence makes it clear that Jones did a good deal of archaeological fieldwork in the area which I call the Upper Dart basin – the boggy, rolling, rather self-contained area between the North Moor and the South Moor, between Hameldown and North Hessary Tor. The Upper Dart basin had recently changed quite dramatically as a result of the efforts of the Improvers, who believed that Dartmoor could be fertile and productive if attention was paid to drainage, liming, reseeding and the building of good stock-proof walls and shelter-belts. Today, the landscape around the prison farm at Princetown shows what the Improvers were trying to achieve – ruler-

straight drystone walls, good-quality grazing land, well-regulated drainage. They changed the landscape, but as Rev. Jones pointed out shortly afterwards, their efforts were a finanacial disaster; Dartmoor 'could not be forced into an unusual produce'.[8]

The Rev. Mason himself was one of the Improvers, enclosing 240 hectares (600 acres) around Crockern Tor, and building himself a cottage there. After Princetown church, built by American and French prisoners of war, had been completed in 1815, Mason had to travel there to officiate at services. He must have known Sir Thomas Tyrwhitt, the most famous of the Dartmoor Improvers, who had founded Princetown (can this be regarded as an improvement?) and lived not far away at Tor Royal. A.C. Shillabeer, the Walkhampton surveyor whom Mason employed at Grimspound, had also surveyed the line of the Plymouth to Princetown tramway, another of Tyrwhitt's projects, and the predecessor of the railway. It was under construction in the 1820s.

The travelling antiquary was able to use the recently constructed turnpike roads. Archaeology benefited from this greater mobility, and to some extent also from the disturbances wrought by the Improvers; sensible antiquaries made it their business to keep in touch with the country people who were carrying out the work. Rev. Jones noted that there had been a reave in the fields near Heatree, where 'it had here sunk in the meadows, and had been frequently cut through, where gutters had been formed for draining the meadows'.[9] In the Upper Dart basin, fragments of old walls were uncovered by people cutting peat and digging drains for Improvement; at times they came across buried trees or wooden bowls.

Now a reave discovered in a peat-bog (fig. 8) looks just like an ancient causeway, constructed to allow

8 A reave buried in peat. This was the kind of context which persuaded some ninteenth century antiquaries that reaves were really intended as causeways across boggy ground, and thus contributed to the myth about the Great Central Trackway. *Photo: A. Fleming*

9 Walkhampton Common Reave, from the south, somewhat foreshortened by the use of a zoom lens. Running not far to the west of the Princetown-Yelverton road, it is a good example of a long, direct 'watershed reave', of the kind which persuaded the early antiquaries of the existence of long-distance 'trackways' across the Moor. For a general location plan, see fig. 24. *Photo: A. Fleming*

people to cross the bog dry-shod. And it was this which confused the early antiquaries. To someone like the Rev. Jones, who realised the similarity between these buried stones and the reaves on Hameldown, they posed a problem of interpretation. We have seen how he hesitated between calling them dykes and calling them trackways; the dykes won, it seems, perhaps after Northmore had delivered a few crisp comments on the subject.

The antiquaries soon noted that there were several stretches of reave in and around the Upper Dart basin. Mason spotted a reave on Peek Hill, on the western side of the Moor; perhaps Shillabeer the surveyor pointed out the long one on Walkhampton Common, which would have been visible to those who were working out the line of the Princetown tramway (fig. 9). Another fairly obvious reave ran over Chittaford Down, west of Postbridge, and up to Lower White Tor, or Waydon Tor as it was called then. There may have been other old walls discovered in drainage or peat-cutting work in the Upper Dart basin, or visible on the ground surface in the areas now covered by the forests of Bellever and Soussons, where fieldwork is now virtually impossible. Somehow, Mason, Jones and Northmore decided that the reaves on Hameldown were parts of much longer boundaries. As far as I can determine, Jones did most of the detailed fieldwork (fig. 10).[10] Hameldown North Reave, he thought, started much further east, at Wingstone, not far from Manaton church, reaching Hameldown via Cripdon Down and Heatree Down. To the west it ran over Challacombe Down, across the area now covered by Soussons Forest, through Postbridge and onto Chittaford Down to Lower White Tor. He decided that Hameldown South Reave went across 'Sowston Commons' (now Soussons Forest), through the farmyard at Pizwell, over Lakehead Hill near Bellever Tor, to the Cherry Brook near the 'turnpike road', and eventually as far west as 'the common adjoining Roborough Down', via Crockern Tor, the traditional site of the old tinners' open-air 'Parliament'. Northmore suggested that this reave must have been a boundary intended to divide Dartmoor into two roughly equal halves.

Jones was quite an observant fieldworker, although it is not always possible to be sure now what he was referring to, or to check his observations on the ground. But by trying to link up isolated stretches of reave separated by extensive blank areas he over-reached himself. It is impossible to agree with him that there were once two major reaves crossing the Upper Dart basin where he claims they did, even taking into account that in some places conditions for fieldwork were better in the 1820s than they are today. The northernmost of the Hameldown reaves is really a short, crossridge boundary; the southern one is longer, but there are no grounds for taking it anywhere near as far as Jones did. And although Jones was evidently persuaded to see the reaves as boundaries, the claims which he made about their length, the fact that when encountered in peat-bogs they looked like causeways, and probably local folklore about former

routes across the Moor, soon ensured that the trackway interpretation prevailed – which was unfortunate for the future of Dartmoor archaeology.

Even to those who know the history of archaeological investigation on Dartmoor, Mason, Jones and Northmore might as well be a firm of estate agents. That is because the first proper account of Dartmoor's archaeological remains was written by someone else altogether. Samuel Rowe had spent nine years as a bookseller before going up as a mature student to Jesus College, Cambridge, where he took holy orders some six months after the appearance of Northmore's newspaper articles. He came to Plymouth as a curate, and then took charge of two successive parishes in the district of Stonehouse, before moving to Crediton in 1935. He soon became involved in Dartmoor archaeology, walking the moors in the summers of 1827 and 1828 with a small group of fellow enthusiasts. The result of this work was a paper which he read to the Plymouth Institution in 1828, the substance of which eventually appeared in book form, as part of Rowe's *Perambulation of Dartmoor*, first published in 1848 and dedicated to Prince Albert.[11]

Rowe offered a classification of the antiquities of Dartmoor, and an account of some of the more notable archaeological sites. His archaeology was mostly a matter of straightforward description and commonsense commentary, mixed with various scholarly allusions, and a little nonsense about the Druids, a hangover from eighteenth-century antiquarianism. In the debate over reaves, Rowe came down on the side of the trackway interpretation, though he was not dogmatic about it, admitting that the boundary line hypothesis had one or two points in its favour. Rowe drew an important distinction between single reaves and systems of parallel reaves, calling them respectively 'trackways' and 'tracklines'. Trackways, he said, 'traverse the moor to a very wide extent, ascending the hills, penetrating the bogs and swamps, and fording the rivers'. Rowe provided a description of the northernmost of Jones' two lines, which, he said, was supposed to run from Hameldown to Great Mistor. His description concentrated on the sector from Hartyland Farm to Lower White Tor. Rowe accepted the notion of a major east-west reave, although he very honestly pointed out that 'a large extent of it rests upon the testimony of tradition, than on existing remains; for this is one of the few relics of remote antiquity which seems to have excited any attention from the moormen'. Despite this admission, seven pages later he calmly refers to the reave on Chittaford Down as 'the grand central trackway'. A legend was in the making.

'Tracklines', which according to Rowe were numerous and looked as if they should be

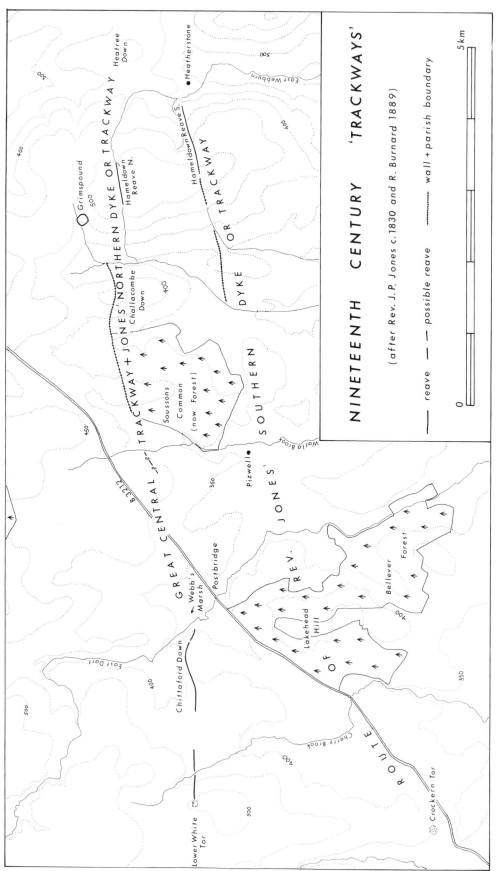

10 The Upper Dart basin around Postbridge, showing the routes of long-distance trackways suggested by nineteenth-century antiquaries. These were based on reaves, which looked like causeways when they were discovered beneath valley bog, as at Webb's Marsh, Postbridge. Both Jones and Burnard extended the routes further east and west than shown here.

contemporary with the 'trackways', were clearly associated with hut-circles and enclosures, and 'in great probability served for bounds or pathways, connecting and enclosing dwellings' (again, that fateful confusion!). Rowe provided a neat description of the reaves forming part of a parallel system near Rippon Tor, on eastern Dartmoor, where 'they intersect each other at right angles in such numbers, that nearly the whole of the eastern slope is partitioned into squares, conveying in a striking manner the idea of an antient rural settlement. This notion is strongly supported by the appearance of hut circles, which are found in many of these primitive divisions'.

By the time Rowe came to write his *Perambulation of Dartmoor*, he was able to mention a good many more reaves; after moving to Crediton he must have got to know northern and eastern Dartmoor much better. He corresponded with the Rev. Mason, who according to Rowe was by then referring to ancient walls by their proper dialect term, reaves, and believed firmly that they were boundaries. Mason had also begun to speculate that the reaves might have been constructed by tin-miners. Seemingly in deference to Mason's authority, Rowe concluded: 'we shall have no difficulty in concluding, that they may have been connected with mining operations, and yet belong to the British period of our history'.

But a careful reading of the *Perambulation* shows how confused and uncertain Rowe was about reaves. He started off by reiterating his 1828 classification into trackways and tracklines, but as the book progresses it is clear that he was unable to distinguish them by their appearance in the field. Nor was he consistent in using their character and context to separate them. Trackways were supposed to be single reaves, tracklines occurred together to make up field systems. Yet his account of Cosdon Beacon described 'one of those ancient paved ways . . . principally exhibiting the characteristics of the trackway . . . but partaking somewhat of the character of the trackline also'. Phrases like this betray Rowe's dreadful inability to decide on the function of reaves. He justified his approach by suggesting that 'trackways . . . were no doubt often made to serve the purpose of boundary lines'. Rowe made some useful observations, but his general remarks on reaves ended up by making no sense at all. It looks as if the *Perambulation* was written in several stages and not revised before going to the printer. So for the rest of the century the standard work on Dartmoor antiquities spread considerable confusion about reaves, especially as most other writers borrowed from it freely and uncritically. The great central trackway turned up on maps; the words 'Ancient Trackway', printed in Gothic script,

appeared on Chittaford Down and to the east of Postbridge. The Ordnance Survey also marked the great central trackway, but they went further, and indicated reaves in one or two places by the trackway convention, a pair of parallel hyphenated lines. When I bought a set of 1:25000 maps at the start of my work I was bemused by what I saw on the Princetown sheet – apparently there was a trackway starting out from the top corner of a block of relatively modern walled fields, straggling up a steep slope for about 300m (330 yards), and ending abruptly amid the piles of rock surrounding Roos Tor![12] In the field, of course, all was made clear; the 'track' turned out to be a reave.

Not very much happened in the study of Dartmoor archaeology between the appearance of Rowe's *Perambulation* and the activities of the Dartmoor Exploration Committee forty years later. The most sensible comments on reaves during this period were made by an Egyptologist, Sir J. Gardner Wilkinson, who published his own classification of Dartmoor antiquities in 1862.[13] He wrote: 'they have sometimes been called "trackways" but as they are evidently single walls, and could not have been used for roads, that appellation does not properly belong to them. Some of the hills over which they stretch bear the traces of early cultivation . . . and it has been conjectured that the hill-tops were often cleared and tilled by the ancient Britons, while the lower lands were covered with dense woods.'

The next major advance was the series of excavations carried out by the Dartmoor Exploration Committee in the 1890s and the first few years of this century.[14] Apparently they did manage to operate as a committee, but their writings hint at strong personalities, and they must often have agreed to disagree. Reading what they wrote, I feel sure that this must have been the case with reaves (which they did not excavate). R.N. Worth (father of the better known Richard Hansford Worth) and Robert Burnard took what can only be called a generous view. According to Burnard, 'the Great Central Trackway is a portion of the Great Fosseway, which ran from Caithness to Mount's bay'.[15] There is a nice flavour of Victorian railways in Burnard's use of initial capital letters. It is not altogether clear why Worth and Burnard believed that this reave was Romano-British in date; perhaps it was simply the general scale of the concept, although as far as I know Burnard's fieldwork on the route did not take him to northern Scotland. But he did read a paper on the Great Central Trackway to the Devonshire Association in 1889; it was based on fieldwork in the Postbridge area (fig. 10).[16]

It is interesting how one fixed idea can influence the direction which archaeological fieldwork and argument will take. Although the 'Great Central' clearly stops at Lower White Tor, Burnard was determined to find evidence for a long-distance trackway. So, after casting around further west, he managed to persuade himself that another reave on Roos Tor, a full eight kilometres (five miles) away, was on the right line, and linked that with two other reaves on the eastern and western slopes of Cox Tor, further west still. The trackway was 'heading straight for Tavistock'. To the east of Postbridge, as he tried to follow the route originally suggested by Rev. Jones, Burnard had to admit that 'it is very difficult to follow the track all through this section'. Indeed, having spent a hot afternoon here, swatting horseflies while casting around fruitlessly in search of the 'trackway', I know myself that one's affection for the memory of the Rev. Jones can occasionally waver. But Burnard made light of the difficulties: 'here and there', he remarked rather airily, 'it can be made out, and the blanks can be filled in'. This approach seems firmly rooted in the J.P. Jones school of archaeological fieldwork. Eventually, however, 'all doubt about it is easily dispelled by . . . the perfect section on the summit of Hameldown'. Further east, on Heatree Down, Burnard said 'the trackway appears to have been heightened by trenching on each side, and piling the stones and earth higher in the centre', which sounds like a good description of a medieval hedge-bank (although such a hedge-bank could, of course, have been built on a much earlier reave). The 'trackway' was then supposed to head for Chudleigh.

In the marshy ground of Webb's Marsh, north-west of Postbridge, peat-cutters had recently come across a reave, and were freely robbing it for wall-building stone. Burnard described it, and took a good photograph, which is still in the possession of his granddaughter, Lady Sylvia Sayer. It was ten feet (over three metres) in breadth, and it did look very like a causeway. How did Burnard account for the fact that, when they emerged onto dry ground, reaves looked much more like boundaries? His explanation was ingenious: 'the effect of the weather on Dartmoor is often underrated, and its action on a raised causeway for very many centuries can hardly be realized'.

Burnard's colleague on the committee, R.N. Worth, was also a Great Central Trackway enthusiast. But he was dismissive about the 'tracklines', the reaves within parallel reave systems, even though they look just like the 'trackways'. This was Worth's opinion: 'they appear, as a rule, to represent enclosures exterior to the immediate surroundings of the huts, and to belong to a more recent date than the so-called pounds . . . . Probably they are among the most modern of the moorland antiquities. They are certainly among the least mysterious.'[17] Worth's view

was evidently passed on to R. Hansford Worth, his son, who was to become the Dartmoor expert for the first half of the twentieth century.

The Rev. Sabine Baring-Gould was more sensible. He would have nothing to do with the 'trackway' interpretation, nor with a Romano-British date for the reaves;[18]

It is very probable that the long tracklines that extend over hill and vale on Dartmoor indicate tribal boundaries, limits beyond which the cattle of one clan might not feed. Some of these lines, certainly of the age of the neolithic men of the hut circles, may be traced for miles.

Clearly Baring-Gould was using the word 'trackline' simply as conventional terminology, and his Neolithic dating for the hut-circles reflected the fact that the pottery found in the Committee's excavations had been recognised as prehistoric, but not yet assigned to the Bronze Age.

So at the beginning of the twentieth century, the Dartmoor Exploration Committee was in total disarray about the date and function of reaves. Depending on whom you talked to, they might be Neolithic, Romano-British, or quite modern. They might be ancient trackways, graziers' boundaries, or tin-miners' bounds. The 1896 edition of the *Perambulation*, revised by a member of the Committee, perpetuated the ambiguities and contradictions of the first edition, published almost half a century before. The Worths, father and son, seem to have had little interest in reaves, as we have seen. Quite a number of reaves had been discovered since the days of Northmore, Mason and Jones, and references to them were scattered through Dartmoor's topographic literature, which had been growing steadily throughout the nineteenth century. Far from fulfilling Northmore's desire for a complete cartographic record of Dartmoor's ancient boundaries, later scholars had scattered snippets of information about reaves through the literature like confetti. Since the heady days of 1825, knowledge of the true historical context of these boundaries had receded.

From 1909 onwards the best information about reaves was to be found not in scholarly tomes or articles in learned journals, but in the most popular guide-book, *Crossing's Guide to Dartmoor*. William Crossing was a freelance writer, who lived off his wits; he died in near-poverty, the costs of a three-year stay in a nursing-home being met by an old friend. Educationally and financially he was at a disadvantage compared to most of those who pontificated on Dartmoor archaeology. But his approach to reaves did him credit. Crossing used the word 'reave' in preference to 'trackway' and argued firmly that the reaves were land boundaries.[19]

Trackline is a name that has been given to them, but not very happily, as it suggests that they were formed to serve the purpose of marking a track, which they certainly were not. There are, however, those who consider that the large examples were roads, and have given to them the name of trackways. I confess that I have never been able to regard them as such, and until it is explained how those who used them contrived to ride through rocks, or immense cairns, I am afraid that I shall be unable to accept the view that they were designed for the purpose of traffic'.

Crossing went on to explain this last comment. Politely but firmly, he refused to accept the traditional view of the Great Central Trackway: 'no explanation has been offered why this so-called trackway should be carried straight into a tor, and none, in fact, could be given unless the tor were its terminal point . . . whatever purpose the reave on Chittaford Down may have served, I am certainly not inclined to consider that a road was one of them.' But, as Crossing pointed out, there is an even less convincing 'trackway' on Ugborough Moor, on the southern part of Dartmoor. Here there is a reave (fig. 20) which was referred to in a sixteenth century document as 'a long conger of stones called Le Rowe Rew'. But as Crossing noted, it is a most implausible road, starting as it does from the head of a stream and ending on the open moor, with no obvious destination. There is a worse problem, however; it runs up the Three Barrows, large Bronze Age burial cairns on the hill above Piles Wood, and incorporates two of them in its line. Remorselessly, Crossing analysed the possibilities:[19]

We must believe one of three things: that the reave and the cairns were thrown up at the same time; that the reave was made first; or that the cairns were built first, and in either case the conclusion arrived at must be that the bank was not a road. If we suppose the first to have been the case this is plain, for nobody would take the trouble to make a road, and then render it impassible by building cairns upon it; if we consider the reave to be older than the cairns we have to believe that those who threw up the latter deliberately blocked the road, which is absurd; and if we suppose the cairns to have been placed on the hill before the bank was formed (and they most certainly were) we must imagine the road makers to have been stupid enough to carry their track towards an obstacle instead of trying to avoid it. No men with a grain of sense would have made a road in the line of this reave. It climbs a lofty hill for no apparent purpose but that of descending its further side.

It is a pity that the intelligence of a Crossing was not brought to bear upon the reave problem earlier. However, Crossing accepted without discussion the notion that reaves were tinners' boundaries. And there the matter rested until the 1950s, since R.H. Worth had little interest in reaves.

As explained in the first chapter, after Worth's death in 1950 the prehistory of Dartmoor was re-examined

by C.A. Ralegh Radford and Lady Aileen Fox. But there was still no place for reaves; we have seen how parallel reaves in places like Foale's Arrishes and Kestor (fig. 11) were described as 'medieval' or 'the result of medieval remodelling'.[20] Yet if we look carefully at the illustrations which Fox and Ralegh Radford themselves provided, we can see that they raise one or two awkward questions. At the Rippon Tor homestead (fig. 1), the obvious interpretation of Fox's plan is that long boundary marked by the reave came first, and that the 'homestead' was attached to it; it is difficult to think as she encourages us to do, in terms of a phase one involving a detached Bronze Age homestead with a curiously straight side then coincidentally used in phase two by the builders of the 'medieval' reave. Another problem is raised by Ralegh Radford's discussion of the ancient fields at Foale's Arrishes not very far away, where, as can be seen from his plan (fig. 11), the long 'medieval' boundaries were apparently laid out before the 'prehistoric' boundaries *which run up to them*. To some extent Ralegh Radford realised that this posed a problem for his interpretation, and he argued that the medieval strips allegedly marked out by these long banks were 'subdivided by cross ridges, over which the banks are humped and which clearly belong to an earlier stage of cultivation'. He seems to be suggesting here that the prehistoric boundaries were re-used as subdivisions of the medieval strip system. This results in a very odd picture of medieval farmers. On the one hand, they laid out these very long strips; on the other, they re-used the small prehistoric fields, taking extraordinary pains to make their long banks line up with the field edges of their Bronze Age predecessors. I'm not sure where Ralegh Radford thought he could see long banks humping over lynchets, but the overall picture doesn't make any sense. And the same problem applies to Lady Fox's plan of the fields at Kestor (fig. 11) where the 'prehistoric' fields are stippled, and the other boundaries are supposed to have been inserted, or remodelled, in the Middle Ages.

With hindsight, we should not have had to wait until 1968 for Gawne and Somers Cocks to produce their careful re-evaluation of the date of parallel reave systems.[21] The evidence which demanded a re-think was there before our very eyes – not tucked away in some obscure county journal, but printed in the *Proceedings of the Prehistoric Society*, the national journal for British prehistorians. In the late 1950s, and in the early '60s, major new prehistoric field systems could have been discovered without so much as putting on a pair of boots or donning an anorak; possession of a library ticket would have sufficed.

Why did Fox and Ralegh Radford prefer more complicated interpretations than those suggested

11 At Foale's Arrishes and Kestor, archaeologists of the 1950s separated the small 'prehistoric' fields (stippled at Kestor, below) from the land division represented by the long parallel reaves, which they suggested was medieval 'remodelling'. The similarity and the close relationship between the two, clearly shown in these illustrations, was not accounted for their interpretations. *After Radford and Fox*

their own published plans? Why didn't anyone notice the problems created by these interpretations? I believe that the idea of small-scale Dartmoor field systems was acceptable, even if it had to be supported by perverse approaches to the field evidence, because it accorded with contemporary views of the simplicity of prehistoric society. Ancient field systems should be small, and not too well organised, especially in the uplands. Admittedly, not too far away from Dartmoor there were impressive ceremonial monuments, like the stone circles at Avebury, and the massive chalk mound known as Silbury Hill; but these were regarded as essentially the product of brawn rather than brain. Stonehenge, of course, was more sophisticated, with its mortise-and-tenon and tongue-and-groove joints, and the carefully contrived visual impact of the uprights.

But Stonehenge, according to archaeologists of the 1950s, did not originate in Britain. The dagger carved on one of the uprights, which made a dramatic first appearance in the viewfinder of Richard Atkinson's camera in the late afternoon sunshine of 10 July, 1953, was immediately claimed by its discoverer to be of early Mycenaean type. Atkinson went further, suggesting that the dagger afforded 'presumptive evidence that the designer (indeed, the architect) of the monument was himself a Mycenaean'. As it happens, Atkinson's comments appeared in the same volume of the *Proceedings of the Prehistoric Society* as Radford's discussion of Foale's Arrishes.[22]

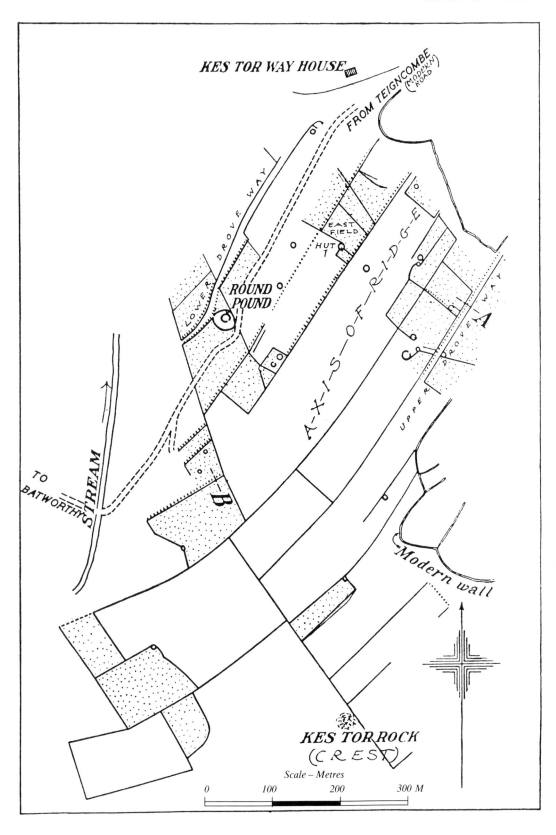

KES TOR WAY HOUSE

FROM TEIGNCOMBE
(MODERN ROAD)

LOWER DROVE WAY

EAST FIELD

HUT 1

ROUND POUND

C

A-X-I-S—O—F—R-I-D-G-E

UPPER DROVE WAY

A

B

TO BATWORTHY

STREAM

Modern wall

KES TOR ROCK
(C R E S T)

Scale – Metres

0   100   200   300 M

By the time John Collis and I appeared on the scene in 1972, the climate of ideas had changed. For one thing, calibrated radiocarbon dates now showed that Stonehenge IIIA (the sophisticated phase in question) was built long before the Shaft Graves at Mycenae. Even if the dagger *is* Mycenaean (which many would dispute) it would carry no more implications for dating than does the signature of Lord Byron on the temple of Poseidon at Sounion, in Greece, as Colin Renfrew pointed out.[24] It was now suggested that prehistoric Europeans were considerably more inventive than had been supposed. More attention would have to be paid to social and economic processes working within essentially tribal societies, processes capable of generating change and complex development without the intervention of outsiders bringing in 'new ideas'. As it happens, John Collis, Elizabeth Gawne, John Somers Cocks and I made up our minds on the basis of the field evidence, rather than because we wanted to appear fashionable. This is a matter of record. But there is no doubt that large-scale land division was a much easier concept to accept when we started to talk about it, than would have been the case twenty years earlier.

I found the results of my researches fascinating. I knew that Kent's Cavern was important in the history of archaeology, but I had known nothing of a group of antiquaries working on Dartmoor at the same time, just after the publication of Sir Richard Colt Hoare's *Ancient Wiltshire* but before most other archaeological enterprises. Some day it would be interesting to find out more about Mason, Jones, Northmore, Rowe and company. It is striking how some of the most perceptive observations and comments were made by people not celebrated for their contribution to Dartmoor archaeology – people like Thomas Northmore (a forgotten man, it seems, in more than

one field) and William Crossing. It has been interesting to note the tyranny of the fixed idea, and its influence not only on the way prehistorians think about the past, but also the observations they make and the way they handle archaeological evidence. Students of reaves have deployed a variety of arguments which can politely be called ingenious – for the existence of the Great Central Trackway, for reaves being trackways, for reaves in field systems being essentially different from single reaves, and for parallel reave systems being medieval in date. Some of these arguments have flown in the face of common-sense and observed facts. The common human habit of accepting the view of a recognised authority has not always been helpful. For example, did anyone worry about the internal contradictions in Samuel Rowe's account of reaves, or the even more confusing version published later by his nephew? Did the person who marked the Roos Tor reave as a trackway on the Ordnance Survey map really fail to notice its most untracklike behaviour?

The Great Central Trackway is a dead concept now. It was an imaginative, not to say grandiose, idea which ultimately could not be supported by the archaeological evidence. The current 1:25000 Ordnance Survey map marks its western end, a perfectly respectable reave, as a 'Boundary Work'. But the Rev. Jones' intuitive belief that widely separated sections of reave might well be part of a single line was not altogether wide of the mark; modern study has revealed that reaves are often longer than appears to be the case at first sight. And the parallel reave systems of Dartmoor present the prehistorians of today with a much greater challenge to their understanding than the Great Central Trackway ever provided for that of our predecessors. That is what the rest of this book is about.

3: The search for a pattern

In the summer of 1972, it seemed likely that reaves would be found to occur widely on Dartmoor – single reaves like the ones we had found in the Plym valley, or 'parallel' reaves of the type which Gawne and Somers Cocks had discussed. Only in the areas covered by modern fields and the intakes of the Improvers would reaves have been totally obliterated; elsewhere, out on the open moor, they should have survived. Since Dartmoor covers a large area, the number of visible reaves should be quite considerable, raising the exciting possibility that they might be not so much recorded as individual antiquities as recognized as parts of a boundary system indicating the pattern of ancient territories. Such a discovery would be a considerable step forward, since ancient land boundaries in areas such as Wessex had not so far yielded much territorial information.

The next step was to seek out as many reaves as possible and put them on the map. There were three ways of doing this – looking through archaeological and topographic literature, scanning air photos, and searching for reaves in the field. A literature search gave me a good start. No one had collected together all the references to reaves and 'ancient trackways' but it was remarkable how many there were. Apart from the work by Gawne and Somers Cocks, who had picked out seven parallel reave systems, the main sources were Samuel Rowe's *Perambulation of Dartmoor* and William Crossing's *Guide to Dartmoor*. Rowe tended to describe sites with reasonable accuracy:[1]

At the foot of the western pile of this conspicuous tor, we shall observe a trackway, running from south-east to north-west, intersected at the extremity by another, tending to the converse points of the compass, and discernible to the extent of two hundred and forty yards. The adjacent commons abound with similar remains of trackways and tracklines. One of these, of very marked character, comes down the hill from Rippon Tor and crossing both the Bovey and the Ashburton road, may be traced for about two miles .... Following the winding course of the trackline mentioned above, we shall find ourselves on the high road to Chagford ....

Crossing, too, refers to a number of reaves, mostly treating them in typical guide-book fashion, as curiosities to be noted in passing or used as route-markers by the rambler. As we have already seen, his comments about some of the wilder claims made for reaves could be quite withering. Here he is discussing a reave on Walkhampton Common:[2]

These reaves have been said to extend for a very considerable distance; one of them, indeed, as far as Chagford. If the visitor considers that a hiatus of a few miles here and there does not render this doubtful, and is quite ready to believe, if he picks up a line anywhere to the north or south of the point at which all traces were lost, that he is still following the same reave, he may, if he cares for a long tramp, satisfy himself that it really does go to Chagford.

One or two of the early antiquaries also noted reaves, in various papers printed in the *Transactions of the Devonshire Association*. The only reasonably competent account of reaves, however, was that by the Rev. Arthur Prowse, in 1890; he was writing about a group of prehistoric enclosures and hut-circles on the eastern edge of Taw Marsh, on the north-east part of Dartmoor.[3]

The best available air photographs were a set of colour prints taken in 1969 under the auspices of the University College of Wales at Aberystwyth. They were commissioned for a survey of vegetation patterns and livestock density, so they didn't show very much detail, and they were taken when the sun was too high in the sky to create the kind of shadow effects which archaeologists find so helpful. I had to make the best of it, poring over the prints with the aid of a magnifying glass.

Looked at in this way, much of Dartmoor appears dark and forbidding, a matt mass of peat and heather, oozing with water in bogs and streams, gutted and gridded by the trenches of nineteenth-century peat-cutters. On some of the hill-tops, large bare cairns glint in the sun; a few prehistoric people, at least, were buried out here. And then as the plane flies on towards the edge of the Moor, the next print takes you into a more pastoral world, where cloud-shadows scud across grass-covered slopes, speckled with sheep, cattle and ponies. Here the impact of man is much more obvious – and much more complicated.

A

12 Reaves from the air: part of the Dartmeet parallel reave system on Holne Moor, east of the valley of the Aller Brook (see fig. 34). Note the large circular prehistoric house, and not far away a less conspicuous D-shaped building attached to a reave (A on photo). *Photo: 846 Naval Air Squadron*

The tin-miners have left lines of pits, each line like the craters of a stick of bombs, and they have turned over the stream-beds and left piles of exposed gravel there. They have dug leats – long aqueducts running sometimes for miles around the contour – and piled up buries, long earth mounds for their rabbits to live in. Then there are abandoned fields and farms and lanes of the Middle Ages; massive 'corn-ditches' to keep out the king's deer, wide droveways to take the sheep out onto the open moor. Quite a few of the medieval fields were re-used in the wetter conditions of succeeding centuries, leaving a pattern of closely-spaced furrows. Then there are the gashes made by the sledges of tinners and peat-cutters, and the ruler-straight walls of the Improvers, the occasional recent bomb crater or pipeline trench.

This outer zone of moorland, just outside present-day enclosed land, was obviously the one to concentrate on. Looking for the first time at air photos of the two largest systems of parallel reaves noted by Gawne and Somers Cocks, I was amazed. The reaves (figs. 12, 13) looked so relentless and uncompromising, crossing streams, scaling rock-strewn hillsides, running up to rugged granite tors and continuing on the other side, the insistent, grid-like pattern emerging where present-day fields give way to a patch of rough moorland. Prehistoric surveyors had to lay out field systems between predetermined limits often some considerable distance apart. One system, already noted by Gawne and Somers Cocks, looks particularly impressive from the air, incorporating as it does the steep-sided ravine of the river Dart just below Dartmeet, and running over the rock-strewn slopes of Yar and Corndon Tors. It is six and a half kilometres (four miles) from one end of the system to

13 Part of the Rippon Tor parallel reave system on Horridge Common. The spacing of the circular prehistoric houses and their relationship with the reaves make them a classic neighbourhood group; the behaviour of the short, narrow lane which approaches one of them (A) is characteristic. *Photo: National Monument Record*

the other – in London terms, the distance from Liverpool Street station to Paddington.

Clearly, these ancient field systems were supposed to be laid out in gridiron fashion and to cover very large areas, but that didn't mean a landscape of ruler-straight lines running from end to end of each field system, as in the American mid-West. Conformity to the prevailing axis was relaxed; for instance, the rugged terrain chosen by the surveyors of the Dart-meet system, where one end is barely visible from the other, meant that the axis had to swerve markedly in

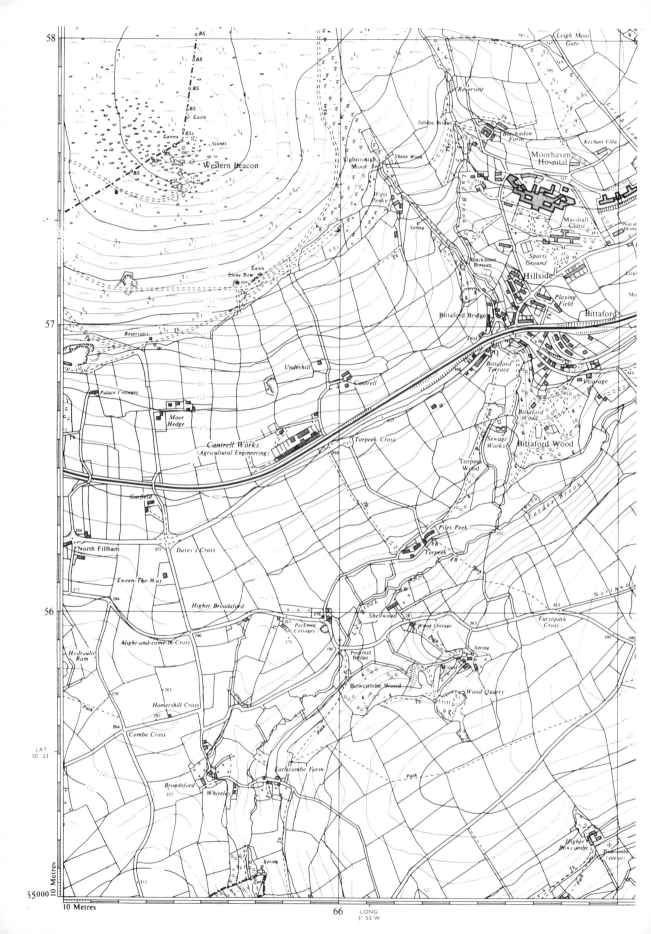

the middle of the system, between Corndon Tor and North Tor, in order to reach its objective (fig.35).

On eastern Dartmoor there are two very large parallel systems, each covering over 3000 hectares (7500 acres), which I named the Dartmeet system and the Rippon Tor system; the latter includes the settlement site at Foale's Arrishes and the Rippon Tor 'homestead' (fig. 1), which I have already mentioned. The other parallel systems have been to a large extent blotted out by the more recent fields which make up the present-day land-use pattern. A case in point is the parallel reave system near Kestor, on north-east Dartmoor. Here the moorland part of the reave system is quite small, but a glance at the map shows that the orientation of the system — roughly east–west — has been followed by quite a few of the present-day field-walls, suggesting that the system probably extended as far as the South Teign river. This is a good example of what I call 'fossilisation' of an ancient field system; another one occurs in the Ivybridge-Bittaford area (figs. 14 and 69).

It soon became clear that parallel reave systems were once present around much of the fringe of Dartmoor, except possibly parts of the north and north-west, and even here the apparent gaps could easily be due to poor survival of the evidence. There were also reave systems on the isolated, bracken-covered hill-tops to the east of Dartmoor. Easdon Down is a particularly good example. There are reave systems to the east, west, north and south of this prominent, outlying hill; the reaves are fossilised by existing field-walls and they are also present among the gorse and bracken of the unenclosed upper slopes of the hill.

If it was relatively easy to pick out parallel reave systems, what about single reaves, of the kind John Collis and I had studied in the Plym valley? In 1973 John and I came to understand more about ancient land division in the area when we were checking up on an 'Ancient Wall' marked on the Six-Inch map and shown as running across Shaugh Moor, just to the south of a hill called Saddlesborough (fig. 5). This turned out to be the end wall, the terminal reave as we later came to call it, of a parallel system whose axis ran roughly south-west towards the village of Wotter. This showed that the reaves we had discovered the year before were located about two kilometres (one

mile) beyond the upper limit of Bronze Age enclosed land, which tended to support the idea that they were subdividing open pasture. What kind of land division could be expected out here? Would the distinction between contour reaves and watershed reaves hold in other parts of the Moor? Could Bronze Age people be expected to have had a systematic approach to the problem of dividing upland pastures? And would isolated reaves, shrouded in peat and moorland vegetation, show up on high-altitude photographs taken in the middle of the day?

There were certainly some quite promising indications on the photographs, linear features well worth following up on the ground. But what was really encouraging was the sight of what were obviously prehistoric enclosures *attached* to reaves, just like the one which John Collis and I had been able to use to argue for a prehistoric date for these boundaries. For example, there was an obvious 'D-shaped enclosure' of this kind on a tongue of land between two streams, in Ruelake Pit, on the north-east part of the Moor. And in one or two places there were 'quadrant' enclosures, as I came to call them – enclosures formed by two reaves meeting at right-angles and a third, curving wall running between them. Soon it was possible to cite more than a dozen examples of D-shaped and quadrant enclosures (see fig. 21), and I felt confident that virtually all reaves must be prehistoric.

It was not long before I had a small card index of apparent references to reaves, culled from various books, and a set of maps with pencil-marks on them, indicating reave-like features seen on air photos. It was time to check these possibilities on the ground. When I started work, in September 1974, I was met by three days of gales and torrential rain, which comprehensively demonstrated the folly of buying a cheap frame tent for working in the British uplands! The city of Plymouth has many famous associations; for me, I am afraid, it will always be linked with tumble-driers. Late summer is not in fact a good time to do fieldwork on Dartmoor, because many of the best sites are located on the drier, bracken-covered areas. The fieldwork season really starts in January, by which time the dead bracken is fairly well beaten down; it is over by the end of June, although some areas may be impossible to work in by mid-May. Most of my later fieldwork was done in April, although in 1978 and 1982 I was able to take advantage of periods of study leave to work in January and March. This is the best time of year for searching for sites. There is something about winter light which can pick out the subtlest of archaeological features, and there is always the possibility that snow cover will add some special effects. For instance, when a heather-covered moor is

14 Most of the evidence for the Bittaford parallel reave system, on the southern edge of Dartmoor, comes from the regular orientation of modern field boundaries. This is what a 'fossilised' parallel reave system looks like on the map; although direct archaeological proof is lacking, this reave system may have been 3-4km from end to end and 2-3km wide. *Copyright: Ordnance Survey*

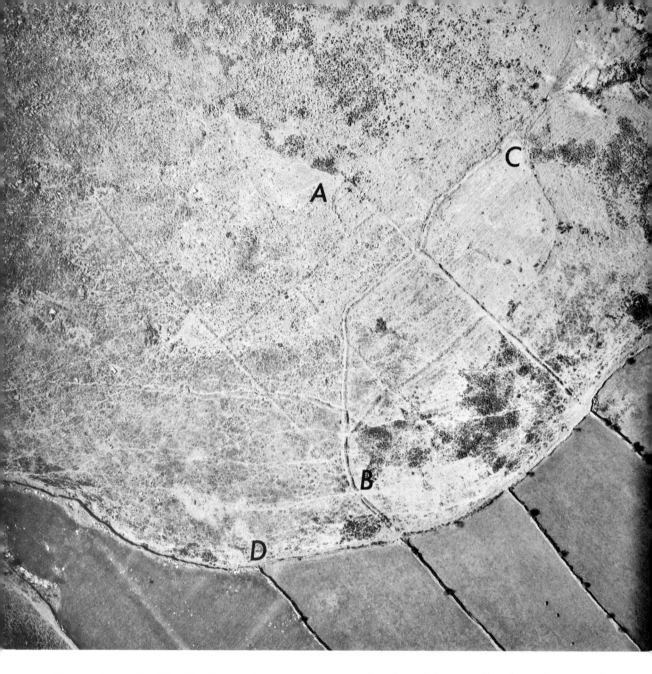

15 A good example of 'fossilised' reaves from the Dartmeet parallel reave system, just north of Yar Tor. Near the centre of the photograph are the reaves, and a prehistoric quandrant enclosure (A); B-C is a medieval ditch and bank, which has followed the course of a reave before diverging from it at B. That the modern walls conform to the axis of the reaves but do not always reflect the original pattern very accurately is shown at D, where the modern wall does not become a reave on the open moor. *Photo: National Monument Record*

blanketed in snow, and a brisk wind springs up, the snow tends to get blown off the more exposed heather stems – including, of course, the ones growing on archaeological features. So a linear feature such as a reave will show up as a dark line against a white background. And when most of the snow has melted, the reave becomes a white line, since the snow along one of its flanks will have been protected from the warmth of the sun.

Over the next couple of years I learnt to distinguish reaves from other features of the Dartmoor landscape (figs 16, 17). I learnt that reaves are low (less than about 50cm (1½ft) in height), broad (about 1-2m; 3-6ft) and made of densely packed stones, which are normally covered by a peaty turf. They are quite frequently faced with large upright stones, just like the walls of many of Dartmoor's well-known settlement enclosures. Reaves are different from medieval hedge-banks, which are made of earth, derived from an accompanying ditch; normally only reaves which have been converted into medieval hedge-banks have ditches running beside them. A ditch running round the contour, with its bank on the downhill side, is a leat (a tinners' aqueduct). In one or two places, walls of turf, probably erected in the early nineteenth century by the Improvers, have decayed and slumped so much that they can be mistaken for reaves, but the absence of stone in their construction eventually gives the game away. In some places where streams of boulders have sludged downhill during the Ice Age's brief and muddy summers, the density of the stones, some of which have been forced by natural agencies into an

upright position, may cause the reave-hunter some momentary confusion. But these streams of clitter, as they are called, are usually very obvious; they tend to radiate outwards and downwards from a hill-top tor.

Many reaves have become overgrown, demolished, or incorporated into later boundary lines. But I found it was usually quite easy to work out what had happened. It is not easy to eradicate a reave completely. Stones were often taken away in quite recent times for road-mending or wall-building; but the robbery has often been incomplete, and even where the reave has been completely removed, the trench made by the robbers can usually be picked out. And when a later hedge obliterates a reave, if you are patient enough to follow it for some distance it will usually swing away, with the reave carrying straight on ahead of you.

When I started my fieldwork, the possibility that other reaves might still lie buried beneath the peat was worrying. Clearly this was not a problem on the

16 A typical reave in the field. This one is on Rowden Down, on the northern side of the Dartmeet parallel reave system. *Photo: A. Fleming*

17 Reaves in the field: Venford Reave, the terminal of the Dartmeet system on Holne Moor, as it scales the hillside above the O Brook. To its left is an enclosure, and some parallel reaves run off it further up the hill. For a plan, see fig. 66.
Photo: A. Fleming

fringes of the Moor, where the blanket peat is quite shallow. But in the Upper Dart basin, the Improvers' country around Postbridge and Two Bridges, the situation was different. This is a badly drained area, chosen by Sir Arthur Conan Doyle to drown Stapleton, the villainous lepidopterist. Here there are certainly ancient walls which have been engulfed by valley bogs and blanket peat. One of the most striking cases occurs about one kilometre (2/3 mile) west of the Warren House Inn, where a reave runs into a broad valley bog. Although it has been completely submerged, its line is marked by a series of tall heather stems, their growth favoured by the slightly drier conditions above the reave. In other places it is possible to detect the presence of a submerged reave by noticing a slight change of level along its expected course, where the drainage has been impeded; in wet times there may even be a little waterfall.

The Upper Dart basin was once a favoured settlement area; the area round Bellever Forest in particular has some fine burial cists, cairns, stone rows, enclosures and field systems. Confused nineteenth-century reports suggest that some buried walling may have been encountered by peat-diggers in the Princetown-Two Bridges area. But there is no parallel reave system in the Upper Dart basin and, deep though the peat is in places, it is hard to believe that a whole parallel reave system could have been buried without trace. The field systems here (fig. 65) have small, irregular fields, with small houses, tending to be rather oval in plan, and situated at wall junctions; in places they are buried, or almost buried, by blanket peat. In one or two places on Dartmoor, as I discovered later, it is possible to show that these field systems are earlier in date than the reave systems.

What about the high moors, where the peat is deep enough to bury a reave completely? I have visited these remoter regions several times, keeping an eye open for reaves, but without result. Perhaps I should have conducted a more systematic search, or used one of the machines which utilise geophysical principles to enable archaeologists to locate buried structures – a resistivity meter, for instance. But I think that there are good reasons for expecting reaves to be rare or scarce on the high moors. For one thing, these areas would have been swathed in peat in the Bronze Age, although the peat would have been thinner and less extensive than it is today. It is also worth remembering that in the nineteenth century a great deal of peat-digging went on on the high moors. If anything interesting was found, local antiquaries would have got to hear about it. As we have seen, they noted the uncovering of the Great Central Trackway. They recorded the finding of wooden bowls, said to be made of oak, in the Two Bridges-Postbridge area, and

one not too far away at Skir Gert.[4] They also remarked on the evocative remnants of Dartmoor's former forest cover; Mrs Bray, writing in 1836, recorded an oak trunk ten feet long and nearly five feet in girth, for example. If reaves had been uncovered on the high moors they would almost certainly have found their way into nineteenth-century Dartmoor literature. Also, many of the peat-cuttings lie open now, and it would not be too difficult to spot reaves if they were present.

So I do not believe that many reaves have been obliterated by the growth of peat. A more serious threat to their survival has been the making of later land boundaries over the last millennium or thereabouts. Some medieval farmers noticed that they were settling on land which had already been divided up. Before I started work, W.G. Hoskins had pointed out[5] that place-names like 'Yelland', 'Yellam' and 'Yeoland', meaning 'old land', were probably coined by Saxon-speakers who noted the presence of ancient land boundaries. I can think of two places, Yalland in South Brent parish, and Yellands, just south of Meldon Hill in Chagford parish, where the names are quite possibly referring to field systems laid out in the Bronze Age.

Some later farmers ignored reaves, or failed to notice them; but others followed them when they constructed their own land boundaries. There are many tell-tale signs of this, apart from grid-like field patterns visible on modern maps. Most medieval hedge-banks, for instance, were made solely of earth, so a hedge-bank with upright stones poking out at its base could well be incorporating a reave. The stone-faced 'Devon hedges' of later times are so thick that it is impossible to see whether they are incorporating reaves or not. When you get to a gateway, it may be possible to observe the bottom course of a reave running through the gap; if there is a well-defined edge it is probably a genuine reave and not just a spread of stones dumped there more recently. Then there are the drystone walls of the nineteenth century, whose builders either used reaves as foundations or robbed them for their stone. The present 'top wall' above the hamlet of Hexworthy is continuing the line of a long reave which runs across Holne Moor; if you follow it along from the O Brook in a westerly direction, you can see a few orthostats from the reave poking out at the base, on the downhill side. Further along, this time on the uphill side, a whole line of stones lean towards the wall, at some distance from it; they were once the facing stones of the reave, which have been rudely disturbed by the wall-builders who were after the smaller stones which were helping to support them (fig. 18).

A modern boundary which has 'fossilised' a reave

18 Above Hexworthy, the facing stones are all that survive of Venford Reave after it has been robbed to build the wall on the left. These orthostats faced out onto open grazing land beyond the Dartmeet parallel reave system; their size may tell us the minimum height of the boundary when it was in use. *Photo: A. Fleming*

has two important characteristics which are immediately obvious on a map or an aerial photograph. First, its line is relatively long and direct, laid out with a distant objective in mind. Second, an ancient boundary which has been preserved as part of the modern hedge-pattern will be *dominant*; that is to say, boundaries will run up to it from either side, and the junctions they make will be staggered. Normally the dominant boundary will be approached by others; only rarely will it do the approaching itself. A good example of a dominant boundary which is almost certainly following a reave line occurs to the west of Hameldown. Here a modern wall, itself continuing the line of a reave, runs down the western flank of Hameldown from Two Barrows to the Rowden-

Grimspound road. West of the road, the line continues through the fields for a distance of about 700m (770 yards) in the form of a dominant hedge-line, with no fewer than ten boundaries staggered along it. This hedge is also a parish boundary, which tends to imply that it is very ancient.

These are some of the lessons which I was to learn during my fieldwork on Dartmoor. In the autumn of 1974, however, the finer points of landscape archaeology were not uppermost in my mind. A few days' fieldwork were enough to convince me that there *were* reaves in many of the places mentioned by writers like Rowe and Crossing; that reaves *did* show up on aerial photographs; and that the work of Gawne and Somers Cocks on parallel reave systems was fundamentally sound. Clearly there was enough material here for a long-term research project, which would seek financial support for the accomplishment of a number of defined objectives. So the Dartmoor Reave Project was born, and from 1974 onwards my work had an annual rhythm – the appeal for funds in December, fieldwork in spring and summer, the

19 Venford Reave, terminal of the Dartmeet system, on Holne Moor. In the distance can be seen a modern wall which has been built on the line of the reave. *Photo: A. Fleming*

20 Three Barrows Reave, a watershed reave between the Erme and the Avon on southern Dartmoor, seen heading north towards the heart of the South Moor from one of the Bronze Age burial cairns from which it takes it name. In the late sixteenth century, however, it was described as 'a long conger of stones called le Rowe Rew'. It was this relationship between reave and cairn which made William Crossing, author of Dartmoor's best-known guidebook, sceptical about the idea that reaves were trackways.
Photo: A. Fleming

writing of a typescript interim report in October.

The work of the next eighteen months or so was rather like doing a jigsaw puzzle. Various fragments made their appearance on my maps. First, there were the parallel reave systems, most of which had already been briefly recorded by Gawne and Somers Cocks. Then, out on the higher moors, beyond the parallel systems, were some conspicuous single reaves. Some of the best examples were to be found on the South Moor, on the watersheds between the main river valleys. On the south-east fringe of Dartmoor a long reave which I christened Pupers Reave runs from Skerraton Gate along the ridge to a large burial cairn on Pupers Hill; it changes direction at the cairn and heads off in a NNE direction towards the Mardle Brook. This one was called 'le Rowe Rewe' in an Elizabethan document – and so was another striking reave some five kilometres (three miles) to the west (fig. 20), which runs out of the head of the West Glaze Brook up to the Three Barrows on Ugborough Moor, along the watershed between the Avon and the Erme[6]. Three Barrows Reave, as I have called it, continues further north, beyond the cairns, before dying out in somewhat mysterious circumstances. Further west, Rook Reave behaves in much the same way, aiming for a cairn and then apparently disappearing somewhere on the watershed between Plym and Yealm. Another reave heading out towards the high moors which I was able to check at an early stage was quite well recorded in 1890 by Rev. Arthur Prowse.[3] This one, Taw Marsh Reave, traverses the south-western flank of Cosdon Hill, skirts the eastern side of Taw Marsh, and then runs over Metheral Hill and down-slope to Steeperton Brook (the current Outdoor Leisure map, incidentally, still marks it as a footpath, leading nowhere!).

So on both North and South Moors there were reaves in the zone beyond the parallel systems, running radially towards the higher ground, sometimes along watersheds. In this zone of open pasture land there were also 'contour reaves', running along hillsides, like the one which John Collis and I had initially located. And in a few places there were what I came to call 'block systems' – single reaves occurring together in an organised arrangement, as if

to make up large blocks of pasture land rather than the relatively small 'fields' found in parallel systems. There seemed to be a block system of this kind in the area to the north and west of Warren House Inn, and we mapped it in July 1975, in the first season of the Reave Project (fig. 21). In this zone of reaves around the southern edge of Fernworthy Forest – which will undoubtedly have destroyed some critical evidence – we seemed to be working with a system of blocks of land demarcated by interconnected reaves which stretched from Stannon and White Ridge in the west across the B3212 to Birch Tor, East Bovey Head and Shapley Common to the east – an area four or five kilometres (c.2-3 miles) across, whose boundaries were impossible to determine.

Single reaves, parallel systems, areas divided by reaves into large blocks of open pasture(?) – could these fragments be integrated in any way? Well, it soon emerged that there was a connection between parallel reave systems and single reaves. It seemed to be the usual practice for the axial reaves in parallel reave systems to run at right angles to the edge of the Moor and end on a single reave whose equivalent in modern Scotland would be called the 'head dyke' and which in the Dartmoor context I came to call the *terminal* reave. Now the concept of the terminal reave was clearly a primary organisational principle of ancient land division on Dartmoor. As the enclosed fields came to the edge of open pasture, they all stopped along one line, usually a fairly straight line – a very different situation from that of today, where the irregular line of the 'top wall' reflects the complex history of the ebb and flow of piecemeal enclosure at the moor edge. In contrast, the prehistoric blocks of enclosed land were systems planned on a large scale.

The longest terminal reave on Dartmoor is Venford Reave, which runs across Holne Moor, forming the southern boundary of the Dartmeet parallel system (fig. 19). Its eastern end emerges from a modern wall corner about two kilometres (one mile) west of Holne village. Tracing it from here across Holne Lee, down to the Venford Reservoir fence, across Holne Moor and down to the O Brook, noting the axial reaves which join it on the northern side, makes an excellent archaeological walk. West of the O Brook, the line is continued by a relatively modern drystone wall; traces of its ancient predecessor can be seen beneath and beside it (fig. 18).

Further west, the axial reaves of the Dartmeet parallel system are discontinued south of Hexworthy, and it is apparently impossible to trace Venford Reave further west. Or so I thought when I first did fieldwork in the area. It was only later, when I was scanning an air photograph, that I suddenly spotted, to my amazement, a reave about one kilometre (2/3 mile)

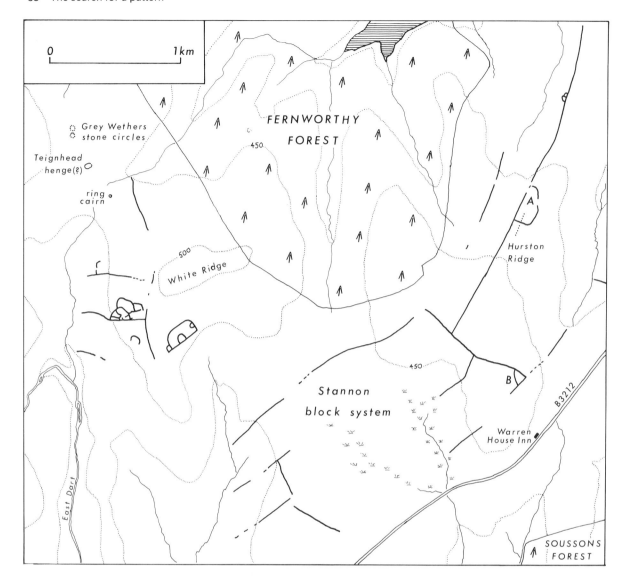

21 Plan of the Stannon 'block system', as investigated in 1975 (there are other traces of it further west). Here land is laid out in a rectilinear pattern largely without the small fields and settlements characteristic of parallel reave systems. Also visible are the Hurston Ridge D-shaped enclosure (A), which has slighted a stone row, and a quadrant enclosure (B). A walk from the Warren House Inn to Grey Wethers stone circles can take in an interesting variety of archaeological sites.

further west, emerging from the modern 'top wall' opposite the ruined house at Swincombe, and heading for the river. Further fieldwork showed that the reave crosses the Swincombe river here and heads in the direction of Moorlands Farm; modern enclosures make it impossible to trace it further west.

Venford Reave is one of Dartmoor's longest reaves,

with a minimum length of 7.5 kilometres (5 miles). For much of its length it forms the terminal reave of the Dartmeet system. But clearly it was designed to do more than this; it had a regional function, involving the southern edge of the eastern part of the Upper Dart basin.

At about the same time, I discovered a reave of a similar kind on south-west Dartmoor. On the west bank of the Plym, on Wigford Down, I knew that there was a small parallel reave system, with its axis running roughly north-west/south-east, and the terminal reave at right angles to the axis, running over the eastern part of the down in the direction of Brisworthy Plantation. An air photograph suggested that a continuation of this reave ran across Ringmoor Down, on the watershed, and then skirted Gutter Tor on its north-west side. It was when I was near Gutter Tor, where the reave apparently ended, that I suddenly noticed that it could be seen about 500 metres (550 yards) further east, running into the distance. I could then follow it to a point near the head of Narrator Brook – where it is interrupted by tin-workings – and on up the hillside through a zone of later destruction to the point where it ends, on the northernmost of the two Bronze Age cairns known as Eylesbarrow.

Eylesbarrow Reave is a classic reave, nearly eight kilometres (five miles) in length, and aiming for a distant Bronze Age cairn. And like Venford Reave, it is performing two roles – a local one and a more regional one. Not only is it the terminal of the Wigford Down parallel system, it is the fourth of the southern Dartmoor watershed reaves, running between the Upper Plym and the river Meavy and its headwater tributaries around the modern Burrator Reservoir.

So by early 1976, fieldwork had demonstrated that some reaves were longer than had been apparent from the literature or the photographs where they had been first picked up; others became longer after a second or third visit. It became clear that I could not rely solely on air photographs; there were zones where a heather-covered reave could not be expected to show up against a heather background, and the same tended to be true for undifferentiated grassland and dense gorse. In these areas reaves tended to be discovered by fieldwork. On the higher moors, and on the north-western side of Dartmoor, reaves seemed to be largely absent. Was this really the case? I had to spend a good deal of time checking the apparently blank areas, deliberately traversing zones where nothing was known and finding vantage points from which I could scan such areas with field-glasses. Sometimes the bank which had looked so promising in the distance turned out to be medieval, or the dark line seen from the other side of the valley proved to be the edge of a modern track. Occasionally there was triumph, as a slight vegetation change spotted from a long way off turned out to be a genuine reave.

This kind of fieldwork was frequently exhilarating. It was usually possible to spot something new – a new site, or a new relationship between sites, like the case I found on Hurston Ridge, where the wall of a big D-shaped enclosure attached to a reave was cutting right across a stone row (fig. 21). Changes in light conditions, in the weather, in vegetation, in the direction from which I approached an area – all these things could make a profound difference. I was learning the subtler points of landscape archaeology. But when would all this walking around and making marks on maps produce the pattern I was looking for?

4: The pattern revealed

The breakthrough came one day in July 1976. The objective was to search the zone between the Erme and the Avon, on the southern part of the Moor. Surely there ought to be more reaves in this zone, and not just the 'watershed reaves', Pupers and Three Barrows? I spent a warm, sleepy summer's day searching these quiet moors. It was frustrating; no new reaves were discovered. That evening I wondered whether a few lines on a map would ever became a meaningful pattern. Then a thought struck me: surely, by this time, fruitless searches like the one in which I had just been engaged carried their own meaning? Could it be that the blank areas really were blank areas in the Bronze Age? For southern Dartmoor that would mean that the pattern displayed by the watershed reaves – Pupers, Three Barrows, Rook, Eylesbarrow and probably Walkhampton Common – could be taken at face value. From this point of view, each river valley would constitute a single 'territory' of pasture land, probably of higher quality than is the case today, judging by the density of prehistoric hut-circles and enclosures there. The 'territories' centred on the Avon, the Erme/Yealm, the Plym and the Meavy were all four or five kilometres (three miles) from side to side, a measurement conditioned, of course, by the drainage pattern on southern Dartmoor (fig. 22).

The more I thought about land division on this scale, the more attractive such a proposition became, because it made sense of a number of other things. The sheer length of some reaves, Venford and Eylesbarrow in particular, was entirely appropriate for territories of this sort of size. These two reaves, by functioning both as terminal reaves and as individual boundaries, had also demonstrated a link between the single reaves and the parallel reave systems. And the latter, presumably blocks of enclosed land, were also conceived on a grand scale. On eastern Dartmoor, much of the Dartmeet system had survived, and it was easy to work out that it once covered over 3000 hectares (7500 acres); the Rippon Tor system to the east seemed to be almost as large. Unfortunately, it soon became clear that in many areas it would be impossible to work out the original size of parallel systems because most of them had been to a greater or lesser extent engulfed by fields in current use.

But there were indications that rather large parallel systems had once existed on the southern fringe of the Moor. In the Plym valley area, Saddlesborough Reave acted as the terminal of a parallel system on Shaugh Moor. Further west, on Shaden Moor, parallel reaves on the same axis running up to a modern wall on the line of Saddlesborough Reave were obviously part of the same system, which must have a minimum width of two and a half kilometres (one mile), and a minimum length of about one kilometre (2/3 mile). In the Avon valley area, I discovered that there are parallel reaves on Corringdon Ball, running roughly NE–SW. However, in this area the dominant axis seems to have been NW–SE, judging by the layout of the modern field boundaries immediately to the east. A conservative view would be that the principles on which parallel systems were laid out here operated over an area approximately two kilometres by one (one mile by 2/3 mile). However, looking at the configuration of present-day field boundaries on the map now, I am inclined to believe that most of the area from South Brent to Corringdon Ball Gate, between the Avon and the East Glaze Brook, was once laid out in this fashion.

Between Bittaford and Ivybridge, on the lower slopes of Western Beacon, the pattern of present-day fields (figs. 14, 69) displays a dominant axis, suggesting that there was a parallel system here, perhaps extending as far as Ugborough. If so, it would have covered an area about two kilometres by three (one mile by two). Vital confirmation of this idea came when I searched just beyond the present-day top wall, near the Bittaford stone row, and found a short stretch of what must have been the terminal reave of this system, preserved on the open moor.

It was beginning to look as if each 'territory' on southern Dartmoor had two components – a large parallel reave system demarcating enclosed land, and a large zone of unenclosed grazing land between watershed reaves and thus based on a major river valley. Perhaps the Upper Dart basin, too, could be fitted into this pattern; after all, Venford Reave,

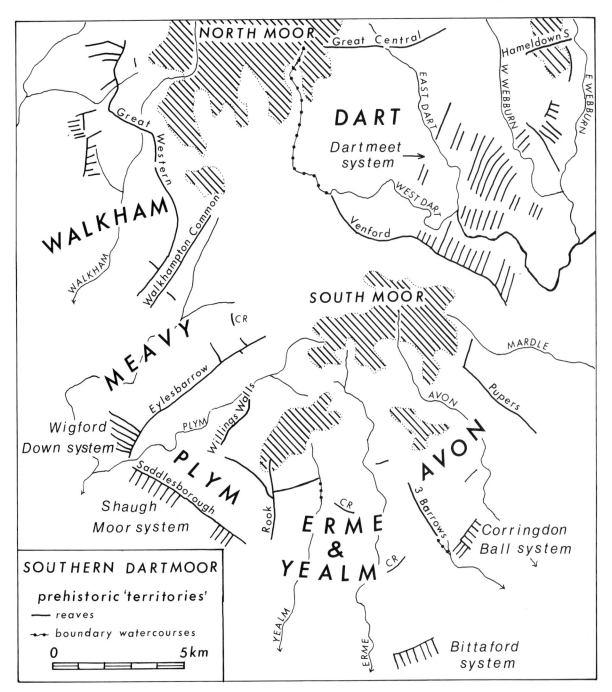

22 The pattern of reaves on the southern part of Dartmoor, as it emerged in 1976. The map shows 'territories' based on river valleys; each territory has a large parallel reave system (a zone of enclosed land) and a grazing zone, separated from its neighbour by a watershed reave (e.g. Three Barrows Reave) and from the high moors by a contour reave (in the Rook Reave area). As can be seen, the contour reave is incomplete; detached sections are marked CR on this map.

continuing in a westerly direction from the south-west corner of the Dartmeet system, suggested that the area around Dunnabridge was included in the unenclosed part of the Dartmeet system 'territory'.

I was beginning to understand the nature of the pattern (fig. 22), and the scale of ancient land division systems on Dartmoor. Now it was becoming possible to predict which reaves would probably turn out to be

23 The Great Western Reave, straggling up the NW slopes of Roos Tor; scenically, this is one of the most spectacular reaves on Dartmoor. *Photo: A. Fleming*

longer, where parallel systems ought to occur, and which areas should prove to be blank. I could hardly wait to get into the field, to see whether my predictions would be fulfilled. Unfortunately, at this time (August and September 1976) I was committed to other activities – helping Dr Geoffrey Wainwright and a team from the Central Excavation Unit at the DoE with some survey work on Shaugh Moor, and then the first season of my own excavations on Holne Moor. That summer the sun blazed down for day after day from a cloudless sky; but my fieldwork was done in the quiet, dew-laden time just after sunrise. And things were starting to fall into place.

One of the most encouraging discoveries occurred on the western side of the Moor. I had for some time been aware of three isolated reaves in this area. One ran just west of the B3212 road from Yelverton to Princetown, near Sharpitor, and then passed to the west of Leeden Tor, across the western side of Walkhampton Common. The second made a dramatic ascent of the rock-strewn north-western

slopes of Roos Tor (fig. 23) and emerged on the other side. Further north, at Whittor, there was a reave which approached the tor from the south and emerged on the northern side.

I had previously assumed that each of these three reaves had a strictly local significance. But now, with larger-scale land division in mind, it occurred to me, looking at the map (fig. 24), that they might all be parts of one and the same reave. It proved easy to demonstrate that the Roos Tor reave and the Whittor reave were connected. Between the Roos Tor reave and the one on Walkhampton Common the gap was greater. Fortunately, however, Hansford Worth's plan of the stone rows at Merrivale marked an 'old bank' running past the eastern ends of the two main rows (fig. 60);[1] this proved to be a very dilapidated reave. It proved impossible to follow it very far in a northerly direction,

24 Map of the Great Western Reave, the longest known single reave, which runs along the western edge of the Moor, defining the lower edge of upland pasture. Three stretches of unfinished reaved beyond the edge of this map suggest that it may have been intended to run some 4km further north. The position of Walkhampton Common Reave (fig. 9) is also indicated.

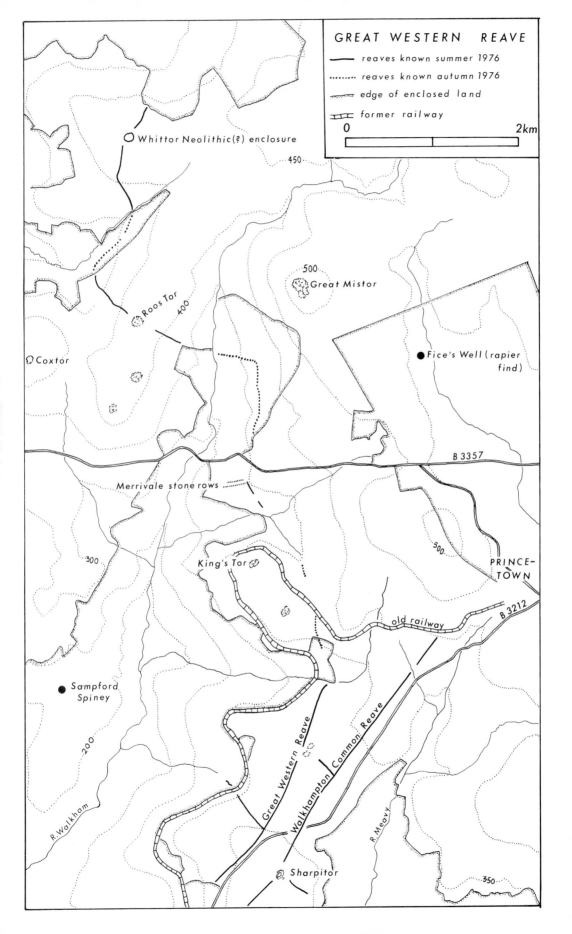

GREAT WESTERN REAVE

— reaves known summer 1976
····· reaves known autumn 1976
‒‒ edge of enclosed land
╫╫ former railway

0   2km

○ Whittor Neolithic(?) enclosure

450

500
⊙ Great Mistor

⊙ Roos Tor   400

○ Coxtor

● Fice's Well (rapier find)

B 3357

Merrivale stone rows

300

500

King's Tor ⊙

PRINCE-TOWN

old railway   B 3212

● Sampford Spiney

200

Great Western Reave

Walkhampton Common Reave

R. Walkham

R. Meavy

⊙ Sharpitor

350

through the Merrivale group of hut-circles. However, now that I was beginning to get some idea of the scale of the Dartmoor land boundaries, I started prospecting further north. Sure enough, just inside the wall enclosing Merrivale Warren, was a reave in just the right position; then, in the middle of the warren, it turned to head for Roos Tor. Half the gap had been closed.

The next day I went back to Merrivale to follow Worth's 'old bank' in the opposite direction. Soon it approached a brook at right angles and stopped. This was disconcerting; projecting the line of the boundary across the brook would mean following the course of a stream barely visible among tinner's spoil-heaps. But by this time I knew that watercourses were sometimes used as boundaries; Three Barrows Reave, for example, runs into the head of a stream. So I followed this stream up, and was glad to see a short stretch of reave beyond the marshy ground at its head. Then came another break, as I traversed the unlovely post-industrial surroundings of Foggintor quarries. Then, just on the other side of the railway track, was a reave running south, in exactly the right direction. Ten minutes later I was on the north-west side of Walkhampton Common. The gap had been closed; I had discovered a reave over 10km (six miles) in length! It seemed appropriate to call this remarkably long boundary the Great Western Reave, a name which simultaneously describes its character, alludes to the fact that it is crossed by a former branch of the GWR, and contains an echo of the 'Great Central Trackway' myth of the nineteenth century.

What was the function of the Great Western Reave? It behaves like a contour reave, like the Cholwichtown and Willings Walls Reaves in the Plym valley area. The Great Western tends to run at about 350m (1150ft) above sea level, except where it rises to cross the 450m (1500ft) summits of Roos Tor and Whittor; it hardly ever dips below 330m (1100ft). Much the same can be said for the Plym valley contour reaves, whose altitude ranges between about 320m (1050ft) and 370m (1225ft).

The discovery of the Great Western Reave, and the comparisons made with the Plym valley situation, suggested that there was a third element in the South Dartmoor pattern – a contour reave, located well beyond the terminal reaves, whose function seemed to be to separate the higher moorlands from the grazing land on the lower slopes. This stimulated me to look for the contour reave in other places. It turned out, however, that on southern Dartmoor no further continuous contour reaves could be found – only a few short stretches of reave behaving in the appropriate manner. Going east of Penn Moor Reave, for instance, there is a reave about 500m (550 yards) long

on the south-western slopes of Stalldown which is in roughly the right position (fig. 5). To the west of Willings Walls Reave, in the Plym valley, the most convincing contour reaves are a spur reave leaving Eylesbarrow Reave, heading in a northerly direction towards Combshead Tor, and another disconnected section of reave just west of the Down Tor stone row and circle. What might have happened between here and the Great Western Reave is unclear. The Great Western Reave itself could easily have continued further north. Although it seems to be impossible to follow it through the enclosed land north of Whittor, there are two separate sections of reave further north, on the southern and western slopes of Standon Hill, in just the right position.

These short stretches of contour reave are all palpably unfinished. It is of course possible that the apparent gaps were filled in by wooden fences, which have left no trace on the present-day land surface. However, taking the situation at face value, it looks as if the contour reave was an important concept which was only fully implemented in the Plym valley and along the centre-west fringe of the Moor. The implication, I think, must be that the grazing land on the higher moors was being set apart somehow from lower-lying pastures.

Soon I was able to write an article, suggesting a pattern of 'territories' for the southern half of the Moor.[2] These were based on the Meavy, Plym, Erme/Yealm, Avon valleys and the Upper Dart basin (fig. 22). There were three categories of land; each territory had a parallel reave system, a river valley or low-lying grazing zone, and access to the higher moors. I suggested that the Upper Dart territory included the Dartmeet parallel reave system, plus a grazing zone bounded by Venford Reave to the south, the West Dart to the west, and the Great Central Reave (the 'Great Central Trackway' rechristened) which survives well from Lower White Tor to the East Dart, and more problematically in the area east of Postbridge. People based in this territory would have access to the higher hills of both North and South Dartmoor.

These territories cluster around the higher moors rather like the medieval parishes, whose people enjoyed rights of common on Dartmoor. I believe that in prehistoric times too the North Moor, the South Moor and probably an East Moor as well would have developed as common pastures used by several social groups. Eventually, a contour reave demarcating the zone of common grazing on the higher hills was completed in some places, and commenced in others. Perhaps the zones where the contour reave was completed were those where there was greatest pressure on grazing land; certainly west and south-west Dartmoor has a high density of hut-circles and impressive-looking enclosures.

Beyond the terminal reave of each parallel reave system, and below the contour reave, where it existed, lay a zone of unenclosed pasture land based on a river valley or basin. These zones – areas such as the Upper Plym valley, for example – contain a diverse range of ruined prehistoric settlement sites: groups of small hut-circles, larger hut-circles inside and outside walled enclosures, and complex enclosures with several additions and subdivisions. Very few of these sites have been dated archaeologically; but if the reaves can be seen as a response to pressure on land, it may be safe to suggest that a fair proportion of these settlements were occupied in the later Bronze Age.

Talking about pressure on land, it is interesting to note that there is some evidence for the subdivision of these zones of pasture. On western Dartmoor, near Whittor and in the Cox Tor/Whitchurch Common area, reaves divide land into a series of blocks which are not 'fields' like the subdivisions within parallel reave systems. Elsewhere on the southern and south-western parts of the moor there are various enigmatic short lengths of reave within the 'pasture zone'. In areas like the Upper Plym valley, tributary streams may have been used as minor boundaries.

At this time I wondered whether the distribution of ceremonial monuments might fit these territorial arrangements. Would it turn out that there was, say, one stone circle or one group of stone rows per territory? It proved impossible to find a good agreement between the reave territories and the circles. However, the relationship between stone rows and reaves is an interesting one, which I was able to discuss in my article. What little dating evidence exists for stone rows suggests that they date from the earlier part of the Bronze Age, and thus pre-date reaves. My fieldwork tended to confirm this, and I was able to suggest several places on southern Dartmoor where stone rows are cut through, impinged upon, or even possibly destroyed by reaves. The layout of the Dartmeet reave system, for example, seems to have ignored the Yar Tor stone row. Yet in other places, stone rows seem to have been respected. It is not uncommon to find a stone row just on the moorward side of a terminal reave; good examples may be found on Holne Moor (fig. 34), Shaugh Moor, and at Cantrell (just above the Bittaford parallel system, fig. 14).

Quite a number of rows are found near terminal and contour reaves. We must therefore take seriously the possibility that these stone rows, and the cairns and standing stones associated with them, were placed in areas transitional between zones of different land use, for example on the edge of an upland common, or perhaps on actual boundaries like the cairns recently excavated at Trelystan in the Welsh border country, where evidence for long fences was uncovered.[3] So the 'respect' shown to stone rows by reaves may be a sign that some boundaries remained in use throughout the Bronze Age. And it must be clear by now that the reave-builders also treated large cairns as aiming-points, and sometimes – as on Pupers Hill – as points where it was appropriate to change direction. Whether this indicates continuity of boundaries is a moot point; large cairns have always been useful boundary-marks, as they were on Dartmoor in much more recent times.

Tradition has it that in the early Middle Ages Dartmoor was available for intercommoning to all the men of Devon, and there is some evidence from those times that some estates in southern Devon had outlying portions on the edge of the Moor, in connection with this custom.[4] It looks as if the prehistoric pattern of land-use was similar to this in some respects – and it is a pattern which has been suggested in other prehistoric contexts. Francis Pryor, working on the ditched field systems at Fengate, just outside Peterborough, and John Coles and Alan Hibbert, discussing the uses of the Somerset Levels in prehistoric times, have argued that the fenlands were valuable seasonal resources.[5] It might be possible to visualise the Dartmoor uplands, too, as a zone of valued summer grazing in prehistoric times.

But there must have been more to it than that. The presence of ceremonial monuments – large burial cairns, stone circles, and some stone rows – beyond the contour reave suggest that the higher moors must have been an important zone of social interaction. People living in scattered communities have to be able to exchange goods and services, to seek marriage partners, to maintain social and economic relation-ships, to know about more distant social and political structures; if a developed social hierarchy exists, those in the upper echelons have to have some institutional means of maintaining their position. Solutions to these organisational problems may well influence the way in which land is used; different zones not only have different uses, they also play different roles in people's view of the world. The ceremonial monuments seen on Dartmoor and elsewhere in the British uplands suggest the important role which these areas played in the ideological or spiritual value systems of prehistoric peoples. In this sense we may well have underestimated the importance of extensive tracts of intercommoning land in prehistoric times.

But what of the northern half of Dartmoor? Would it be possible to find a similar pattern there? By 1978 I had quite a good general knowledge of the location and character of reaves all around the fringe of the

Moor. There were numerous reaves all the way along the Moor's north-east side, from Hameldown, where the south Dartmoor survey had stopped, all the way to Cosdon. They included the parallel system near Kestor, which had become quite well known since Lady Fox's excavations at the Round Pound in the 1950s.[6] There were also reaves and parallel systems on most of the outlying heath-clad hilltops to the east. Reaves had been found not just on nearby hilltops like Meldon and Easdon. Parallel reaves had been picked up towards Lustleigh, south-east of the hillfort at Hunter's Tor; on Butterdon Down; near Willingstone Rock; and on the eastern sector of Mardon Down, to the north-east of Moretonhampstead. John Collis and I, on an evening visit to the Iron Age hillfort at Cranbrook Castle, overlooking the gorge of the river Teign, had spotted a couple of single reaves just outside the hillfort; one of them apparently preceded the hillfort, as one would expect.[7] So it looked as if this form of land division was once widespread in the general area of Moretonhampstead and Lustleigh, being found up to about nine kilometres (7½ miles) from the edge of Dartmoor proper.

Northern Dartmoor, desecrated by army ranges and a military road which for some reason is open to private cars, is rather a wild, bleak region. According to the map produced by Gawne and Somers Cocks in 1968, there were no parallel reave systems at all on the fringe of the North Moor between Throwleigh Common in the north-east and Wigford Down in the south-west. I soon located reaves beside the river Taw and on Whittor; but it was clear that in this area the search for reaves was going to be a struggle. The source of the problem seemed to be the nature of the terrain. On southern Dartmoor, the gentler relief has permitted the edge of enclosed land in prehistoric and historic times to fluctuate across a fairly broad zone, providing many opportunities for the landscape archaeologist. On northern Dartmoor, on the other hand, the hills rise abruptly from the surrounding lowlands, so that fields are driven as close as possible to the edge of the zone of steeper gradient; the upper edge of enclosed land is always in much the same place, so that the prehistoric boundaries are frequently masked or destroyed by their successors.

King Wall, to the east and north-east of Lydford, illustrates this point very well. It is a top wall today, a conspicuous feature on the map (fig. 25). For most of its length it looks like a wall which has been built and repaired within the last two or three centuries. But it must surely be much older than that, since it is used as a boundary by three parishes, Sourton, Bridestowe and Lydford. Furthermore, it behaves much more like a reave than like a medieval top wall, following a very

direct line over a distance of four kilometres (2½ miles), respecting the general nature of the terrain rather than the local disposition of parcels of land. I feel that King Wall must have started life as a reave, yet despite an assiduous search for evidence, looking closely at the base of the wall and in gateways, I have been unable so far to prove it; the original character of the boundary seems to have been completely masked by its successors.

It seemed easier to try to sort out the pattern on the east and north-east fringes of the Moor, and this is what I did the next time I had study leave, early in 1982. I knew already that there were many reaves here, mostly grouped in parallel systems or at any rate demarcating rectilinear parcels of land. If the lessons learnt on southern Dartmoor could be applied here, it could be expected that reaves would turn out to be longer, parallel systems more extensive, and 'territories' bigger than at first seemed to be the case. I knew also that watercourses could act as boundaries. Also, the parallel reave systems, presumably on the most highly valued land, should prove easy to pick out, with their dominant axes of orientation and their tendency to become 'fossilised' by later field boundaries. So I was quite optimistic about the chances of picking up a pattern on this side of the Moor. These general expectations turned out to be correct; it did prove possible to suggest a territorial pattern for North and East Dartmoor, which was in general terms similar to the one devised for the southern half of the Moor.[8]

The largest parallel reave system on the East Moor was undoubtedly the one which I had labelled the Rippon Tor system (fig. 26), which was apparently second only in size to the Dartmeet system, its fairly near neighbour. The Rippon Tor system was orientated roughly NW–SE, and lay mainly between Rippon Tor itself and Buckland Beacon. However, when I got down to work in 1982, I realised that I had been too cautious in my approach to this system. In the first place, reaves and present-day field boundaries on the same axis as that of the Rippon Tor system could be found further west, on the other side of the East Webburn valley, on and just below Dunstone Down. I had cautiously assigned these to a

25 King Wall, on western Dartmoor, is something of an enigma. The wall itself is not particularly old, but it is remarkably long, dominant to all other field boundaries which meet it, and has been used by those who laid out parish boundaries (in early medieval times?). The normal fieldwork strategy for this situation is to look into gateways and gaps for traces of reaves. In this case it is impossible to prove that King Wall has been built along a reave line, though there are one or two indications.

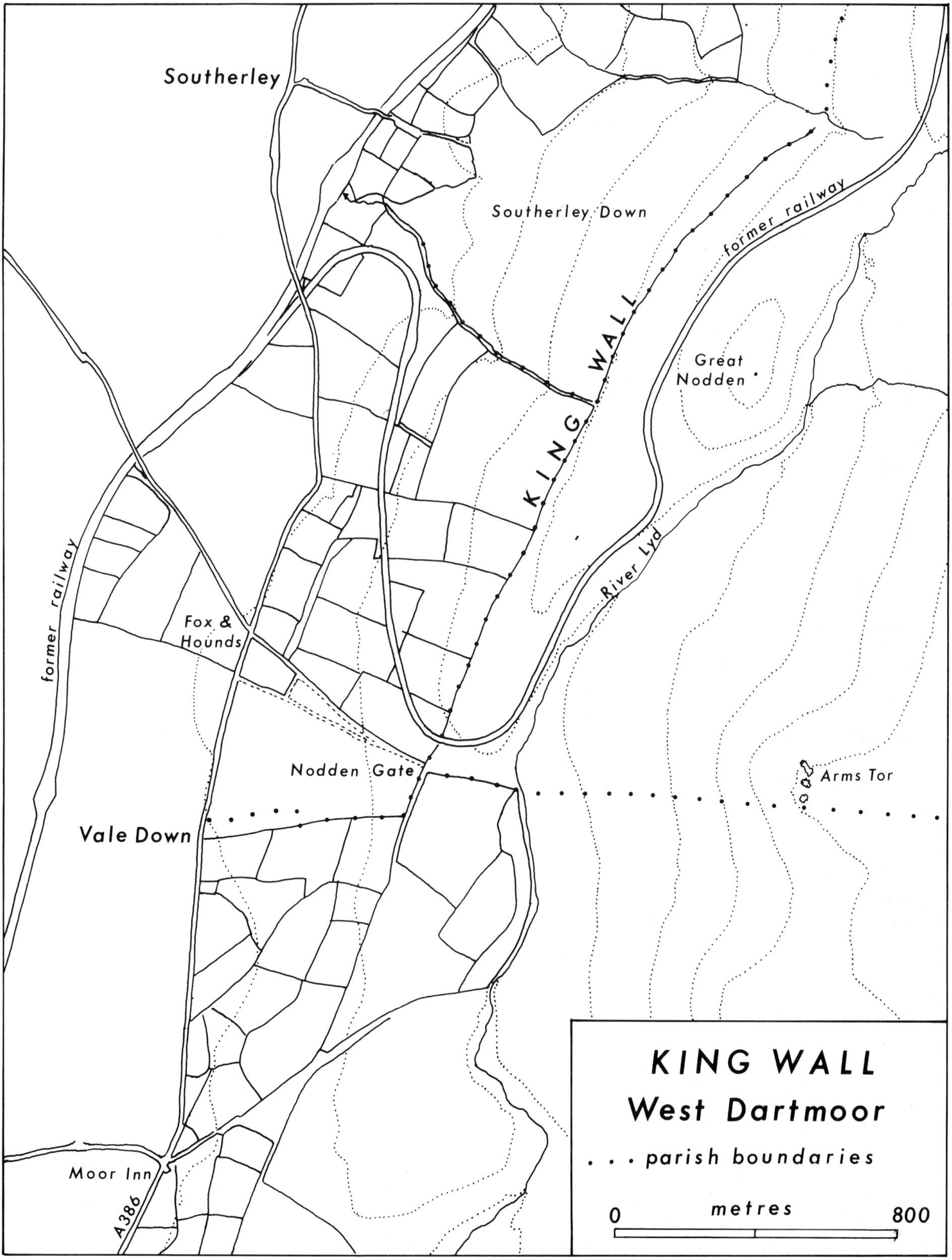

Southerley

Southerley Down

former railway

K I N G   W A L L

Great
Nodden

River Lyd

former railway

Fox &
Hounds

Nodden Gate

Arms Tor

Vale Down

Moor Inn

A386

KING WALL
West Dartmoor

. . . *parish boundaries*

metres

0   800

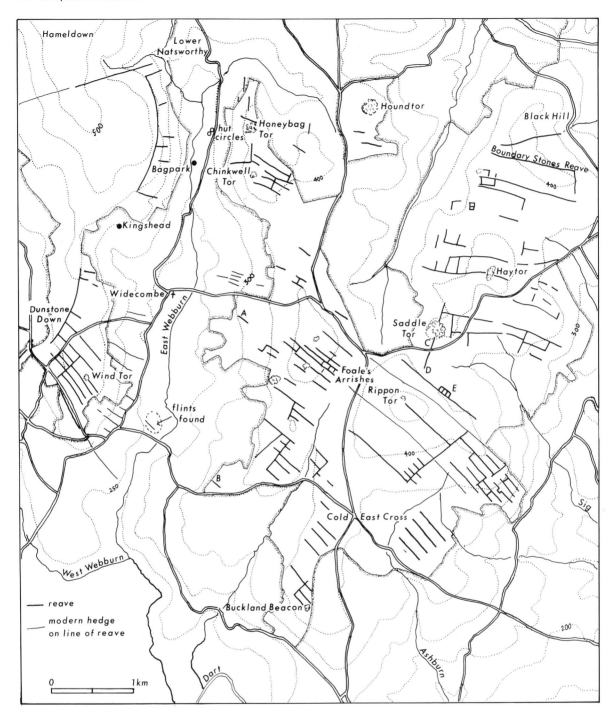

different system; perhaps the shared axis was a coincidence, after all. But I was forced to think again. Following the Dunstone Down reaves in a north-westerly direction, to the north of the Southcombe–Dockwell road, I eventually managed to sort out the position of their terminal reave, which was mixed up in a complex pattern of more recent fields. It was heading NNE, and was soon interrupted by the modern fields of Kingshead Farm. However, I knew better than to give up at that stage, and heading further north I managed to pick it up again, running round the contour on the south-eastern flank of Hameldown,

26 This sketch map of the western part of the 4500-hectare Rippon Tor parallel system does scant justice to the detail of the layout (see fig. 13). The system included the area of the present-day village of Widecombe; evidence for this includes the Bagpark hut-circles, reaves like A and B which comes close to the edge of enclosed land, and flints located in low-lying fields between Cockingford and Great Dunstone. The reave C-D is important because it links the layout around Haytor, with its slightly different orientation, with the rest of the system. Note the location of Fox's Rippon Tor 'homestead' (E).

above Bagpark. That made sense for another reason; a few days earlier, as I was driving down the Natsworthy-Widecombe road, the soft sunlight at the end of a March afternoon had suddenly picked up a couple of reaves, breasting the 20 degree slope towards the reave I was following. Clearly, this reave must have been their terminal. So the reaves on the hillside below must have been part of the same system as those on Dustone Down, with which they shared a terminal.

And then something else fell into place. To the east of where I was standing, on the other side of the valley, lay the craggy summits of Honeybag and Chinkwell Tors. I had visited that area a long time ago, tipped off by a mention of reaves in Crossing's *Guide to Dartmoor*.[9] So I knew there were reaves there; and what was more important, that their orientation was much the same as that of the reaves on my side of the valley. So it was apparent that reaves on much the same axis of orientation could be found on opposite sides of the East Webburn valley in two areas – here in the Bagpark area, and further south on the other side of Widecombe, in the Dunstone–Venton area. Furthermore, they had a common terminal. There could be only one conclusion – the Rippon Tor system was a good deal larger than I had originally been willing to contemplate. It had been laid out right across the East Webburn valley onto the south-east flank of Hameldown, and must have taken in the area now occupied by the village of Widecombe. The boundaries themselves probably came right down to the river, so that in the later Bronze Age the lovely valley in which the core of Widecombe parish lies would have had much the same kind of open land-scape of fields and farms which we see today.

The north-west corner of the northern boundary of the system apparently runs across the northern flank of Honeybag Tor; so the Chinkwell Tor and Honeybag Tor reaves are in the extreme north-western part of the Rippon Tor system. In 1982 the addition of these reaves to the system posed something of a problem. They should surely continue further east, across the extensive block of moorland around Haytor, yet there was no obvious parallel

system here. However, there were some reaves, spaced at fairly broad intervals and following an orientation not very different from that of the Rippon Tor reaves further south. Could the Haytor reaves perhaps be considered part of the Rippon Tor system? It would after all have been very hard for prehistoric surveyors to have standardised the orientation of the field system over such a large area, with such dissected terrain.

As it happens, the block of moorland around Haytor is separated from the Rippon Tor area by the marshy headwaters of the river Sig, and by quite a narrow saddle above that – not the best conditions for seeking links between the two areas. Fortunately, however, I was able to find a reave running across this zone, linking the Rippon Tor reaves with the Saddle Tor area. The existence of this link, plus the fact that the northernmost reave on the Haytor massif which respects the local axis – Boundary Stones Reave, two kilometres (one mile) to the north – lines up quite well with the northern boundary of the Rippon Tor system on the northern side of Honeybag Tor, suggests quite strongly that the reaves around Haytor are part of the Rippon Tor system. It seems to be an under-developed part of the system, however; there are not many transverse reaves, small fields or farmsteads within it.

The Rippon Tor system is an awesome piece of land division, starting out on the fringe of Hameldown, taking in the broad East Webburn valley, and then the six-kilometre (four-mile) long ridge from Black Hill to Buckland Beacon. I have not yet tried to find out how far it extended into present-day farmland to the south-east. However, the configuration of the present-day hedges suggests that it could well have extended as far as the area of the modern A38, just north-east of Ashburton, some nine kilometres (six miles) from its north-west terminal. This would give it an area of about 4500 hectares (10,000 acres), making it substantially larger than the Dartmeet system, and one of the largest prehistoric field systems in Britain.

One of the most intriguing things about the Rippon Tor system is what happens at its south-western corner. The reaves of the system, as they run from Wind Tor towards their own terminal on Dunstone Down, lie just beyond the terminal reave of the Dartmeet system, and run parallel to it. In other words, the two systems meet at right angles. Unfortunately, by some kind of Murphy's Law of Dartmoor archaeology, it is quite impossible to locate the position where the terminals of these two massive systems must once have met! It may well have been in the spot where there is now a disused stone quarry beside the road, some 250m (275 yards) south of

27 A reave which is apparently subdividing open pasture land – Leather Tor Reave, a short reave running between Sharpitor and Leather Tor (seen on the right) in the area just north of Burrator Reservoir. *Photo: A. Fleming*

Rowden Cross. Which system came first? Did the Rippon Tor system use the terminal of the Dartmeet system as its south-west boundary? Or did the surveyors of the Dartmeet system run their boundaries up to the edge reave of the Rippon Tor system? Alas, the site which might have allowed us to decide the question has probably been quarried away. But there is another possibility. The neat junction of the two large systems, each one over six kilometres (four miles) long, must raise the possibility that the arrangement was the product of an agreement between two neighbouring communities, if not part of an even wider regional plan. I will return to this question later.

Some of the characteristics of the Rippon Tor system, I discovered, were repeated elsewhere on the north-eastern part of the Moor. Just to the north of Grimspound is the Shapley Common parallel system (fig. 28), which like the Rippon Tor system has a terminal which runs around the contour on the fringe of Hameldown; it then skirts the northern edge of Birch Tor before reaching the North Walla Brook. There are indications that some of the reaves of the Shapley Common system ran from their terminal on the lower slopes of Hameldown right across the valley in the Vogwell-Lower Hookner area to a terminal on the side of Easdon Hill (Easdon Hill itself is a marvellous place to visit; it is a meeting-place for three or possibly four reave systems, which converge upon it first as 'fossilised' modern hedges, and then, on the heath-clad summit, as reaves, some of which were re-used as boundaries in the Middle Ages).

The tendency for land to be divided into large rectilinear blocks, often arranged side by side since the reaves which delineate them all run up to the same boundary, seems to be more strongly developed on the north-east side of the Moor. These arrangements I have decided to call 'block systems'. The best example of a block system is the one which I have called the Stannon system (fig. 21), which stretches from a reave between Water Hill and Assycombe Hill (just north of the Warren House Inn) across to the East Dart, a distance of about three kilometres (two

28 Reaves on eastern Dartmoor. Main reave systems are named in capital letters, the most important individual reaves in lower case. Reaves within parallel systems are shown schematically. Note the two very large systems (Dartmeet and Rippon Tor) and the way in which all the major systems run up to 'terminal reaves' (Venford for the Dartmeet system, Widecombe for the Rippon Tor system, Shapley for the Shapley Common system). Easdon Hill is the meeting point of three or four reave systems. Both Hameldown and the plateau around Haytor also had 'cross-ridge' reaves (Hameldown North and South; Yarner Reave and Haytor North) which do not fit in with the other reaves, and may indicate an earlier pattern of boundaries.

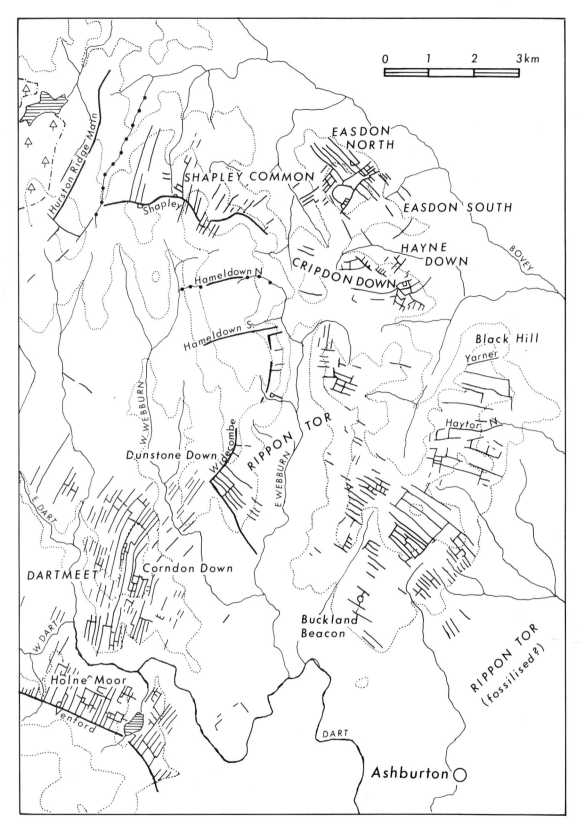

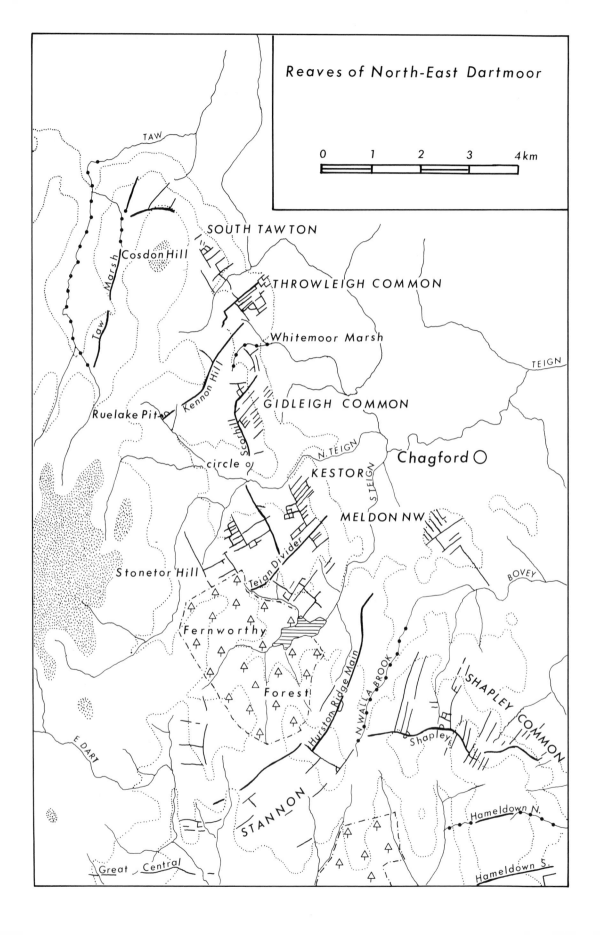

Reaves of North-East Dartmoor

0   1   2   3   4 km

29 Reaves of north-eastern Dartmoor. Main reave systems are named in capital letters, the most important individual reaves in lower case. Reaves within parallel systems are shown schematically. Some important reaves (Hurston Ridge Main, Teign Divider) run along watersheds, as on southern Dartmoor, but others, like Taw Marsh and Kennon Hill, do not. The Kestor and Gidleigh systems could well be part of a single system, judging by the line taken by their terminal reaves. This map shows how watercourses were used as boundaries or parts of boundaries (dotted); note the relationship to streams of Taw Marsh Reave, Hameldown North Reave and the two which flank Hurston Ridge Main Reave.

miles). This is not a parallel reave system, because it has only a few, generally widely-spaced reaves, and few if any related settlement sites. However, the way it is laid out, with the boundaries heading towards distant objectives with few concessions to difficult terrain, is very reminiscent of normal parallel reave systems. Block systems also occur on the north and west sides of White Ridge (a little to the north of Stannon) and on the northern slopes of Cosdon Hill, where two reaves run up to a high-level contour reave which runs round the hill at over 450m (1500 feet) above sea level.

It is possible, I believe, to pick out 'territories' on the same general scale as those on southern Dartmoor (figs 28, 29). There are no watershed reaves here, but there are two obvious long-distance reaves (Taw Marsh and Kennon Hill) which do head away from the edge of the Moor towards the centre in similar fashion (fig. 29), suggesting that they are major territorial dividers. For some peculiar reason both of these reaves come to an abrupt end on the banks of streams. The only way one can relate them to the topography is to suggest that they are running roughly parallel to watercourses – respectively the Taw and the stream running through Whitemoor Marsh. The watercourses themselves would then be the territorial boundaries, and the reaves would be marking the edges of 'buffer zones' which could also perhaps have served as through routes for people taking stock through onto the North Moor.

To the south of Whitemoor Marsh, Scorhill Reave, the terminal of the Gidleigh Common reave system, corners and heads north-east well before it reaches the Whitemoor Marsh stream, perhaps respecting the hypothetical buffer zone. Further south, the North Walla Brook can be regarded as a watercourse boundary running through a buffer zone. The reaves of the Shapley Common system stop well to the east of it, while their terminal, Shapley Reave, stops on it, and possibly steps up the stream a little to continue over Water Hill as the southern (?) boundary of the Stannon block system. West of the brook, on the other

side of a reave-free corridor, is Hurston Ridge Main Reave, which looks like another major territorial boundary a little like Taw Marsh or Kennon Hill Reaves; it may have gone all the way out to Meldon Hill. The only other major territorial boundary is the one I have named the Teign Divider. There is no buffer zone here, but the reave does bisect the triangle between North and South Teign, and since the land division system to its north is clearly not the same as the system to the south, it seems reasonable to suggest it as an intergroup boundary.

So going from north to south along the north-east shoulder of the Moor, five major territories seem to be identifiable (figs 28, 29). The first was located between the Taw and Whitemoor Marsh, based on Cosdon and edged by Taw Marsh and Kennon Hill Reaves; its enclosed land is not particularly well preserved. Then comes a territory based on the North Teign river, and bordered to the south by Teign Divider Reave. This territory would have the Kestor and Gidleigh Common systems as its enclosed land. These systems should perhaps be regarded as one; they appear to share one terminal, Scorhill Reave. Scorhill Reave has an interesting relationship with the Scorhill stone circle; it swerves, apparently in order to leave the monument on its moorward side. Evidently the circle was already in existence, and worth respecting, at the time when the reave was under construction.

The enclosed land of the North Teign territory will have included the Kestor parallel reave system, whose terminal runs from Kestor Rock to the area just west of the Round Pound. Some fields have been laid out *beyond* this terminal, which seems to have been a rare occurrence on Dartmoor. To the west of Scorhill Reave is a large area, extending right out beyond Stonetor Hill and almost as far as the North Teign, which contains some very well-preserved reaves forming a large block system, part of which has been laid out like a small parallel reave system. It looks as if these fields, too, represent some kind of expansion beyond the boundaries as originally envisaged.

Further south is the South Teign territory, between Teign Divider reave and the 'buffer zone' along the North Walla Brook, and further south still are the distinctive blocks of enclosed land fringing Hameldown – the Shapley Common and Rippon Tor parallel reave systems, which I see as indicating the territories of two further communities. It is not altogether clear where the Stannon block system fits into this scheme; it apparently contains few small subdivisions and settlements, and it could have been the subdivided lower pasture land of the South Teign group.

The picture is not so clear-cut as it is on southern

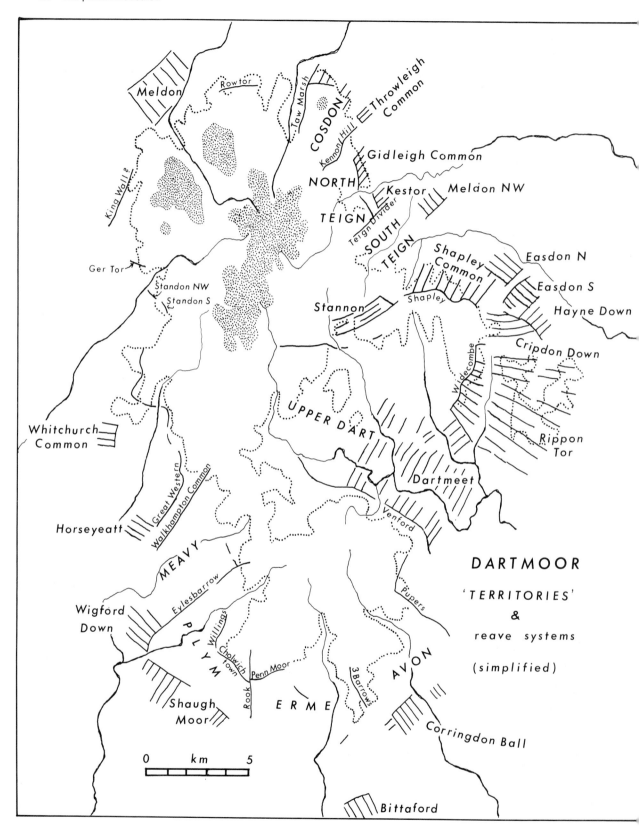

Meldon

Rowtor

Throwleigh
Common

COSDON

Kennon Hill

Gidleigh Common

NORTH

Kestor

Meldon NW

King Wall?

TEIGN

Teign Divider

SOUTH

Shapley
Common

Easdon N

Ger Tor

TEIGN

Easdon S

Standon NW

Stannon

Shapley

Hayne Down

Standon S

Cripdon Down

Widecombe

Rippon
Tor

Whitchurch
Common

UPPER DART

Dartmeet

Great Western
Walkhampton Common

Venford

DARTMOOR

Horseyeatt

'TERRITORIES'

MEAVY

&

Eylesbarrow

Pupers

reave systems

Wigford
Down

PLYM

Willings

(simplified)

Cholwich
Town

Penn Moor

Rook

AVON

ERME

3 Barrows

Shaugh
Moor

Corringdon Ball

0   km   5

Bittaford

30 The pattern of reaves on Dartmoor as a whole, simplified. Note the three short reaves Ger Tor, Standon NW and Standon S which may have been planned to continue the line of the Great Western Reave. The pattern as defined by large blocks of enclosed land and radial boundaries such as the watershed reaves works quite well, but there are some mysteries, notably which unenclosed grazing land was used by the inhabitants of the giant Rippon Tor system.

Dartmoor. But it does look as if five communities were settled on the fringe of Dartmoor between Ashburton and Cosdon Hill (fig. 30), a distance of about 25km (15 miles), compared with eight parishes occupying this area in more recent times. If the territory of each prehistoric community was roughly square, so that it measured about five kilometres (three miles) each way, the inference is that each community was settled on about 2000-3000 hectares (5000-7500 acres) of land.

The pattern on north and north-west Dartmoor, however, is still unclear. The reaves are sparse and it is impossible to find a pattern. The most convincing contour reave, unless there was one beneath King Wall (fig. 25), is Rowtor Reave, not very far south of the Okehampton army camp. It is nearly two kilometres (one mile) long, and its general position

suggests that it was some kind of contour reave, probably an unfinished one. The gap between Rowtor Reave and King Wall contains Branscombe Reave, in the saddle between Corn Ridge and Sourton Tors; it runs up to a conspicuous burial cairn, and is overlain by a rather impressive linear earthwork of unknown but obviously later date. Evidently even the north-western heights of Dartmoor were the object of some sort of territorial claim.

However, one of the most important discoveries of 1982 was made in this region. Immediately to the north-west of Meldon Quarry and Meldon Reservoir, the tendency of many of the present-day field boundaries to follow a north-west/south-east orientation is very striking on the map and in the landscape. This applies both to the small fields around Meldon and Youlditch and the larger ones to the north of the A38. I was very fortunate to find an air photograph in the National Monuments Record in London which provided proof that this pattern has fossilised a much older field system. In a field not far

31 This pattern of modern hedges, near Mel Tor, just above Poundsgate on eastern Dartmoor, takes its orientation from that of the Dartmeet parallel system. This may be roughly what the Bronze Age landscape looked like. *Photo: A. Fleming*

from what used to be Meldon railway junction, elements of what is obviously a prehistoric field pattern can be recognized from the air; and not very far away, medieval field boundaries on Sourton Down also conform to a north-west/south-east axis. To judge from the map, the Meldon system, as I have called it, must have been quite a large one, about two kilometres (one mile) long and nearly four kilometres (two miles) wide – about 800 hectares (2000 acres) in area. On the map, it looks as if it is possible to pick out the terminal which ran along the north-west edge of the system.

The Meldon system is important because it is the first Bronze Age field system to be discovered on the north-west side of Dartmoor, extending the distributional area recognised by Gawne and Somers Cocks in 1968. In principle, then, the entire periphery of Dartmoor could have been surrounded by these large field systems in the Bronze Age. Here and at Bittaford, on the other side of the Moor, the finding of a very small fragment of evidence was enough to show that a distinctive pattern of present-day field boundaries really is a fossilised parallel reave system. In one case, a few markings on an air photo, in the other, a short length of reave just beyond today's top wall, are enough to provide the proof required. Perhaps we should develop the self-confidence to look for similar patterns among the modern field boundaries further away from the periphery of the Moor, and be prepared to identify them provisionally as prehistoric field systems (see figs 31 and 69).

Looking at the general results of my fieldwork on both northern and southern Dartmoor (fig. 30), I was heartened to realise that the size of territories, and the general 'behaviour' of reaves, as single boundaries or within parallel reave systems, was really quite uniform and predictable around the fringe of the Moor as a whole. It might be thought that when things become predictable they become rather boring; but for an archaeologist it is often a good sign, an indication that a kind of understanding has developed, that what is in

his mind is aligning itself with some kind of past reality. Or so it seems . . . .

This raised in my mind the question of the interdependence of the boundaries. Could a reave like Three Barrows Reave, on the Avon-Erme watershed, really have any meaningful existence unless its counterparts on neighbouring watersheds were in use as boundaries at the same time? Was the meeting of giant reave systems at right angles to one another on Dunstone Down just a casual happening – or was it part of a master plan, a major reform of land division systems which affected most of south-east Dartmoor? Did the Great Western Reave, over 10 kilometres (six miles) in length and arguably once intended to run from Meavy to Tavy or even beyond, just happen to result from the piecemeal land division concepts of several little local communities – or was it part of some regional scheme affecting the whole of Dartmoor's western fringe? And why did Eylesbarrow Reave, after a normal existence as a watershed reave, run onto Wigford Down and then suddenly swerve south, plunging down through what is now Cadworthy Wood to meet the river Plym – at exactly the spot where Saddlesborough Reave, approaching from the other side, hits the river? Coincidence – or the result of a master plan?

If it could be shown that most of the reaves were built in one major episode of planned land division, with each parallel system conceived as part of a larger territorial system affecting the whole of Dartmoor, this would be very good news; in theory, good dating evidence obtained from any reave could be transferred with some confidence to the whole of the system! But it was the social implications of a regional system of land boundaries which intrigued me most. I had to think about what large-scale land division might have meant to the Bronze Age people of Dartmoor – and indeed to prehistoric people in general. This problem could not be solved by further fieldwork; it needed a much more wide-ranging kind of enquiry, as we shall see.

5: Anatomy of a field system

When I started the Dartmoor Reave Project I was hoping that the survival of numerous ancient land boundaries would mean the preservation of Bronze Age territorial patterns. I felt that systems of land division ought to reflect the social and economic organisation of prehistoric communities. And it seemed a fair assumption that most information would come from the most highly valued land, the land which required the most careful regulation and subdivision – namely the enclosed land in parallel reave systems. The parallel systems contained fields, droveways, houses and domestic enclosures of various kinds, clearly visible on the ground surface in the form of reaves. So at quite an early stage, sometime in 1977, I decided to make a detailed study of the Dartmeet parallel reave system.

Why the Dartmeet system? Well, by 1977 we were already excavating on Holne Moor, at the southern end of this system, and I needed a good plan of the areas close to our excavation sites. But a much more important reason for my choice was that Holne Moor appeared to be the best-preserved sector of the best-preserved reave system on Dartmoor. (At this time, before I realised the true size of the Rippon Tor system, I also thought that it was the *biggest* system on

32 On the western slopes of Holne Moor, just beside the road and above Saddle Bridge, two Bronze Age houses (A and B) are associated with a characteristic set of small fields or paddocks; their relationship to the axis of the Dartmeet parallel reave system can be clearly seen. For a plan of this site, see fig. 39b. *Photo: A. Fleming*

the Moor.) Holne Moor, I felt, made an ideal research area; here were examples of all the different kinds of site and surface relationships that one could possibly want to excavate.

Strangely enough, the superbly preserved archaeological landscape on Holne Moor, full of intricate detail (fig. 32), seems to have attracted little attention, until Gawne and Somers Cocks drew attention to the 'parallel reaves' here in 1968. Crossing's *Guide to Dartmoor* refers vaguely to 'the lands of the forest settlers', marked out by 'long lines of grey walls that spread over the heath like a net-work', and Lady Fox in 1954 noted four locations here where hut-circles and fields could be found.[1] That seems to be all, as far as the pre-1968 literature is concerned. Yet it is here, more than anywhere else on Dartmoor, that one is most starkly confronted with the reality of parallel reave systems and the challenge to the imagination which they represent. To stand on Combestone Tor in the winter sunshine, preferably when there is a light covering of snow, and to observe a dozen or so reaves coming down from the rugged heights of Yar Tor and over Vag Hill to the edge of the Dart gorge, always on the same insistent axis, is quite an experience (fig. 33). The reaves on Holne Moor itself, seen from various points on the Dartmeet–Poundsgate road, can look very striking too, particularly on a summer evening.

Over the next ten years I was to find out a good deal about the Dartmeet parallel reave system. Our surveying season was normally the first two weeks in April, a time when, in most years, Dartmoor seems to have barely emerged from the winter. The task was to make a map of the system, at a scale of 1:1000, picking up as much detail as possible. Most of the work involved running long base-lines, laid out by eye with ranging-poles, along the reaves, and plotting with tape-measures using off-set measurements. Towards the end of the work, when the Sheffield Archaeology Department had obtained an EDM (Electronic Distance Measurer), we used this to establish accurately the positions of the main junctions, and other critical features. It proved to be rather a slow method, but at least this way it was possible to gain a close acquaintance with detail on the ground. As I walked around, sometimes checking my sketch-plan, sometimes supervising the work, I would cover a lot of ground. Frequently I would revisit areas I had been to before; but I often found myself approaching from a different direction, or in changed light conditions. It is surprising how different a site can appear on a second or subsequent visit. In landscape archaeology there is always something new to notice. Given the right level of organisation and resources, we could perhaps have plotted the Dartmeet system from air photos and field-checked it in a couple of seasons. If we had done

it this way, our checking would have been essentially working outwards from a piece of paper, our provisional plot; the method which we actually developed, though slower, was much more responsive to what was actually on the ground.

The Dartmeet parallel reave system covers over 3000 hectares (7500 acres) and measures over six kilometres (four miles) from its southern terminal on Holne Moor to its northern terminal on Dunstone Down, just south-west of Widecombe. Its eastern and western boundaries are more problematic. To the east, its boundaries may well have followed the course of the Dart, the Webburn up to Lizwell Meet, and then the East Webburn; the fields certainly covered the Poundsgate area and may have come almost as far east as New Bridge. On the western side, there is a prominent edge-boundary running across Riddon Ridge; further south, the system extended almost as far west as Outer Huccaby Ring, and somewhere to the west of Hexworthy. So the maximum width of the system, in its southern half, was also more than six kilometres (four miles), though further north it was less. What is not clear is the route of its northern terminal to the west of Rowden, that is to say in the zone around Cator.

The best vantage-point for viewing the Dartmeet system is Corndon Tor, which is in the most dramatic central zone of the system, where the reaves scale the heights and run across saddles between the summits of Yar Tor, North Hill and Corndon itself (each one over 400m (1300ft) above sea level) as well as Sharp Tor to the south. About 800m (900 yards) to the north-west can be seen a group of modern fields, to the south of Sherril Farm. It is immediately apparent that these modern hedge-banks are conforming to the axis of the reave system (fig. 15). To the north, on North Hill, two great cairns dominate the skyline. But in reasonable light conditions some correctly orientated reaves can be seen across the West Webburn on some enclosed rough pasture land near Shallowford, and the conforming orientations of the modern hedges between here and Rowden Down, a little further north, give a fair impression of the character of the northern sector of the system. To the south can be seen the gorge of the river Dart, and beyond it Holne Moor. In some lights the Holne Moor reaves may show up quite well, but normally the most prominent feature is the modern top wall above Saddle Bridge, which follows the line of Venford Reave, the system's southern terminal (fig. 18). Usually it is possible to see the reaves which run up to it just here. Beyond Holne Moor can be seen the northern fringe of the South Moor, with hills going up to over 450m (1500ft) above sea level.

One of the first thoughts which occurs to the visitor

33 The Dartmeet parallel reave system just above Dartmeet, seen from Combestone Tor; in the background are Yar Tor (left) and Corndon Tor (with a burial cairn on the skyline, to the left of the tor). Some of the reaves were enlarged in the Middle Ages. The orientation of the system shows well, with two reaves climbing the steep slopes of Yar Tor. *Photo: A. Fleming*

is that the system must have been laid out in a fairly open landscape, and pollen analysis, as we shall see, confirms this. When these boundaries were laid out, the natural tree cover had been largely depleted, mainly by browsing livestock. The surveyors of the Dartmeet system would also have been aware of ceremonial monuments dotted around the landscape, most of them probably dating from the earlier part of the Bronze Age. The line of the southern terminal of the system across Holne Moor (fig. 34) was probably determined to a large extent by the position of a triple stone row 150m (165 yards) long, which I think was deliberately left on the moorward side of this boundary, along with a group of cairns further west, near Horn's Cross. But further north another rather insignificant triple row, running up to a small cairn in the saddle between Yar Tor and Corndon Tor, has been ignored completely by the reave builders; the boundaries run straight through at an angle to the axis of the row. A third row within the system once existed on Sherberton Common, but it was comprehensively destroyed by road-menders in the 1890s.[2]

Then there are burial cairns. The most con-
spicuous ones, three massive piles of stones each 25m (80ft) across, are on the rugged summits near the centre of the system – Corndon Tor and North Hill. There must have been quite a large one just south of the road running past Combestone Tor; it was destroyed by road-menders in the late nineteenth century, but the crater which they have left can still be seen, not far from a reave which has been gutted in the same way. At the other end of the scale, there are small cairns, 3-4m (10-13ft) in diameter, some of which have been dug into so that the stone cists within them are visible. There are also ring-cairns, four of them on Holne Moor (fig. 34) and one on the other side of the Dart near Aish Corner. A ring cairn is a stony bank enclosing a roughly circular area, which may well have contained a burial or burials. The best example, commanding a fine view of Holne Moor, lies to the south of Horn's Cross, beside the track leading to Holne Ridge. There is another ring-cairn in the group of monuments near the cross, and three others in the reave system. The evidence that the ceremonial monuments preceded the reaves comes largely from other parts of Dartmoor; some of it I have already mentioned. It also seems quite likely that one or two walled enclosures within the Dartmeet system were built a considerable time before the boundaries were laid out.

If you look at an air photograph of part of the Dartmeet system, the sight of the reaves running side by side, in conformity with the main axis, is very

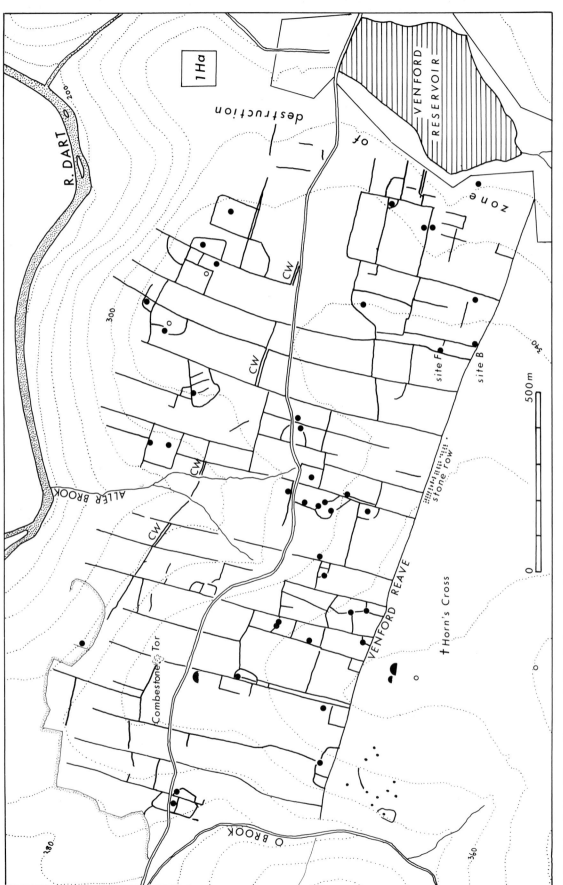

34 Provisional plan of the southern part of the Dartmeet parallel system, on the western part of Holne Moor. Note how the houses (filled circles) tend to cluster into 'neighbourhood groups'. Ring-cairns (open circles) and large cairns (mound symbols) occur both within the system and just beyond the terminal reave. A triple stone rows lies just beyond the terminal and may have helped to determine its position. Note also a transverse through route name the Combestone Way (CW), a line of four separate stretches of lane.

35 In the central part of the Dartmeet system, near Sherril, the axis swerves markedly, which it has to do if the reaves are to hit both the terminal reaves at right angles. The points where the angle change occurs are marked at A, B, and C. Note the two large Bronze Age burial cairns at X and Y. *Photo: National Monument Record*

impressive. To think about the achievement which this system represents, one has to keep in mind the immense area covered by the system as a whole, and the rugged nature of the landscape upon which this layout was imposed. I have had to coin a word – 'terrain-oblivious' – to describe this kind of field system. Only in the Corndon area, near the centre of the system, would the surveyors have been able to consider their plan in relation to the form of the land.

But they had a problem. The end boundaries were not parallel to one another, so that a straight axis could not run from end to end of the system on the same axis *and* meet both terminals at right angles. The solution

which they adopted (fig. 35) was to put in quite a sharp angle change, twenty to thirty degrees, in the centre of the system, just south of North Hill, with a switch of more like ten degrees further west, in the Sherril-Babeny area, as far as one can tell from the orientation of the modern fields. This angle change also tended to keep the system's axis roughly at right angles to both the Dart and the West Webburn valleys, so that many of the long boundaries ran across the contour. From this point of view, it is pretty clear that in this area of steep-sided valleys, where the river pattern is quite complicated, the axis chosen for the system as a whole, in the N-NNE/S-SSW sector of the compass, is the best one; the system is also at right angles to much of the West Dart and even a portion of the East Dart.

The idea that the orientation of parallel systems was chosen carefully so that as much valley terrain as possible was intersected at right angles by the axis, with a preference therefore for boundaries running straight up the hillsides, is supported by the behaviour of other systems. The Rippon Tor, Shapley Common, Meldon and Bittaford systems are all quite good examples of this kind of layout preference. Of course, with systems as large as these, it is inevitable that some reaves will have to be laid out *along* hillsides, which is rather awkward on concave slopes. On Holne Moor, on the east bank of the O Brook and of the Venford Brook (north of the reservoir) the reave-builders bowed to common sense and took the boundaries around the contour.

The dominance of the Dartmeet system's axis may give the impression that many of the axial boundaries run from one end of the system to the other. However, I soon found out that this is not so; however long and direct an axial reave may appear to be, sooner or later it stops on a *transverse* reave (that is, one at right angles to the axis of the system). To follow the axis of the system further, you have to walk along the transverse reave – perhaps for two metres, perhaps for fifty – to find the next axial reave continuing into the distance. (Axial reaves and transverse reaves do not very often make a junction in the form of a cross; almost always, in the terminology which I have had to develop, one or the other is 'dominant', with the others 'staggered' on it.) The axial pattern of the reaves is deceptive, giving the impression that the local boundaries had to be fitted in almost as an afterthought to the surveyors' grand design. But in fact some of the most significant boundaries are the transverse ones, and they suggest rather different formation processes for the layout.

It was clear from the first that the 'hut-circles' within the Dartmeet system, and in other parallel systems, were not distributed evenly, but in clusters (figs. 34, 36) and the fields at some distance from the clusters of houses tended to be relatively large and rectilinear; near the houses they were much smaller and more numerous, and the reaves enclosing them were more likely to be curvilinear or irregular in plan. It was these small fields and enclosures close to the houses which an earlier generation of prehistorians set apart as prehistoric, in opposition to the 'medieval' reaves.

Within the Dartmeet system, the settlement clusters – or neighbourhood groups, as I have come to call them – are mostly quite clear. On the western part of Holne Moor, between the O Brook and the Venford Brook, there are four neighbourhood groups (fig. 34). Across the river Dart, there is a zone of settlement on the southern slopes of Vag Hill, stretching from the edge of the modern fields at Rowbrook Farm, around the south-western slopes of the hill opposite Combestone Wood, and along the western part of the hillside, above the Dart. The crown of Vag Hill, or Yartor Down as it is called on some maps, is clearly outside the settlement zone. So

is the exposed summit plateau around Corndon Tor, and the southern slopes of Sharp Tor. But there is a settlement zone in the relatively sheltered saddle to the west and north of Ollsbrim. Another one lies further north, on the lower north-east slopes of North Hill; it probably went right down to the West Webburn near Shallowford (fig. 36). And there was a settlement zone around Sherril. One or two of the hut-circles lie among the modern fields here, having survived the remaking of the field boundary pattern (in the early Middle Ages?) into a network of small, irregular parcels, and then a vigorous assault by a bulldozer in the late 1970s.

On the south-western slopes of Yar Tor, the distinction between settlement zone and non-settlement zone is less clear-cut. Here there are a few single houses, fairly evenly distributed among fields of larger size. But some of the houses have their own 'domestic enclosures' built into the corners of existing fields; so they are unlikely to have been part of the initial settlement pattern. And considering that this hillside would almost certainly have been the most exposed part of the entire system, apart from the tors and hilltops themselves, this idea makes sense. Perhaps the fact that this area *was* eventually settled may indicate that, at some time in the Dartmeet system's history, other areas were fully occupied, with interesting implications for population estimates.

If the loose clusters of hut-circles and their associated fields and enclosures could be distinguished from the zones of larger fields without settlements, the next question was – what happens at the junction between the two kinds of land division? It gradually became clear that this is where some of the transverse reaves came in. Now transverse reaves never run right across the system, from one edge to the other; only the terminals do that. Many transverse reaves in the Dartmeet system are in fact quite short; they are simply the east-west boundaries of individual fields, running across from one axial reave to another. But in some places there is a longer transverse reave,

36 Plan of the northern slopes of Corndon Down, on the southern edge of the valley of the West Webburn near Shallowford. The plan is provisional and simplified. It shows the scattered distribution of houses (A–E) in a neighbourhood group; the increase in field size going south, away from the houses; the apparent outer boundary of the group's fields within the Dartmeet system; and the kinks (marked x and y) showing that no attempt was made to keep axial reaves straight as they crossed the brow of the hill (the boundaries may well have been built by two different gangs working from different ends). The area has been thoroughly enclosed in the Middle Ages, but in most places it is easy to work out which medieval banks must have been built on reaves.

road

modern enclosed land

A

B

C

D

E

F

X

Y

0   metres   100

which is used as an east-west boundary by *several* fields, so that it is locally dominant over axial reaves. In other places the axial reaves are dominant, but short transverse reaves are staggered on them within a very narrow zone running at right angles to the axis of the system, forming a kind of boundary zone.

A recurring relationship soon emerged between the settlement zones and the longer, locally dominant transverse reaves, or the narrow zones of short transverse reaves. These distinctive reaves evidently indicated the boundaries of the land closely associated with the settlement clusters. In some places, two of these boundaries can be seen – forming, in relation to a settlement cluster, an 'inner' and an 'outer' boundary. This is most noticeable in the central part of the Dartmeet system, especially on the northern side of North Hill (fig. 36) and around Ollsbrim, and it provides independent confirmation that the settlement clusters really do represent significant entities within the field system as a whole.

Fig. 36 shows a fairly typical 'neighbourhood group' in the northern part of the system, south of Shallowford in the West Webburn valley. The reaves have been extensively re-used in the Middle Ages, but the locations of houses (A–F) in their typical dispersed pattern can be picked out; there were probably others further north, now destroyed. Transverse reaves define small fields near the houses, and larger fields further away; the largest fields, however, are on the hill to the south, beyond the southern edge of the plan in the no man's land between here and the Sherril neighbourhood group. The kinks in the axial reaves (X and Y) suggest that in each case no attempt was made to ensure that the boundary went over the brow of the hill in a straight line, as if it was built from both directions, perhaps by two different gangs.

Sometimes, transverse reaves and the relative size of fields can give valuable clues about the location of settlement clusters which have been obliterated by more recent land enclosure. There is a good case in point on the lower portion of the south-facing slopes below Sharp Tor. Here, the presence of a long transverse reave, plus the evidence for some smaller fields, in an area of thick gorse and considerable post-prehistoric activity, suggests that there was probably a settlement zone around Rowbrook. The lack of 'hut-circles' on the eastern side of Holne Moor can also be explained in this way; there is an important long transverse reave here, which must be the outer boundary of a settlement zone in the area around West Stoke Farm. The striking layout of the Stoke fields is very noticeable from the other side of the Dart; they are a wonderful example of recent hedge-lines fossilising a prehistoric layout. They lie mostly on a well-sheltered hillside, and it is quite

understandable that the more exposed eastern side of Holne Moor lay outside the Bronze Age settlement area.

So we had apparently located a recurring pattern of boundaries, fields and 'hut-circles' which seemed to show that 'settlement zones' formed distinct entities within the overall Dartmeet system. It seemed to me that it was worth trying to find ways of investigating the question of land 'ownership'. There were obviously several possibilities. At one extreme, all land in the Dartmeet system might have been 'owned' by the group which laid out the system as a whole, and available for distribution and perhaps periodic re-allocation among various families or other social groups. At the other end of the scale, each 'family' or 'household' could have had its allocation of land within the system, to be held in perpetuity. There could have been a 'mixed' system, with some land in 'private ownership' and some held by the community as a whole; or the whole of the field system could have been a very large private estate.

Historical geographers, working in periods with documentary sources, have shown that settlement and boundary patterns do not necessarily provide a direct reflection of social patterning. So it seemed unlikely that relations of ownership could be unambiguously determined from the field evidence. Any conclusion reached would be a provisional hypothesis, a model based on the field system, not revealed truth about Bronze Age land division.

But it did seem to me, around 1978, that the *initial* system of land division and settlement was bound to bear *some* relationship to the way land was intended to be used and controlled. A hopeful circumstance was that the Dartmeet system, unlike some of its counterparts in other parts of Britain, looked as if it had not gone through too many complicated changes, thus preserving many of its original layout principles. Perhaps I could develop some simple methods of analysis. For example, if there was an inheritance system which specified that land should be divided between heirs, one might expect some parcels to be split into equal portions; the German scholar Müller-Wille was able to demonstrate this for some field systems in northern Germany.[4] If the system was designed to contain numerous single farms, such farms might show up as distinct entities, in some parts of the system at least. So, taking the part of Holne Moor betwen the Venford Brook and the O Brook, I tried a simple analysis.

Holne Moor has quite a number of axial reaves running all the way from the terminal to the edge of the Dart gorge, especially in the area between the O Brook and the Aller Brook, by Hangman's Pit. I decided to produce a map which included just the

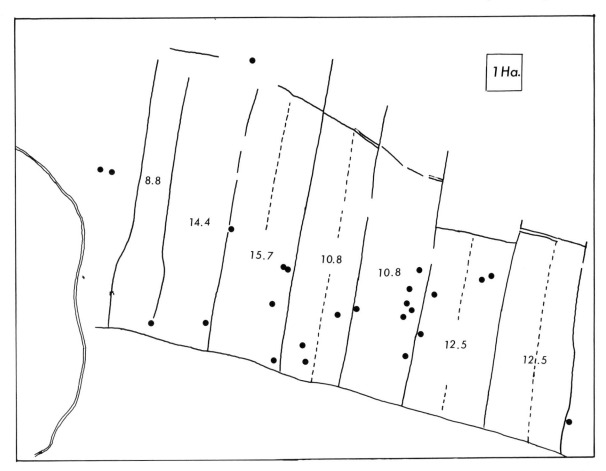

1 Ha.

8.8

14.4

15.7

10.8

10.8

12.5

12.5

37 Plan of the western side of Holne Moor, with detail removed leaving the main parcels of land and the houses. The loose relationship between the houses and the parcels is striking, and suggests that the main reave lines are not to do with setting out individual 'allotments'. The areas of the parcels in hectares are shown, and the hyphenated lines indicate reaves which might be said to divide a parcel into two halves. The rarity of this kind of subdivision (see also fig. 34) also suggests that subdivision of land for inheritance purpose was not practised, or at any rate not common; an obvious explanation would be that land was held by the community.

houses, the main blocks of land – as defined by the reaves which went as far as the Dart valley – and those boundaries which could be seen as dividing fields into equal or roughly equal parts (fig. 37). The first aim was to investigate the inheritance question – by seeing how common subdivision into equal parts might be; as can be seen from fig. 37, this kind of subdivision is not particularly common, and there is no compelling reason to believe in subdivision of land between heirs as a common practice – at any rate from the surface

evidence provided by the reaves.

My second purpose was to look at the relationship between houses and blocks of land. Here the results were quite startling. There seems to be no correlation whatsoever between individual houses – or, for that matter, groups of houses – and blocks of land. This is true whether you count the number of houses per block, or – since the blocks vary in area – the number of hectares per house within a given block (fig. 37). In fact a look at the plan suggests two quite unrelated patterns, and that the locations of the houses have been decided with little or no reference to the main blocks of land in the field system! One or two people, looking at the loose relationship between the houses and the main blocks of land, have even suggested that the two may be of different dates; but once the minor boundaries have been restored to the plan, the links between the houses and the reave system are undeniable – here and elsewhere.

As a general rule, the houses have been placed in open clusters, with each house or house pair lying perhaps 200m (200 yards) from its nearest neighbour; a 'neighbourhood group' of perhaps six to fifteen settlements of this kind is separated from the next such group by some considerable distance. It is a dispersed settlement pattern, not just within the field system as a whole, but within each neighbourhood group's area. I believe that, broadly speaking, the position of each house was determined in relation to that of other houses, and not to blocks of land. In one or two places on Holne Moor it is possible to see a boundary swerving slightly to go past a building (fig. 40); naturally, several houses would have been built before boundaries. But there are also houses and enclosures which have clearly been *attached* to reaves, and therefore represent later additions to the settlement pattern (fig. 12).

By following these different lines of evidence, I was led inescapably to the conclusion that the community which laid out the Dartmeet system was an aggregate of smaller units, 'neighbourhood groups' in my terminology. This suggests a social pattern which is not entirely unexpected. The truly isolated, independent family farm is a historical rarity; even when quite small families have their own land, have access to labour-saving machinery, and operate in many respects as separate economic units, they need their neighbours, whether they live in a hamlet or in dispersed farms. The literature about the rural history of Scotland, Ireland and Wales is full of illustrations of how this kind of community operated. Two from Wales are particularly memorable.

In the early years of this century, the old Welsh social unit known as the *trefgordd* was described as 'aworking unit of co-operative dairy farming . . . the natural group of homesteads of relatives or neighbours acting together as a single community as regards their cattle and their ploughing'. The *trefgordd* as legally defined was supposed to include 'nine houses and one plough and one oven, and one churn and one cock and one bull and one herdsman'[5] which is the most concise statement I have ever come across of the co-operative use of resources and labour which is one of the main advantages of belonging to this kind of social group. The inhabitants of such a little community are, of course, frequently related to one another by birth or marriage as well as by everyday social and economic ties, and it is much more than economic self-interest which holds them together. There is normally a strong sense of community, which is well captured by the recorded statement of an old Irish countryman: 'even though you had your own corn cut and stooked you wouldn't feel fully satisfied until all your neighbours' were done as well'.[6]

Alwyn Rees, writing twenty years ago, conveyed very well how dispersed settlements can nevertheless form a kind of community:[7]

There exists in upland Wales a diffused form of society which is not only able to function without a unifying social centre but seems to be opposed to all forms of centralisation. The hearth of the lonely farm itself *is* the social centre. The farms are not outlying members of a nucleated community, but entities in themselves, and their integration into social groups depends on the direct relationship between them rather than upon their convergence on a single centre. The traditional social unit does not consist of the environs of a town or village: it is *cefn gwlad*, the neighbourhood in the countryside.

This kind of small, dispersed community is present to some extent today on the fringes of Dartmoor (you soon become used to a farmer referring to somebody who lives the best part of a mile away as his neighbour) and has probably been quite common since at least the Middle Ages. The Domesday Book's entry for the manor of *Estocha* or Stoke, within the Dartmeet system, mentions the main tenant, Winemer, holding the land from William de Falaise, plus 4 villeins, two bordars and a serf; until quite recently there were five dispersed farms here, all with 'Stoke' forming part of their names. Stoke is probably a good example of a medieval neighbourhood group, with origins going back before the Norman Conquest, when Ulveva held it.[8]

Some anthropologists have argued that such a small-scale human group has to be large enough to take advantage of the benefits of group living and social and economic cooperation, but that above a certain size the increasing frequency of disputes and rivalries is likely to damage its ability to make decisions and limit the effectiveness of cooperation between its members. Hunting bands, for instance, tend to contain between about fifteen and fifty persons, and there is talk of a 'magic number' – that is, one which tends to occur frequently – of twenty-five.[9] Judging by the number of houses in the neighbourhood groups of the Dartmeet system, most of these social groups may have been no bigger than large hunting bands, and thus quite close to the historically 'natural' size for human groups.

Neighbourhood groups are likely to have played a key structural role in the social organisation of the Dartmeet community. Their social cohesion would have given them considerable local political strength, and there must at times have been tension between individual neighbourhood groups and the larger Dartmeet system community. But it is also likely that individuals and households living in such a dispersed settlement pattern would have been part of a continuous network of social and economic relationships, in some sense linking large tracts of countryside. Reading the Irish literature, I came across an amusing account[10] of an old man whose sons used to hide the newspaper from him until after the evening meal, in order to cut down his attendances at the distant funerals of even more distant relations! Presumably families within the Dartmeet system, which is only six kilometres across, would have had links of various kinds with many other families living within the system.

There is evidence that the neighbourhood groups regarded themselves from the outset as members of a wider community, and that they accepted the principles governing the layout of this community's land. Our plans of the Dartmeet system show that in many areas the fields around the houses are likely to have been among the earliest boundaries to have been constructed. One can legitimately draw this conclusion from a number of field observations. Sometimes, for instance, an axial reave will change course, almost imperceptibly, where it intersects the transverse reave or reaves which form the outer boundary of the fields around a neighbourhood group. This suggests that, whatever the overall *plan*, the building sequence took the axial boundary only as far away as the junction with the transverse boundary, and only later was it extended further. This can be seen in the area of the excavation sites on Holne Moor (fig. 40) where the axial reave which goes past the site F house swerves away markedly once it leaves the northern boundary of the neighbourhood group's area. On the plan of the area south of Shallowford (fig. 36) the enclosure near house F is not D-shaped; it has probably been built with one straightish side, anticipating the line of the boundary. Individual cases are always debatable, but the cumulative evidence for this kind of 'anticipation' of the system is quite strong.

One of the most striking cases occurs on Holne Moor, where Venford Reave, the terminal of the system, takes a pretty direct course across the moor from Venford Brook to the O Brook. Here if anywhere, it seems, we have a *primary* boundary; after all, the axial reaves all run up to it. Yet there is one place where Venford Reave does have a distinct kink. It is not simply a surveyor's error. This is a place (fig. 39a) where the terminal forms the southern boundary of a very small field, only 0.14ha. (0.35 acre) in area, with a house at north-west corner, its doorway facing into the field. Comparing the heights of the land surfaces on either side of the terminal reave, one can see that the southern edge of this little field is also a negative lynchet – that is, the terminal reave has been build along the pre-existing upper edge of a cultivated field, where soil creep has created a slight step in the surface contours. It seems clear here that the little field was laid out by people who knew the general line of the southern edge of the field system, and its axis; later, when the terminal reave came to be constructed, its

builders respected the position of an existing parcel of land – and the result was the kink which we see today.

Some people adhered more closely than others to layout principles. A few of the axial reaves are so straight that they must have been laid out using rods lined up by eye at regular intervals, and in one or two cases the ends of these very straight lines are not intervisible – as with the axial reave which runs right over the top of Vag Hill. But there are also cases like the one on the northern edge of Corndon Down (fig. 36), where an axial reave changes course awkwardly just below the brow of a hill, as if it was laid out both from above and from below, and no-one bothered to get some rods to make sure it was straight. There are areas where the reaves are relatively straight and parallel to one another, and other places where the layout is less meticulous. But the discipline overall was quite good. Very few reaves can be plausibly described as 'unfinished'. And although an individual axial boundary may conform badly with the system, for example leading off at thirty or forty degrees to the axis, the irregularity is not usually copied by the next axial reave; eccentricities were confined within the basic framework of the system. This is why I believe that the system did not 'grow organically', as one or two people have suggested to me; if it had done so, adherence to the axis would surely have been much less strict than is the case.

The system certainly contains some oddities. There is one place on Holne Moor, for example, where a single reave forks to become two reaves separated by 3-4m (9-12ft), and it looks as if there has been a deliberate correction to its line (fig. 39c). And then there is what I call the Foxworthy Block. On the north-western part of Sherberton Common is a whole block of reaves, apparently following the layout principles of a typical parallel reave system, but with an axis completely at variance with that of the Dartmeet system. The axis of the block is perpetuated among a small group of modern fields to the south of Foxworthy, but not to the north of the farm, where the predominant axis is that of the Dartmeet system. It looks as if we have here a small block of fields on a different axis which have been incorporated within the Dartmeet system – possibly a case where a 'neighbourhood group' had not only its own area but also its own axis?

If we can distinguish areas occupied by neighbourhood groups from other zones within the field system, what about individual farms? I did wonder whether it would be possible to approach this question by finding gateways, to discover which fields gave access to which other fields. Unfortunately, although there clearly are original gateways, usually about 1-1½m (3-5ft) wide, and flanked by upright stones on one or

38 This pair of upright stones, on Whitchurch Common on the western edge of Dartmoor, is probably a Bronze Age gateway, set in a reave which has been later remodelled. Most gateways are much less prominent than this one. *Photo: A. Fleming*

both sides (fig. 38), they are in very short supply. It is possible that in the Bronze Age they were closed with stones; with a subsequent covering of peat, such a blocked gateway would be invisible. However this may be, I obviously had to give up this particular approach.

As I mentioned above, if there were 'single farms', each composed of a block of land going with a house or pair of houses within a neighbourhood group, it is not easy to identify the blocks of land in question. It is fairly common for a house to have an identifiable 'domestic enclosure', but this is not large enough to feed a family. And there are other houses which simply stand apparently alone, in small or medium-sized fields. In fact when we come to consider the 'homesteads', the enclosures and other features near the houses, their variability is fascinating (figs 34, 39).

Why is there this variability in the surroundings of the houses? It may be that individual households were less conformist than archaeologists like to imagine. It suits us, after all, to talk about the typical, the characteristic, the predictable; it makes us feel that we are firmly in control of our material. Perhaps if we

could see the wooden fences and other features the differences betwen the homesteads would be less marked. But the variability could also be explained by my ideas about land ownership. It the land around a group of houses was being farmed by a *group* of people, no one house would be an independent production unit, and it would not need to be accompanied by the full range of buildings and enclosures necessary to the farming economy, as has to be the case on a modern farm. Such facilities could be distributed through the neighbourhood group as a whole; not every household would need a sheep-pen, for instance, and the house of the group's shepherd might have its own distinctive character. Perhaps the social status of a household within the neighbourhood

39 Four plans which show the variability of the surroundings of Bronze Age houses on Holne Moor: **a** shows how a kink in Venford Reave, the terminal of the Dartmeet system, is probably respecting a pre-existing field edge (marked by a negative lynchet) which was itself probably planned to anticipate the position of the terminal; **b** is the settlement pictured on figure 32; **c** is a house apparently by itself in a large enclosure (note the way the course of a reave has apparently been re-aligned here); **d** a complex which shows a characteristically short, narrow lane leading up to a house, and another house which, like the one excavated on site F, has had a small hut built in the ruins.

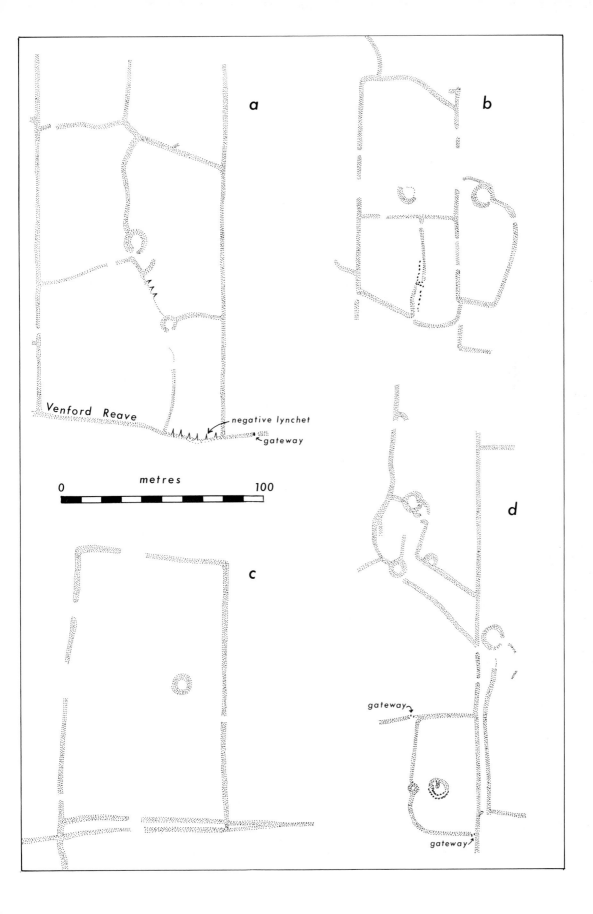

a

b

c

d

Venford Reave

negative lynchet

gateway

metres

0   100

gateway

gateway

group also had an effect on the layout of a house's surroundings.

One interesting feature of the Holne Moor landscape is the near-absence of lanes and droveways. Occasionally there is a short, narrow lane, perhaps 60m (65 yards) in length, approaching a house (fig. 39d). The obvious explanation for a lane like this is that it was to drive livestock to and from the house, helping to control them and perhaps keep them out of nearby enclosures. Yet if an interpretation in terms of normal farming practice is correct, why are these lanes so rare? Is this fact perhaps telling us something important about patterns of stock management or land ownership in the Bronze Age? It may be that lanes were unnecessary because most livestock were kept well away from growing crops, perhaps being sent off to summer pastures on the high moors. At other seasons, if the 'ownership' of land by individual families was a non-existent or very weakly-developed concept, there may have been no 'other people's land' for animals to be driven through, hence no need for closely defined routeways.

One would imagine that a very large field system like this would have been a major barrier to local movement. There is indeed one 'lane' which might be described as a through route. On the northern edge of Holne Moor are four separate stretches of narrow lane, all fairly short and conforming to the layout of the Dartmeet system. On the map (fig. 34) it is obvious that they form disconnected parts of one routeway, which I have christened the Combestone Way, which would have led *across* the system from east to west, from the area of Venford Reservoir across the Aller Brook and then below Combestone Tor towards the Dartmeet area. The route may have led from the Holne area to the Upper Dart basin.

On Throwleigh Common and near Kestor, on the north-eastern side of Dartmoor, there are one or two longer lanes or droveways which follow the axes of reave systems, and some of these are variously long

enough, or wide enough, to be seen as routes for taking livestock through the parallel systems, and out onto open pasture land. At Kestor (fig. 11)[11] there is a broad 'droveway' which runs just below the Round Pound, and a narrow 'lane' some 250m (275 yards) to the south-east (which doesn't, however, run quite as far as the terminal reave of the Kestor system). It may be that here we have the best evidence so far for the proposition that livestock were moved onto the higher parts of Dartmoor from peripheral areas, presumably during the summer.

Perhaps the most important conclusions to emerge from my work in the Dartmeet system involve the *collective* aspects of Bronze Age land-holding; the notion of a community which had control over terrain perhaps more extensive than the average medieval parish, and within that community a federal structure of small neighbourhood groups, each with its defined area of regularly used land and presumably access to the land controlled by the larger community. This model led me to ask a whole series of questions. How did a community of this kind take decisions about how its land should be used? If agricultural operations took place within a group framework, how did this differ from a set-up involving individual peasant proprietors? In a society of commoners, how do radical changes in agricultural technique or economic behaviour come about? What, if any, was the role of social and economic competition, against this background? And in what circumstances do major field systems come to be required and laid out? By the early 1980s, it was becoming more and more obvious that the answers to these questions would not necessarily emerge from further survey and excavation, however conscientiously carried out; thinking about these problems, and having some historical and sociological insight into the nature of certain kinds of community and social process, was becoming more and more vital. But that is another story.

6: Excavation

From quite an early stage in my work, it became clear that there were limitations to what could be achieved simply by fieldwork and survey; there were certain questions which could only be answered by conducting an excavation. One of the most important questions concerned the date of the reaves. John Collis and I had suggested a Bronze Age date because of their close relationship with enclosures and hut-circles like those which had produced Bronze Age pottery when they were excavated around the beginning of this century. But this was not the same thing as saying that the early excavators had dated the reaves. Leaving aside the question of their inadequate recording of what they did, many of the sites they chose were unrelated in any way to reaves, being in the zone of permanent pasture located beyond the parallel reave systems.

Also, it seemed that no reaves had ever been excavated. In the field they sometimes looked like proper walls, with vertical facing-stones; but what were they really like, shorn of their mantle of peat and vegetation? All kinds of unexpected features might be visible. Perhaps the reaves would turn out to overlie earlier boundaries, and details of layout methods and construction techniques might be discovered. It ought to be possible to find out something about environmental conditions when these boundaries were laid out; for example, the reaves might prove to overlie a layer of peat, in which pollen would be preserved.

So in September 1976 I started, with a group of student volunteers, to excavate on Holne Moor, at the southern, best-preserved end of the Dartmeet parallel reave system. I decided to start on two sites. Site A lay SSW of Combestone Tor, at the place where Venford Reave, the terminal of the Dartmeet system, was joined by two parallel reaves which were only about 17m (55ft) apart, enclosing an unusually narrow field some 220m (250 yards) in length. I thought that by laying out a trench along Venford Reave at this point I would be able to take a good look at a long stretch of reave, and at the same time see what happened at the two junctions. The other site, site B, was also located on Venford Reave, but nearly 500m (550 yards)

further east (fig. 40). Here I had discovered the low, ruined wall of a small, rather inconspicuous hut-circle tucked into the angle between the terminal and one of the parallel reaves. These walls must have been standing, and presumably in use, when the building was constructed; therefore any dating evidence from the interior ought to give us a minimum age for the date of the boundary walls.

September 1976 was a difficult season. On site A, 24m (80ft) of reave and associated surface stones had to be cleaned for photography and then meticulously planned in detail – a tough assignment. Then we had to confront a mass of tumbled stones, which had to be judiciously removed, one by one, to try to locate a wall-face which might turn out to be non-existent or patchy! It was not easy. In some places no face could be seen, in others it was very rough. The wall-face was best preserved on the side facing the open moor, where it included some substantial upright stones. The inner face was more difficult to define, and this side of the reave was perhaps the product of rough and ready field clearance, with a couple of long, rather pointed stones propped nearly upright against the 'face'. The whole thing looked as if it had been put up by gangs and individuals with varying standards of neatness and competence. Not very much stone had fallen off the reave; even here, where Venford Reave is at its most massive, it could barely have exceeded 1m (3ft) in height, and 60cm (2ft) seemed a fairer average. This would hardly have made it a very effective barrier to livestock, and we were left wondering whether the reaves were originally surmounted by turves or hedges.

Although we had made limited progress on site B, there was quite a lot of interest in our work, and on site A we were able to take some photographs which were quite effective for publicity purposes, showing a length of rather a massive reave, exposed for the first time, with a modern wall on the same line snaking away into the distance. Shortly afterwards, a lucky break, in the form of a Leverhulme Trust research grant, meant that I now had the resources to tackle a large hut-circle, which might reasonably be expected to produce diagnostic pottery, and charcoal for some

40 Plan of main sites excavated on Holne Moor (except for site A, on Venford Reave but much further west). Note the way the reave swerves to avoid the house on site F (a relationship which was confirmed by excavation) and the critical relationship between the reaves and site B. The positions of three timber buildings and a fence, discovered by excavation, are also indicated. The 'dog-leg' indicated at X may betray a system of earlier boundaries; it might be 'fossilising' the line of a north-south fence almost all of which went out of use when the east-west boundaries which approached it were converted into reaves. In the absence of excavation one can only speculate.

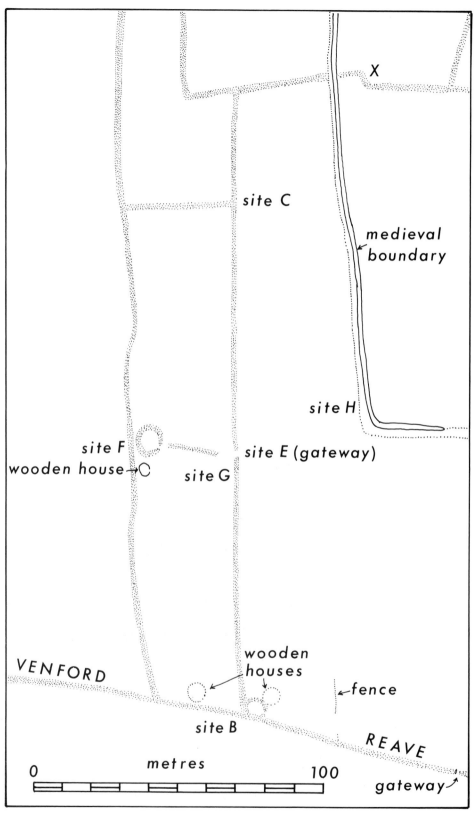

X

medieval
boundary

site C

site H

site F
wooden house→

site E (gateway)

site G

VENFORD

wooden
houses

fence

site B

REAVE

metres

0

100

gateway↗

radiocarbon dates. But I couldn't tackle any hut-circle; it would have to be one with a demonstrable relationship with the reave system, so that the boundaries could be dated as well. This, after all, was why I had started on site B – which had so far produced just one flint scraper and various flint flakes and chips.

Fortunately, while we were making a plan of the area surrounding site B, I had noticed a very interesting relationship. About 100m (100 yards) to the north of site B was a large hut-circle, its interior apparently full of stones and earth, immediately east of a reave running from the terminal to the edge of the Dart valley. About 20m (68ft) north of the building, the reave kinked sharply to bypass the hut-circle. The inference was that the latter had been a standing building when the boundary was laid out – so any dating evidence from this structure, almost certainly a house, should also date the boundary.

I decided that in 1977 we would discontinue the work on sites A and B, for the time being at any rate, and work on this major hut-circle site, which was to become known as site F. We would have a preliminary season at Easter, putting a small trial trench through the reave near site F, and two small trenches at reave junctions not far away. I was interested in trenches at junctions; where one reave meets another at right angles there is an opportunity to use a single trench to look at two or three reaves, which may well have different histories. Perhaps there will be something at the intersection to indicate how the system was laid out (a post-hole, for example) or there might be a blocked gateway. A trench at an intersection also gives the excavator a chance to look at the surfaces of three different fields.

An important influence on my thinking was Nic Ralph, a former film director who had come to Sheffield as a mature student, and had just taken a First Class degree in the department. For his doctorate[1] he wanted to look at the relationship between different farming techniques and soil characteristics, and I had managed to persuade him that an abandoned field system with an archaeologist working in it was a good place to start. In the years which followed, Nic carried out an intensive study. He immersed himself in the literature of soils, and

41 Plough-marks as they appeared at the time of discovery – soft dark peaty stripes against the hard grey-brown soil which lies immediately below the peaty humus on the surface. As the ground dried out on exposure they became much more difficult to see; it became normal practice to mark their edges with coloured pins immediately, so that they could be recorded on plan. *Photo: A. Fleming*

agriculture, and the behaviour of livestock. Perhaps the aspect of his work which most caught the imagination was his attempt to find out which animals had been present in the field system (the soil is too acid to preserve their bones). Previous studies had shown that cows, sheep and horses do not excrete all over a field at random; the different species of livestock have different 'camping' behaviour in relation to field edges – sheep, for example, preferring field corners. Thus in fields where sheep have been, there should be higher phosphate levels in the corners. After discussions with Nic, I was soon noticing the little clumps of nettles in field corners in the Peak District! Nic talked to local farmers, and sometimes helped them out in the fields. He dug soil pits on Holne Moor in a carefully calculated pattern, and got some pollen analysis done. Over the next few seasons, I came to rely a good deal on Nic not just for information about soil conditions on Holne Moor; we had a whole series of stimulating discussions and arguments about what had gone on there in the past.

That Easter, amid flurries of late snow, came a discovery which excited both of us immensely. We opened a trench called site C, at an intersection of field boundaries. As usual, we had taken off the turf and the peaty humus below it, to expose the fairly hard, grey-brown surface of the mineral soil. It was while we were cleaning this surface that we suddenly noticed some dark stripes, only 4-5cm (2in) broad and roughly 30cm (1ft) apart – ploughmarks! They looked quite fresh when the surface was being cleaned with our trowels, but were much more difficult to see when it dried out and loose soil particles started blowing around. We hastened to photograph them while they could still be seen, and then to mark the edges with nails so that they could be put on the plan even if they disappeared from sight.

The dark stripes turned out to be shallow grooves filled with peaty humus. Similar marks turned up elsewhere that Easter, on site E, just to the east of the main hut-circle, where we had discovered a reave in which was a narrow gateway, about 1.5m (4ft) wide. It seemed natural to assume that these must be of Bronze Age date; they were after all in Bronze Age fields. And they were sealed by a peaty humus which, we assumed, must have grown around 700BC, when according to Ian Simmons' 1969 account of the environmental history of Dartmoor,[2] a good deal of blanket peat was spreading. If the marks dated from the Bronze Age, they would have been made by an ard, the simple wooden 'scratch-plough' which did not turn a furrow, and was depicted on various prehistoric rock-engravings in Europe.[3]

The following summer we started work with a larger team on the main house on site F. Once again,

we found 'ard-marks' all over the surface of the mineral soil, the A horizon as Nic had taught us to call it by then. They dried out very quickly as usual, but for the site photographs I purchased a roll of white cotton tape, lengths of which we pinned into place to show the position of each mark (fig. 43).

The 'ard-marks' evidently respected the position of the hut-circle and the reaves, so it seemed that they were late in the prehistoric sequence. But it seemed a bit odd that a field only about 35m (115ft) wide had been ploughed from east to west, across its width; surely the oxen would have spent most of the time turning round? Yet the headlands on sites C and E were much too narrow for that, not much more than one metre in breadth. Collin Bowen, an expert on ancient agricultural techniques who visited the site, suggested a solution to these problems. What if the ard had been drawn by human traction? I gratefully accepted this suggestion, and the idea of an ard drawn by human beings sometime in the later Bronze Age was born. Alas, it was to be discredited a couple of years later, as we shall see.

The rest of site F was shaping up very well. As we cleaned the peaty humus off the stones of the reave, it became clear that the section behind the house, although low, had been beautifully built, well faced on both sides, with a core of carefully-chosen stones, many of them an attractive blueish colour in the sunshine (fig. 42a). The reave was sitting on top of a low earthen bank (fig. 42b), as we had noted when we cut a trial section across it the previous Easter. As we were cleaning up the stones for a photograph, I noticed that just to the SW of the house there was a marked 'notch', about one metre wide, in the surface of the bank, and that this notch had been carefully blocked with stones when the reave was built. Evidently the bank was not made simply as a platform for the reave; it must have been a boundary in its own right, and the notch must have been where a path went across it. It may be that people wishing to reach the field to the west came out of the house, turned right and went straight round to the back, wearing down the bank at this particular spot; but it is also possible that there was a hedge on the bank, with a gateway in it here. We looked for the post-hole for a gate, but we were disappointed. Of course, there might simply have been a movable hurdle here, placed across the gap.

So perhaps there was a pre-reave phase of boundary-making, a phase of earthen banks and maybe hedges, and we would only be able to get at it by removing the existing reaves. This was rather a sobering thought. If the reaves were constructed at a somewhat later stage, there might have been all sorts of changes of plan – after all, we had seen how the

42(a) Most of the reaves excavated turned out to be broad, low walls with properly constructed faces, like this one behind the house on site F on Holne Moor; (b) the same reave, a few metres further south, with stones partially removed to show the bank (? hedge-bank) on which it was built. In the background is the short length of wall with which the reave-builders blocked the notch in the bank, which previously gave access to the field behind the house, where the photo tower is. *Photos: A. Fleming*

notch in our possible hedge-bank had been neatly blocked by the reave-builders. Perhaps one or two of the odd kinks and dog-legs in the reaves had arisen because the reave-builders had perpetuated some parts of the early boundary system but not others. It might not after all be possible simply to look at a plan of a reave system and assume that one was looking at an essentially unchanged original layout!

43   The site F house from the west at an early stage in its excavation. The arc of boulders is a recently constructed structure built of stones taken from the northern side of the house; nearer to the camera, a small structure (a prehistoric shepherd's hut?) built in the ruins of the main house is beginning to emerge. In the background, the white tapes indicate the positions of medieval plough-marks. *Photo: A. Fleming*

Perhaps the house on site F would also turn out to have an earlier phase of construction. But our first preoccupation was with its more recent history. An arc of boulders (fig. 43) just inside the entrance – perhaps a fairly recent shepherd's shelter? – had to be recorded and removed. The boulders had obviously been taken from the outer face of the wall of the house on its northern side. Then, as I stared down from our photo-tower, I realised that the inner edge of a structure, much smaller but still roughly circular, could be picked out from among the jumble of stones inside the house (fig. 43). It lay in the south-western quarter of the interior, just against the wall of the main house. It was only about 2½m (8ft) across, and the narrow entrance faced into what must have been by that time the ruins of the main house; presumably the

area enclosed by the wall of the older building would have formed a convenient yard. This little building was probably put up in the prehistoric period, but it is impossible to tell whether this means three or four generations or three or four centuries later than the occupation period of the house whose ruins it utilised. The structure may have been a herdsman's hut, put up at a time when the field system had been largely abandoned and turned over to pasture; it seems almost symbolic that two pieces of querns, relics of a time when grain was being ground into flour, had been incorporated into its wall. One of them lay right in the entrance.

The most dramatic discovery of the 1977 campaign came late in the season. The area to the south of the house had been cleared down to the surface of the mineral soil, exposing quite an impressive array of

44 Site F house, at a later stage, with the small hut clearly distinguishable. Note the paving slabs near the entrance of the main house, and the arc of stones just inside the house wall, which were probably packing stones for an internal wooden cladding of upright planks. *Photo: A. Fleming*

plough-marks; then we left it, in order to concentrate on the house. Nic Ralph had dug a small soil-pit at the southern edge of the trench, into the yellowish 'B horizon' below; he had taken some samples and recorded the nature of the profile.

A couple of days later we noticed a very distinct brown stripe, about 20cm (8in) wide, on the floor of the soil-pit, and standing out in sharp contrast to the dirty yellow subsoil. At first its significance did not

45 In 1977, we found, beside the house on site F, a dark 'ring-groove', the fill of a narrow trench dug to support upright planks for the wall of a circular building. A few packing-stones can be seen; the building's entrance was at bottom left. *Photo: A. Fleming*

register. We had had some rain. The pit had filled with water and got very muddy. The edges of the stripe seemed very sharp; perhaps Nic had been sitting on a short length of rather dirty plank when he took his samples? But the mark was still there next day. Then, taking a closer look, I could see that it was not a *straight* stripe; it was slightly curved, as if part of the circumference of a circle. It was then that I noticed one or two small stones set on edge, projecting above the surface nearby. How ridiculous not to have spotted their significance before! We were clearly dealing with a narrow, circular palisade trench – a slot cut into the ground to take a timber wall of some kind, whose footings had been carefully wedged in with upright packing-stones.

The end of the season was almost on us; the next couple of days were quite hectic, as we removed the A horizon material and exposed the subsoil beneath. It was true: there was the palisade trench, or 'ring-groove' as it is frequently called, a precise brown ring against an orange/yellow background (fig. 45). There were several packing-stones; impressions of timber uprights were occasionally visible on the floor of the ring-groove when we emptied it of material. The building had been about 4.5m (14ft) in diameter. Not quite all of it was picked up in the 1977 season. The following year we searched for the remaining arc of its circumference. Knowing exactly what we were due to find, we were able to pick up all the packing-stones (fig. 46). In one or two places they were paired, allowing us to see how thick were the planks which they had held in position. Lower down, on the floor of the ring-groove, the plank wall, as it must mostly have been, had left an elongated brown stain.

It seemed clear that our newly discovered wooden house had stood beside the circular house to the north, with its stone-faced wall-base. Both buildings were both close beside the boundary to the west, and faced away from it; they were less than 3m (10ft) apart, and if the use of the buildings was contemporary with the notch in the boundary bank at the back, a path between them would have led straight to it.

In the 1977 season we also discovered how to pick up ancient ditches. Obviously the material for the low earthen bank to the west of the house must have come from somewhere. But it was only when we had removed the bank and taken off the mineral soil that we saw the dark brown linear stain which we were looking for, below where the tail of the bank had been. Just to the north-west of the house, the search for the ditch proved more difficult. We were picking up the colours and textures which ought to indicate ditch silts. But they were not really shaping up into the neat linear feature which we had picked up further south; they seemed to be more extensive than that. After a couple of days of incomprehension I had had enough; I went up to the site by myself, one evening after work. With trowel, pickaxe and shovel, but, above all, the chance to work without distraction, I worked out the stratigraphy, as the shadows lengthened. When I left the site it was dimsey, as they say locally. But I had sorted it out; there were in fact *two* ditches intersecting here, and one of them was curving away to the north-east, around the northern side of the house. Here was another ditch feature which had been invisible on the ground surface and on the surface of the mineral soil.

46 Returning in 1978 to complete the excavation of the ring-groove building discovered the previous year, we were rewarded by the discovery of a fine set of packing-stones. *Photo: A. Fleming*

We were beginning to understand something crucial about the soils of Dartmoor – podsols, as many of them are technically known. Because humic material and various minerals, including iron, have been leached – that is, washed down through the soil profile – archaeological features rarely show up in the compact grey-brown mineral soil immediately below the surface peat. To pick up the more ancient ditches, pits and post-holes, you have to take off the A horizon, preferably quite quickly with a pick. Just below will be a yellowish or orange-brown B horizon. The colour comes from iron staining; sometimes there is an iron pan. The first few centimetres tend to be heavily flecked with brown patches of humic material, so that even when the surface has been scraped clean and fresh the colours are very confusing. It is only when you have gone down a little deeper that this welter of contrasting colours can be reduced, and you may start to pick out archaeological features.

The next season we came back to finish off the excavation of the site F house. On the northern side of the house we picked up the ditch, which did indeed prove to be neatly wrapped around the edge of the building (fig. 47); it was about 1m (3ft) wide and about 50cm (1½ft) deep where we encountered it, low down at the top of the B horizon. Presumably the ditch's main function was to act as a drain or sump for rainwater from the roof. The previous season we had picked up a narrow, stone-lined channel through the thickness of the wall – probably a drain leading into this northern ditch. For some reason there was no ditch on the southern side of the house.

Much of the 1978 season was occupied in trowelling down the earth in the interior of the house. The upper part of the B horizon was pretty 'dirty', flecked with a good deal of humus and charcoal, but we started to notice that some of the patches of humus were small, up to 10-12cm (4in) across, and roughly circular. Could they be stake-holes, indications of the places where poles and stakes had once been driven into the ground? One would expect some wooden fittings inside a house. Or could these circular patches simply be pockets of humic material? There was only one way to find out – take out the fill and see what happened. Six-inch pointing trowels were no use; I went off to get some spoons – tea-spoons, dessert spoons, even a long-handled pickle-jar spoon or two, later to be greatly prized by the diggers. There has been rather a dearth of spoons in my caravan ever since!

We soon worked out how to deal with the 'stake-holes'. They had to be carefully marked with nails with large, painted heads as soon as they were spotted. Then each digger would take a spoon and go to work on one of them, starting in the middle, working

47 The site F house at a late stage in its excavation. Note the ditch (split into sections by our excavation method) running round the northern half of the building; it could not be seen on the surface. The wall has been partially robbed on this side; its true thickness is seen on the southern side of the house (to the right), where the wall's earthen core is noticeable. *Photo: A. Fleming*

outwards and downwards, gradually removing the soft, usually brown fill to try to find harder edges. Sometimes the feature would turn out to be shallow, with an irregular outline – presumably a natural pocket of humus. Quite frequently a digger would break through into a little tunnel, sometimes running horizontally, sometimes plunging down at an oblique angle. Clearly this was the work of a burrowing animal; the obvious candidate, it seemed to me, was the short-tailed field vole. I had seen dead voles on the moor. A couple of years later, as we were demolishing a reave on site B, we were distressed to disturb some baby ones, squeaking away inside their beautifully constructed spherical nest of grass stems, while their mother scurried around distractedly.

A true stake-hole, on the other hand, would reveal itself as a circular or nearly circular pipe, going down straight, or at a slight angle to the vertical. We recorded these genuine stake-holes on the site plan, measuring their depths and diameters. It might seem that we had only to carry out this operation with the spoons once. Unfortunately, however, we found that there was no one level at which all the stake-holes could be picked up, however carefully we stared at the soil colours and kept the trowelled surfaces clean and fresh. Some stake-holes only showed up when they had dried out, so that they would put in an annoyingly late appearance after several hours, or maybe a couple of days. We couldn't afford to stop staring at the surface just because we had finished a tea-spoon session! Also, the greater density of pockets of humic soil, iron-pan and animal tunnels in the upper part of the B horizon undoubtedly tended to confuse the eye and obscure the stake-holes.

We soon found that we had to take off another spit, and then another, and probably a fourth, with the sub-soil becoming an increasingly pure yellow or orange-brown colour, before we could be sure that we had gone through the stake-hole horizon. So the plan that we produced took shape gradually, and every photograph was a compromise, which left out the stake-holes which had yet to appear, and any shallow ones which had already been recorded and removed in previous spits. I think that the changes which have

48 Inside the house on site F we found relatively large, deep post-holes for the upright timbers which supported the roof (two sets, for successive buildings) and stake-holes for various internal wooden fittings. In the foreground is the narrow trench dug for an internal cladding of upright planks, wedged in with packing-stones. *Photo: A. Fleming*

taken place in the soil since prehistoric times, plus the different histories of individual stakes and posts – some left in position to rot, others pulled out for re-use elsewhere – have led to a situation where the apparent 'tops' of the stake-holes occur at varying levels.

Anyway, despite these difficulties, we found so many stake-holes that on the site plan and in the final photographs parts of the main house on site F have a more than passing resemblance to a Gruyère cheese! Work in the interior of the house (fig. 48) also began to reveal the deeper post-holes for upright timbers to support the roof of the house, which would presumably have been conical and thatched. They were arranged roughly in a circle. Another feature of the interior was a group of beautifully laid floor-slabs (fig. 47), just inside the doorway (which was also paved) and continuing for a short distance in a northerly direction, beside the eastern sector of the wall. This 'partial paving' is hard to understand; it occurred in other Dartmoor hut-circles, according to old excavation reports.[4] Perhaps the front part of the house tended to get particularly muddy; one could imagine the odd sheep being brought in for milking in wet weather conditions, for instance . . . .

We were gaining a greater understanding of the history of this building. We knew that the wall of the house overlay the ditch which ran beside the early boundary-bank to the west. This ditch had also been cut through by the ditch which had been dug around the northern half of the house. Now we had noted in our preliminary fieldwork that the *reave* apparently kinked slightly to avoid the hut-circle; but the same could not be said for the underlying earthen bank, since its ditch was covered by the hut-circle's wall. So, if the kink was also a feature of the earthen bank, we could only come to one conclusion – there must have been an *earlier* building on the site of the hut-circle, presumably a wooden one, for the bank to swerve around!

Then we discovered another reason for believing that the main house had a predecessor. Within the bank, just north of the house, we came across a cluster of large potsherds, obviously all parts of the same vessel. Since many of them were on edge, they had obviously been chucked in – by someone carrying the Bronze Age equivalent of a dust-pan? – as the bank was being constructed. Now if these sherds came out of a building, that building could not have been the hut-circle itself, because the latter was built over the ditch from which the bank's material was derived; again, a predecessor was indicated.

So the search was on for an earlier house. Perhaps it was under the wall of the main hut-circle? We removed the wall in two areas, looking for stake-holes – without success. But we did get a chance to examine something which had intrigued us for some time, a ring of small stones set on edge just inside the wall (figs 44, 48). It turned out that they were packing-stones, rammed into the inner edge of a ring-groove, presumably the bedding-trench for a circular wall of upright planks. I am inclined to suggest that we are dealing with some kind of internal wooden cladding, perhaps put up sometime after the construction of the main wall of the house.

Then, just inside the wall of the house, a few distinctively large stake-holes started to appear, not very close together but apparently forming a ring. Could these have held the timber uprights of the wall of the early house? If so, there should be at least one stake-hole beneath the paving-slabs to the north of the doorway. We lifted them, and our efforts were rewarded. And by now we had found so many deep post-holes in the interior of the building that we had to think in terms of two successive sets of roof-supports, not one (fig. 48). So it seemed safe to conclude, taking all these lines of evidence into

account, that phase 1 on site F involved a circular timber house, which was in occupation when an earthen bank was constructed behind it. After a certain interval (it depends how long we can expect a timber building to last on Dartmoor in the Bronze Age – fifty years? A hundred?) this building was replaced by a house with a stone-faced, earthen wall, a ditch on its northern side, and an internal wooden cladding of upright planks. The similarity of the ring-groove and packing-stones method used here to that employed for the timber building to the south makes it tempting to suggest that the latter building was put up at this time. At some stage – perhaps later, if the gap in the earthen bank is seen as related to a pathway between the two buildings – the reave was built along the top of the bank. Finally, a good deal later, a small hut was built in the ruins of the house.

The 1978 season also saw the opening of site G, just to the east of site F. This was at the spot where a ditch, thought at the time (wrongly) to be part of a pre-reave field system, appeared to meet a parallel reave at right angles. The reave proved to be very well-constructed. It had a very neat dry-walled face with several courses surviving (fig. 50), and a densely-packed mass of stones piled against one face, presumably during field clearance (fig. 49). But the really spectacular thing about site G was the character of the 'ard-marks' – 15-20cm (6-8in) broad, and standing out well, in the wet conditions, against the pinkish-brown mineral soil. These grooves proved to be much deeper than usual (fig. 51), and we had a wonderful time photographing them in low sunlight, and taking plaster casts of their profiles in the belief that we might be able to draw some conclusions about the implement which made them.

This, however, was to be the ard-marks' finest hour! I had suggested that they were prehistoric, but there were problems with this idea. Most of them ran in only one direction, east-west; if they were really prehistoric, should they not run 'criss-cross', in two directions, as in the famous case from Gwithian, in west Cornwall? Further fieldwork had shown that they were not after all, as I had supposed, *outside* the area enclosed in the Middle Ages. So the following season, 1979, I determined to try to demonstrate their date stratigraphically.

Our sites lay just beyond the south-west corner of quite a large, roughly square medieval field, marked out by a sturdy earthen bank with a ditch on its western side (fig. 40). I decided to put a trench on the western edge of this ditch. If we could establish the presence of 'ard-marks' in the area, the next step would be to extend the trench to the east, remove the bank, and see whether we could find the marks underneath it. If we could, that would not prove that they

49 A reave on site G, with Bronze Age clearance stones packed against its eastern face. These stone are packed too tightly against the face to represent 'tumble' or to have been placed there in the Middle Ages. *Photo: A. Fleming*

were prehistoric, but at least it would put them before about AD 1200-1300.

So we opened site H, not far to the north-east of site G. The first part of the operation went as planned; the 'ard-marks' were indeed present in the area. Then came the moment of truth. We duly extended the trench and took away the medieval bank, which proved to overlie a peaty layer up to 10cm thick. We carefully stripped this layer away – no 'ard-marks'! It looked as if the marks might be medieval after all. And as we drew the plan of site H, I realised that there was an 'ard-mark' running along beside the western edge of the ditch, at right angles to the others. And at one point it was cutting through the base of a scoop in the mineral soil, a kind of shallow extension to the ditch which must have been made by the bank-builders. So the cultivation-marks were made *after* the construction of the hedge-bank; they were medieval plough-marks after all.

50 The reave seen in fig. 49, with clearance and tumbled stones removed. Most reaves investigated were proper walls, low but with evidence for facing on both side. *Photo: A. Fleming*

51 Ploughmarks on site G, after remove of their peaty fill. These plough-marks were at first thought to be prehistoric, but it was later realised that they date to *c.* 1300 AD. In other places these plough-marks are sealed below the spoil-heaps of tinners' trial-pits, themselves old enough to be covered by several centimetres of peaty humus. *Photo: A. Fleming*

And then various other things started to make sense. I realised why the 'headlands' were so narrow; in the Middle Ages the reaves would have been much as they are today. The oxen would simply have walked over them, and the ploughman would have left the plough-share in the soil until an encounter with one of the stones fallen from the reave reminded him to halt the oxen and lift it out. No need, then, to postulate a plough pulled by human traction. One of the plough-furrows was only 85cm (33in) from one of the facing-stones of the site F house; the hut-circle is a pretty solid obstacle, and it is hard to believe that a large ox-team could have come that close. We could conclude, I think, that the medieval plough was not pulled by more than one or two oxen. The plough's job must have been to improve soil texture by grooving the surface of the mineral soil, improving the drainage and throwing up sandy particles into the peaty humus on the surface.

Our main task in 1979 was to continue the excavation of the hut-circle on site B, picking up where we had left off in 1976. It proved a disappointment, in terms of finds and in terms of interior stake-holes or other features. This was rather an inconspicuous hut-circle, just over 5m in diameter; it did at any rate seem to have been built later than the reave. The interesting discoveries were made outside this building, however. Having learnt lessons from site F, we made sure we had a good look in the zone outside the house. And it was here, in one corner of our trench, that we found a roughly linear scatter of stake-holes, including two quite deep post-holes. They were just to the north-east of the building, not very far away from the doorway (fig. 53). What could this be? It was quite likely that many of the activities of the people who lived in the building – if it *was* a house – took place out of doors, just outside the entrance; we might easily have picked up the edge of a Bronze Age 'farmyard'. There might be pits, fences, post- and stake-holes for wooden structures, working areas, rubbish deposits, hearths, and so on – a wonderful opportunity to study such an area for the first time on Dartmoor.

So although we had completed four seasons' excavation, and finished work on the hut-circle, we could hardly leave site B. Next year we came back, and went through a routine which was to become very familiar over the next few seasons – scraping the B horizon, marking the features, taking out their contents with teaspoons, putting them on the plan, and recording their dimensions and levels. Then we would take off a few more centimetres and go through the same procedure again – and then again. It was only towards the end of the season, however, that I realised that the deeper post-holes which we had picked up during the previous season were part of a ring of six such holes, the roof-supports for another circular timber building (fig. 54). The inner part of the timber building, within

52 Venford Reave, the southern terminal reave of the Dartmeet system, seen under excavation on site B. Judging by the amount of tumble on the site, the reave can never have been much higher; it might, however, have been the base for a hedge (see fig. 70). *Photo: A. Fleming*

53 Site B during excavation in 1979, from the west. The relationship between the building and Venford Reave can clearly be seen, as can the neatly-built character of the reave itself. In the background, white markers show the positions of post- and stake-holes; the following year it was realised that these were traces of a circular wooden house. *Photo: A. Fleming*

the ring of roof-supports, was 3m (9 ft) across; further out was a ring of widely-spaced stake-holes, presumably for the upright poles which held the framework of what was probably a wattle-and-daub wall. The house was about 5m (16ft) in diameter, with a 'cooking-hole' near the centre; the pattern of stake-holes suggested a prominent porch of some kind on its SE side. It is clear from the plan that this building must have been put up before the hut-circle, which might have been its replacement.

We had to think about stakes and poles and planks, and houses which would not have been out of place in the lowlands; the more stake-holes came to light, the more one began to wonder about coppices. After all, evidence for coppice management well before 2000BC, and woodland crafts like hurdle-making had recently come to light from not very far away, in the Somerset Levels. And the post-holes of a fence, some

of them 10cm (4in) in diameter, had recently been discovered beneath a terminal reave on Shaugh Moor, in the Plym valley, by the Central Excavation Unit from the Department of the Environment.[5] (We had a good relationship with the archaeologists of the Central Unit, whose exuberant life-style was legendary. For me, their most exciting discovery came the next year, when they discovered a mass of hoof-prints trodden into the base of a Bronze Age ditch.[6] They were mainly of cattle and sheep, with a few of horse; they looked as fresh as if the livestock had walked up the ditch last week. They were invaluable because Dartmoor's acid soils destroy bone, so that it is normally impossible to find out about domestic livestock.)

My own team spent six more seasons on site B, searching for more stake- and post-holes, trying to sort out what appeared to be a Bronze Age 'farmyard'. At the end of each season we realized that we had not reached the edge of the site; we extended to the east, north and finally west, in the hope of finding more stake-holes that would help us to make sense of those discovered during the previous season. I was also hoping to get a large enough number of holes, covering a reasonably extensive area, to try to work out what wooden structures were present on the site.

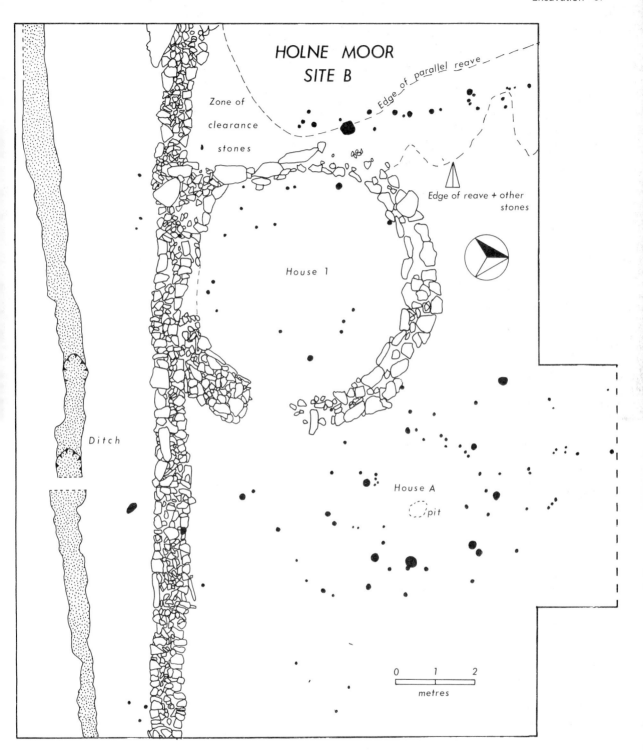

HOLNE MOOR
SITE B

Edge of parallel reave

Zone of
clearance
stones

Edge of reave + other
stones

House 1

Ditch

House A

pit

0   1   2
metres

54 Plan of site B after the 1980 excavation season, showing the circular timber house, with a ring of holes for roof-supporting posts, and a small number of stake-holes, probably to support a wall based on panels of hurdlework.

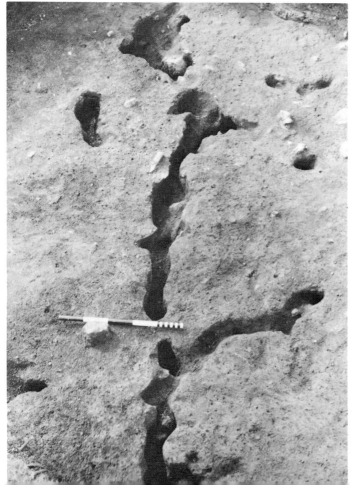

55 Tunnels made by animals during, or immediately after, the time when site B was occupied; I believe that they were made by moles, and that they are evidence for better soil conditions in the Bronze Age.
Photo: A. Fleming

As on site F, we had to cope with numerous animal tunnels. One thing we noticed about them on this site was their tendency to contain charcoal – usually fresh-looking charcoal. We started joking about an ancient civilisation of voles which had discovered the use of fire! In 1982, however, I began to worry about the vole theory. When the animal tunnels contained more than air, the earth which filled them was just like the fill of the stake-holes. By now we now had a fairly good understanding of the soil history of Holne Moor. The 20-25cm (8-10in) of peaty humus on Holne Moor, we knew, had formed *after* the main Bronze Age settlement episode which we were investigating. We knew that reaves were not built on peaty soils, and that ancient ditches here filled up with silt, not peat. Since very few of our animal tunnels contained peaty material, most of them must have been dug at least as far back as the Bronze Age. In fact the presence of fresh charcoal in them suggests that they were made while the settlement on site B was occupied, or very soon after its abandonment.

As far as I can see, the size, depth and general character of the tunnels suggest that they were made by moles. The tunnels also have vertical shafts of the kind which moles use to eject their spoil to form the familiar molehills. Moles don't live on this part of Holne Moor now; for one thing, in today's acid, peaty humus the earthworm population is very low. But thinking about moles made sense of something else. Sometimes we had found spreads of charcoal, with well-defined edges, right down in the B horizon. Presumably these had once been equally clearly-defined charcoal patches on the original ground surface, and had 'percolated' down through the soil profile. Charcoal scattered on the surface today would certainly not get buried in this wholesale fashion. The most likely way for this to happen would be swift burial by an active population of earthworms, followed by gradual descent through the soil profile as the worm tunnels collapsed, in the fashion explained by Charles Darwin over a century ago. Also, thinking about the depth of the stake-holes, and hence the depth to which the stakes were driven into the ground, I am inclined to believe that the soil must have been more friable than it is today. The behaviour of the charcoal and stake-holes imply earthworms, the tunnels imply moles, moles imply earthworms . . . . The picture is one of an active soil fauna, and a less acid, peat-free soil.

One of our best seasons on site B was in 1985. We had cut a long, narrow trench, with its long axis roughly north–south, on the eastern side of the site. As soon as we got down just below the iron pan and humus horizon, we picked up a few stake-holes, most of them on a rough line running straight up the middle

of the trench. A fence, perhaps? We started to take a little more off the surface. A few more holes appeared. As the sun rose in the sky, on a lovely September morning, its growing warmth dried the slight dew which had fallen overnight. And suddenly, as the ground dried out, little brown spots started making their appearance along the central axis of the trench. They had retained their moisture just a little longer than the orange-brown earth in which they were set. I rushed around sticking in lots of yellow-topped indicator nails.

Within threequarters of an hour we had a line of stake-holes, many of them quite small and close together, running straight up the middle of the trench (fig. 56). So we had a fence, presumably made by driving in stakes and creating a continuous line of hurdlework by weaving brushwood or split laths between them. Alternatively, the stakes might have been the upright members of a laid hedge, although they were closer together and more upright than examples from recent British hedge-laying traditions. The orientation of the fence was of considerable interest; it followed the axis of the parallel reave system within which we were working. It could have been an 'early' boundary, not perpetuated by a reave, or a subdivision of the reave system, perhaps inserted quite late. We now had to ask ourselves how far we could take the shapes and sizes of the fields in a reave system at face value, if parcels of land demarcated so clearly by reaves might once have been subdivided by fences?

The long fence made a satisfactory eastern boundary for our excavation area, allowing us to conclude our operations in this area. This was good news, since after several seasons of promising, over-optimistically, that I was just about to finish, I was unlikely to be able to raise enough money for another full excavation season. But further west, in our other 1985 trench, the stake-holes came thick and fast. And towards the end of the season, in the south-west corner of the trench not far away from the terminal reave, we found a pair of deep post-holes, accompanied by one or two quite deep and large stake-holes. Evidently we had stumbled upon another roofed building, perhaps a second circular house. It seemed wrong to leave the site without coming back to check this possibility.

Fortunately we were rescued from our financial impasse by the generosity of two individuals, who managed to find the money for us to continue in 1986. It turned out that I was right about the timber house. Very soon, clusters of packing-stones appeared, indicating the positions of the deep post-holes for the roof-supports. There were seven of them (fig. 57). Then we started to pick up the stake-holes of the house wall. The stakes had been thicker and closer

56 The stake-holes of a fence, discovered on site B during the 1985 season. The human figure stands just behind Venford Reave. The fence, whether it was an early boundary or a late sub-division, followed the axis of the Dartmeet system. *Photo: A. Fleming*

together on the western side of the building, the direction from which the worst of the weather comes, at any rate in today's climatic conditions. The wall here might well have been strengthened against the gales – or repaired after one of their onslaughts.

As can be seen from the plan (fig. 58), this house was a little over 6m (19ft) in diameter. It faced south-east, and the combination of two of the roof-posts plus two deep door-posts suggests the presence of a sturdy porch, probably with its own thatched roof thrusting out from the cone-shaped roof of the building itself. The most vulnerable parts of the building would have been the places where the porch met the roof, especially on the weather side to the south-west. It may be no coincidence that the roofing-post in this position is the only one to have been renewed. It is interesting that the post in the corresponding position in the house on site F, probably the one relating to its early, timber phase, was also renewed.

There were quite a number of stake-holes within the building; one day, by comparing them with others in the house on site F and perhaps with other sites on the south-western moors, it may be possible to find recurring patterns, and gain some idea of the wooden fittings regularly found within these houses. Ideally we need houses which were not in use for too long, otherwise replacements and internal changes will presumably have created an indecipherable pattern. On site B in 1986 we encountered a tinner's pit, and a neat rectilinear trench filled with rusty tin cans, but fortunately neither had obtruded too seriously into the area of the building!

The relationship of the building with Venford Reave, which runs only 2-3m (7-10ft) past its doorway, is a matter for debate. It might be argued that, since having a wall running close to a house's entrance would have been inconvenient, the house must have gone out of use before the reave was built. On the other hand, the relationship might have been planned; indeed one could regard both timber buildings on site B as having been set beside the reave.

57 The final season on site B, in 1986, saw the discovery of traces of another timber building on the western side of the site. On this photograph the clumps of packing-stones on the right mark positions of two of the post-holes for the ring of roof-supporting timbers; letters A-E mark the positions of the others. *Photo: A. Fleming*

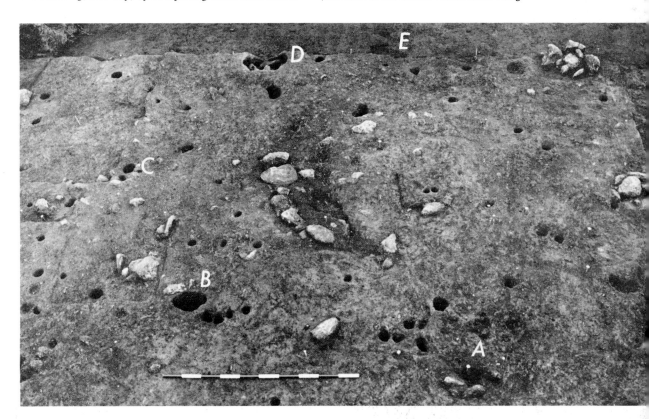

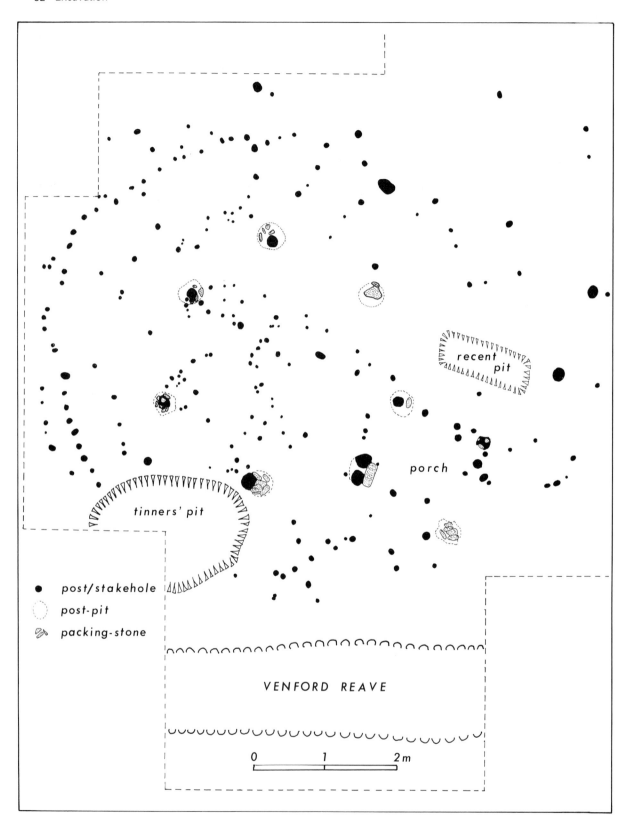

recent pit

porch

tinners' pit

- post/stakehole
- post-pit
- packing-stone

VENFORD REAVE

0   1   2m

58 Plan of the circular timber house discovered on the western side of site B (photo fig. 57). The western side of the house has been strengthened against (or repaired after?) the onslaughts of the elements. The porch at the SE did not project beyond the wall of the building but may have had a hipped roof; if so, the junction of the main roof and the porch roof, facing south-west, would have been vulnerable to storm damage, and it may be significant that this post was the only one to be replaced.

If there was a hedge on the reave it could have provided some shelter, and helped to control the movements of livestock and small children near the house.

Once again we had demonstrated that despite the prominence of reaves and hut-circles in the field, there is much that is not visible on the surface; once again, the importance of timber in Dartmoor's prehistory had been underlined. As we finally left site B, after a campaign which had taken up nine excavation seasons, I could not help reflecting that there were still questions which needed to be answered. Was there anything to the west of the newly-discovered house? How far did the fence go in a northerly direction, and what exactly happened to it? What timber features might lie to the south of the terminal reave? It seemed that in spite of so much work we had uncovered quite a small area – and so we

had, by the standards of excavators who have much greater resources to dispose of. But the site had provided a good deal of new information about the prehistory of Dartmoor, at very low cost. With a larger team and a lot more money, we might have sorted out site B in two or three seasons; but I believe that in those circumstances our understanding of the site would have been a good deal shallower.

The visible Bronze Age landscape of Dartmoor is impressive enough on the surface, with its well-preserved field-walls, enclosures and houses. One or two conservationists have argued that the only justification for excavation is a response to some threat which cannot be averted – mining or forestry, for instance. However, it is impossible to understand this landscape, and so explain it properly to Dartmoor's many visitors, from surface indications alone. To do that, and to understand the opportunities and problems which are likely to crop up when a site does have to be excavated under 'rescue' conditions, we have to excavate. The excavations on Holne Moor, and those carried out by the Central Unit on Shaugh Moor, are just a beginning, showing us something of Dartmoor's rich potential as an archaeological resource, and giving us intriguing glimpses of the period when the Bronze Age land boundaries were first laid out.

7: Reaves and the prehistory of Dartmoor

Reaves are now on the map – literally, marked on the Ordnance Survey's 1:25,000 Outdoor Leisure map of Dartmoor, as 'boundary works'. The work of the Reave Project, when fully published and assimilated, will have shown that some prehistoric inhabitants of Dartmoor lived in very large walled field systems, beyond which lay pasture land subdivided into large areas by long reaves. It can be shown that fences and banks were also used as boundaries at this time. Those which have been found beneath reaves must have preceded them. The importance of wood, and woodland management, has been highlighted by the finding of timber buildings beneath and beside stone-based 'hut circles', and numerous stake-holes at site B on Holne Moor. This indicates that, however well-preserved these 'ancient landscapes' may be, excavation is necessary for a fuller understanding of their character and development. This was a point I had to make when, in 1977, a prominent local conservationist tried to have my excavations stopped. It is perfectly possible, I argued, to enjoy a Shakespeare play without having the faintest idea about the author, the times he lived in and the conditions in which he worked; but that is hardly an argument for closing down research on the Elizabethan theatre!

Behind the concrete results, the hard-won archaeological observations and the more obvious lessons of more than ten years' work, lies the quest for greater understanding of prehistory. Archaeology is not just a matter of collecting new 'evidence'; the past is modelled rather than observed. The project was intended to clarify certain issues. As the work progressed, new questions were raised, conventional wisdom was subjected to closer scrutiny, and new generalisations emerged. Part of this ferment of ideas involved general issues like territoriality, early social organisation, and the concept of marginal land. Part of it was concerned with models of Dartmoor's remote past, and that is what I am concerned with in this chapter. I had to devote a good deal of thought to what I came to call the 'context' of Dartmoor's episode of major land division – the social and economic conditions leading up to the making of the boundaries, the history of the landscape in previous centuries, and the

possible motives of the reave builders. I hope to make clear, in the following explanatory sketch, that many questions remain to be answered. Working out how to do this is a challenging question for the future.

Not very much is known about the onset of farming in the Dartmoor area. This process took place shortly after 4000BC. It is not clear which model is to be preferred – a movement of intrusive 'colonists', or indigenous hunters and foragers who gradually acquired domesticated plants and animals from farming peoples living at a distance. More complicated scenarios can be envisaged. What interests me is the physical appearance, at that time, of the granite hills which later came to be grouped together and known as Dartmoor. David Maguire, who did some pollen analysis on Holne Moor, and Chris Caseldine have recently discussed this question.[1] They conclude that most of Dartmoor would have carried trees, except for the most exposed hill-tops, which would have been species-rich heathland. As I understand it, much of the forest was dominated by oak: the Dart itself is 'Oak River', from a Celtic word which has given us the Derwent and the many Irish place-names in 'derry', and the oak is the main tree found in the two old woodlands on the Moor today, Wistman's Wood and Blackator Copse. In the wetter places alder and willow would have been common, and peat would have been growing here too. Rowan would also have been present in the woods; at higher altitudes, the oak would have given way to hazel and to some extent birch, and it seems likely that the woodlands would have gradually thinned out to become a good deal more open on the higher hillsides.

So around four or five thousand years before the birth of Christ, there was really no such thing as 'Dartmoor' – in this region there were just some disconnected patches of upland heath among fairly open hazel woods, with a few tracts of blanket peat beginning to grow on badly-drained cols and saddles. This would have been good country for hunting red and roe deer and perhaps wild cattle, especially in the summer months. There is plenty of evidence in the form of 'microliths', the flint barbs and tips of hunting weapons, that people came here in the period before

the onset of farming;[2] we found one or two microliths during our excavations on Holne Moor. There are some indications from pollen analysis[3] that these hunting communities were changing the pattern of vegetation, perhaps by burning the undergrowth as hunting peoples frequently do. This in turn may have encouraged wild animals to congregate in particular places, browsing on young tree seedlings and keeping some areas fairly open.

These hills are classed as marginal land today, but early farming peoples would probably have found it quite convenient to settle in a zone where there was extensive browsing and grazing for their cattle, and the possibility of some good hunting. Their stone axe-heads have been picked up here (again, we found one during our Holne Moor excavations) and a few of their burial monuments have survived. Like some other Neolithic peoples in the British Isles, they buried a selection of their dead in box-like 'chamber-tombs' made of large stone slabs, such as the one known as the Spinster's Rock, near Drewsteignton. These chamber tombs were encased in cairns, some of them rather impressive 'long cairns', like the one near Corringdon Gate, on southern Dartmoor. Probably only a small proportion of the ceremonial monuments originally built have survived and been recognised.

Most of the chamber tombs are found on moorland, just beyond the edge of present-day enclosed land, so it looks as if their builders had some interest in the hills now known as Dartmoor. Pollen analysis suggests that clearances made in the woods at this

59 A fine example of a stone row, in this case a triple one, on the eastern shoulder of Cosdon Hill, north-east Dartmoor. *Photo: A. Fleming*

time were probably quite small and short-lived,[4] although there are technical reasons for believing that the pollen record may have underestimated the extent of cleared land.

By about 2500BC, after perhaps a thousand years of small-scale hunting and grazing in the uplands, pressure on this land seems to have intensified. At this time (though the dating evidence is very thin, and the chronology depends partly on comparisons made with the archaeological sequence in other parts of southern England) over seventy stone rows (fig. 59) were constructed.[5] Nothing is really known of the beliefs and rituals associated with these ceremonial monu-ments, which were probably constructed at about the time when copper was coming into use in the British Isles. A very high phosphate reading from one of Nic Ralph's soil pits at the Holne Moor stone row suggests that a burial may have taken place there.

The stone rows vary considerably. Some of them may have undergone several episodes of construction, or may even have been put up gradually, stone by stone, over the years. They quite frequently lead to small cairns, many of which tend to be demarcated by kerbs of upright stones. Most rows are less than 200m (220 yards) in length, but there are one or two longer ones, including the remarkable row in the Erme valley, which is over three kilometres (two

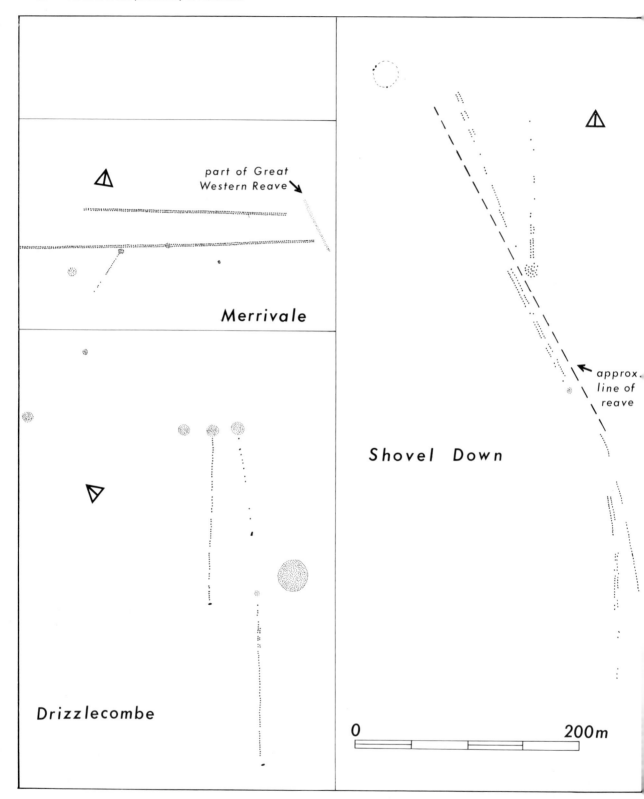

60 Ceremonial centres on Dartmoor. *Drawings after Worth*

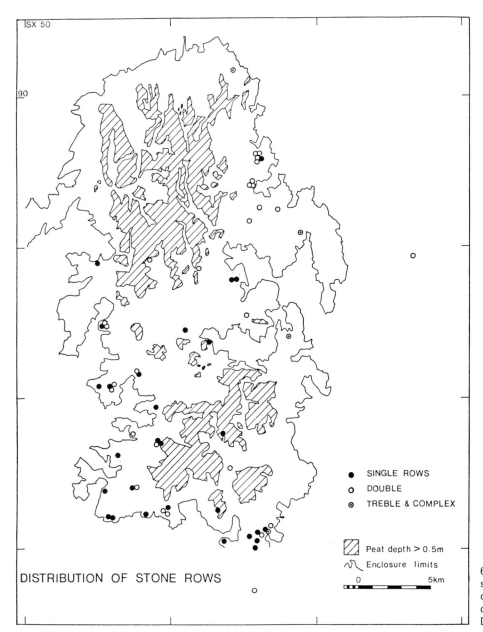

DISTRIBUTION OF STONE ROWS

● SINGLE ROWS
○ DOUBLE
◉ TREBLE & COMPLEX

Peat depth > 0.5m
Enclosure limits
0   5km

61 Map of stone rows, showing their widespread occurrence on most parts of the fringe of present-day Dartmoor. *After Emmett*

miles) long. Some stone rows are grouped together to form ceremonial centres, as on Shovel Down, on north-eastern Dartmoor, Drizzlecombe in the Plym valley, and Merrivale on the western side of the Moor (fig. 60).[6] In each of these places it looks as if the monuments were carefully grouped and positioned to create what prehistorians have come to call a 'ritual landscape'. More elaborate and famous ritual landscapes existed at about this time further east, on the chalklands of Wessex.

What is interesting about these stone rows is their distribution pattern (fig. 61). No rows have been found on the north-western fringes of Dartmoor. To the east of the main moorland massif, more recent agriculture has probably decimated them (during my fieldwork I discovered a new one, almost totally destroyed, in a medieval field to the east of Hameldown). However, in most areas they are spaced quite regularly around the edge of the Moor. If they *were* put up by different, contemporary human groups, each working within the framework of beliefs and rituals associated with stone rows to create its own distinctive sacred place, we can safely conclude that most of the fringe zone of the Moor had been claimed,

62 A cist, which probably contained an early Bronze Age burial, near Willings Walls Reave, in the Plym valley; its capstone has been pulled off and the small cairn in which it was encased has been destroyed. The reave runs through the middle of a group of these small burial cairns.
Photo: A. Fleming

in some sense, by about 2500BC.

Quite a number of the stone rows are associated with small cairns, only three or four metres in diameter. Some of these cairns have stone cists (fig. 62) which would have contained burials. If these small cairns were roughly contemporary with the stone rows, their distribution pattern would extend the areas of human activity at this time, bringing the north-western part of the Moor into the picture.

In the centuries which followed, broadly around 2000BC, other ceremonial monuments were built here – many medium-sized and large burial cairns, and a few stone circles (fig. 63), such as those at Scorhill and Brisworthy and Grey Wethers. There were also ring-cairns, some of them associated with burial cairns. A ring-cairn is a bank of stone, or a faced wall, enclosing a circular or slightly oval area; if finds from other parts of Britain are reliable guide, the enclosed areas within

the Dartmoor ring-cairns would have contained cremation burials. Since hardly any cairns, circles or ring-cairns on Dartmoor have been excavated, the dating is very rough and to some extent extrapolated from parts of Britain where our knowledge is fuller.

The large burial cairns make magnificent landmarks, scattered as they are along ridges and watersheds and on some of Dartmoor's most conspicuous hilltops. They are quite frequently over 20m (22 yards) in diameter; the biggest one is Broad Barrow, on Hameldown, which measures 40m (44 yards). From a cairn not very far away, nineteenth-century excavations[7] produced a bronze dagger with an oval amber pommel decorated with tiny gold pins, indicating that Dartmoor too participated in the exchanges of precious goods which were so important in the Bronze Age. To this we can now add the remains of seven faience beads found with the base of a pottery vessel in a pit within a small ring-cairn on Shaugh Moor, in the Plym valley, during the Central Unit's 1977 excavations.[8]

Leslie Grinsell's recent analysis of Dartmoor barrows[9] concluded that the majority of the larger cairns – prestige cairns, as he called them – were deliberately placed on summits, ridges or saddles.

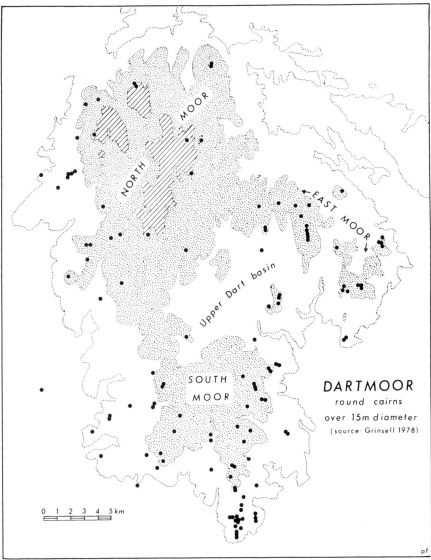

63 Stone circle at Grey Wethers, near Fernworthy Forest on north-east Dartmoor. This is one of a pair. The construction of numerous ceremonial monuments of this kind suggests that in the Bronze Age Dartmoor meant a good deal more to people, in social and ideological terms, than simply a tract of upland grazing land. *Photo: A. Fleming*

64 Map of large burial cairns. Most of these were probably constructed in the two or three centuries immediately before the reaves were built.

DARTMOOR
round cairns
over 15m diameter
(source: Grinsell 1978)

Like the stone rows, the prestige cairns are widely distributed (fig. 64), though they tend to avoid the central core of the North and South Moors. If it is assumed – and it *is* an assumption – that people placed burial mounds in such conspicuous positions in order to assert or maintain some kind of claim on the surrounding land, then most areas were at one time or another subjected to this form of control, actual or attempted. If prestige cairns are defined arbitrarily as those over 15m (50ft) in diameter, there are 130 prestige cairns in the area; if they were built at regular intervals over a period of 500 years, a new one would have been put up every four years. However, this reckoning excludes the smaller cairns, and undiscovered or destroyed ones, which naturally do not feature on Grinsell's list. We also have to take into account the probability that most cairns originally covered more than one burial, that some are the product of more than one phase of construction and had later burials put into them, and that 500 years is a somewhat generous estimate of the time period over which large cairns were put up. Clearly, ceremonial cairn burials in the earlier part of the Dartmoor Bronze Age were quite frequent occurrences; most people would have encountered the beliefs and rituals associated with the custom.

So the density and spacing of the stone rows and small cairns, and that of the larger burial cairns which succeeded them, suggests that, as in a number of other upland regions in Britain, the level of human activity was greater in the Bronze Age than had been the case earlier. The picture provided by pollen analysis suggests that the landscape was gradually becoming more open. At Cholwichtown, about 250m (800ft) above sea level (fig. 5), there is evidence for the making of a small clearing in what was mainly an oakwood, with some hazel and 'a grassy ground flora', and for the growing of cereals here. Bracken, heather and grasses were also present in the cleared area, and they took over after the cultivation episode; the clearing remained open, and at some later stage a stone row some 230m (250 yards) long was constructed in it – now, alas, buried under china clay waste.[10]

Presumably the builders of the Cholwichtown stone row intended and expected that the clearing would remain open, presumably under the grazing and browsing pressures exerted by livestock, and probably deer. Other rows, like the one in the Erme valley, which is over three kilometres (two miles) long, and the one on Butterdon Hill (1.9km or one mile) were presumably designed to run through larger stretches of open country – again, with implications for the expected grazing pressures.

Pollen analysis has been carried out by Stephen Beckett and Nick Balaam in the area of the Shaugh Moor parallel reave system, about two kilometres (one mile) from the Cholwichtown stone row.[11] They have identified two horizons in the pollen record which correspond to this period. In the first, their 'late neolithic', there was an acid grassland vegetation with occasional patches of hazel scrub, with oak woodland not too far away; there was some heathland on the higher ground. In the later period, both hazel scrub and heath seem to have been expanding, and so was alder, though this was perhaps a very local effect, as there was badly-drained ground nearby. On the northern part of Dartmoor and in the Upper Dart basin, the pollen evidence suggests episodes of clearance and grazing, with some increase in the amount of open country, and blanket bog starting to develop and spread on higher ground, to the detriment of any trees still growing there.

Around 2000BC, then, it looks as if these hills were developing steadily as upland pastures, with a few cereals being grown in some places – a shifting mosaic of woodland, scrub, heath, blanket bog and grassland, coming under pressures which probably fluctuated over the years. This was land which was under increasing demand; but its limited value and its very long perimeter together make it unlikely that any one community would require, let alone be able to defend, more than a fairly modest portion of it. I believe that in these circumstances intercommoning would have developed naturally, with different human groups exploiting different areas. How far we are talking about people from lowland Devon bringing livestock to the Moor in summer, as happened in the early Middle Ages, and how far these were people living on the fringe of Dartmoor, is hard to determine. There is a group of small-scale field systems, mostly in the Upper Dart basin around Bellever, which probably date from this period. They consist of small, irregular walled fields, with small houses, circular or ovoid, set at the intersections of the field boundaries (fig. 65). The size and character of these settlements makes one wonder if they were the antecedents of the 'neighbourhood groups' of the later reave systems.

It is tempting to think of the people of the Upper Dart basin exploiting the nearest pastures, on the North and South Moors. These pastures were best approached from this self-contained area between the two moors; here there was no real competition from outsiders. It is interesting that no large cairns are visible on the northern and southern skyline of the Upper Dart basin. This would fit quite well with my idea that the large cairns are partly to do with claiming rights to a portion of the commons. It there was no threat from competing 'outsiders', there would be no need for conspicuous cairns.

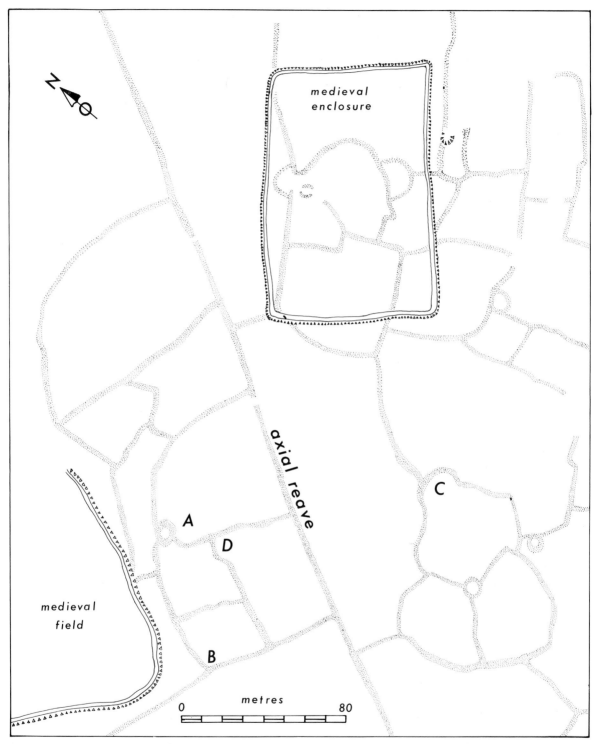

65 On Riddon Ridge, east of Bellever Forest, the Dartmeet Reave system incorporates what are probably earlier fields. The enclosure around house A looks later than the axial reave; but the straightness of its southern side suggests that it was conceived as part of the parallel system. Then one of the transverse reaves of the system was built to join it at B (but badly aligned). To the east, the complex field system has apparently been joined to the axial reave. C and D may once have been locations of timber buildings.

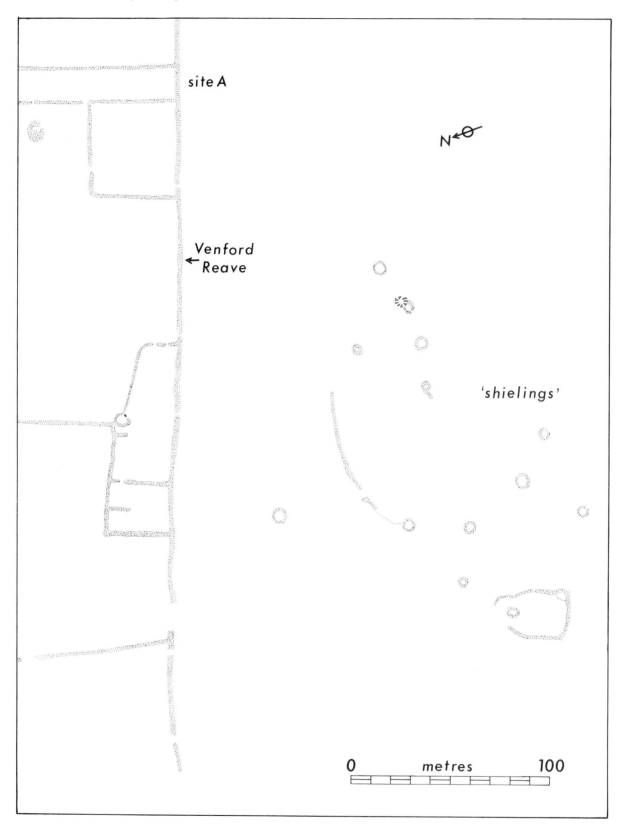

site A

N

Venford
Reave

'shielings'

0   metres   100

There is an interesting settlement site on Holne Moor, on sloping ground above the eastern bank of the O Brook (fig. 66). The 'hut-circles' are circular or slightly ovoid, and only 3-4m (9-12ft) across; they occur in ones and twos. Two of the buildings are associated with a walled enclosure, near the base of the slope, and there are traces of another enclosure further up the hillside. But most of the hut-circles were apparently in the open. This site is representative of a number of others found on Dartmoor; it resembles one of the shieling sites of eighteenth-century Scotland,[12] with buildings looking much more like the temporary abodes of shepherds or dairymaids than permanently occupied houses. Paired buildings may, on the Scottish analogy, have included a dairying hut. These 'shieling' sites, too, may date from the earlier part of the Bronze Age, as may some of the simple roughly circular or ovoid enclosures which were incorporated into reave systems.

The idea that prehistoric people travelled to Dartmoor from some distance away to exploit the summer pastures is a difficult one to support directly, from archaeological evidence. Only two 'pastoral' settlements have been excavated in modern times – a site on Dean Moor, in the Avon valley, and another on Shaugh Moor, in the valley of the upper Plym (fig. 67). The Dean Moor site, an enclosure containing eleven stone-based buildings, was clearly something more than a collection of shielings; it produced evidence for quite a wide range of activities, including spinning (with stone spindle-whorls made from Devonian shales), pottery manufacture, grinding (of grain, presumably) and possibly cheese-making (the excavator, Lady Aileen Fox, suggested that pots sunk in 'cooking-holes' had contained milk set to curdle for cheese). Broken whetstones were found in every building, suggesting the regular use of bronze tools here. The whetstone materials originated from the Brent/Buckfastleigh area. The doorways of the houses were orientated towards various different points of the compass, suggesting a relaxed attitude to prevailing wind directions which might argue for a summer-only occupation.[13]

The other enclosure, Shaugh Moor site 15, was excavated by the Central Unit while we were working on Holne Moor. This was a near-circular walled

enclosure, 60-70m (70-80 yards) across, containing five hut-circles. The enclosure had no identifiable entrance, and the excavators suggested that a pronounced bulge in its wall could have been a base for some kind of wooden stile; certainly the phosphate levels suggested that animals were not normally kept within the enclosure. The wall was quite heterogeneous in character, not unlike the reaves on Holne Moor; presumably various different work-gangs were free to do the job in their own way. All the houses within the enclosure contained saddle-querns (there were 32 on the site as a whole) so evidently some grain was brought here at some stage; all but one of the houses contained one or two whetstones as well. The excavator, Geoffrey Wainwright, suggested 'occasional visits by small groups as part of an economic cycle involving trade in metal and agricultural produce' and he stressed that the radiocarbon dates and artefacts implied an occupation period of perhaps a thousand years, down to about 600BC. However, it is possible to take a slightly different view, on the evidence available. The houses were built around 1600/1700BC, and the enclosure wall was built quite soon afterwards. Two or three hundred years later there was a significant refurbishment of the buildings, most of them being provided with projecting stone porches. It can be argued that most of the 'occupation' (and it is impossible to be sure how frequent or how permanent this was) took place during a period of three or four hundred years, and that the enclosure was only visited occasionally thereafter, notably around 600BC.[14]

Not very much pottery survived on the Shaugh Moor site; most of it was tempered with fragments of volcanic rock whose origin lies off the Moor, at least 10km (6 miles) to the north-west. This recalls the work of Hansford Worth, in the closing years of the nineteenth century.[15] He examined pottery from three separate Dartmoor sites, using a microscope, blow-pipe and reagents, and concluded that it was made from clays derived from non-granitic areas. Clearly it would be pushing the evidence too far to suggest that the various non-Dartmoor materials found at Shaugh Moor and Dean Moor implied that Dartmoor was being visited by transhumants, but the possibility should certainly be borne in mind.

It is a mistake, however, to imagine that Dartmoor in the Bronze Age was regarded simply as an extensive tract of poor-quality pasture, as in more recent times. For one thing, the grazing was better than it is today. And the Moor probably played a key role in the social lives of the people who used it, especially if most of the occupation was in the long days of summer. Not only were the illustrious dead laid to rest here; the stone rows and circles show how this landscape was intri-

66 A group of 'shielings' on Holne Moor, just above the O Brook and beyond Venford Reave, the terminal of the Dartmeet system. These may relate to a period of upland transhumance which preceded the reaves, though this has not yet been proved. The presence of a small enclosure, with most huts outside it, is typical of similar sites in the Plym valley and in the Upper Dart basin.

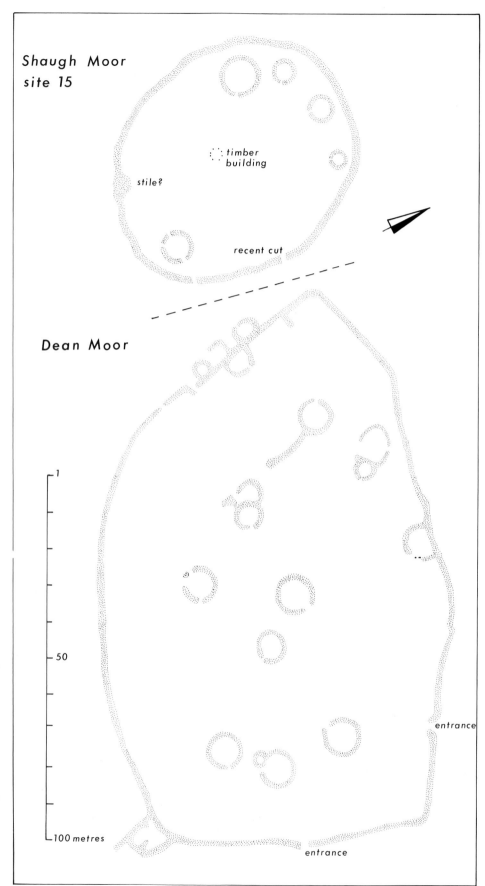

Shaugh Moor site 15

timber building

stile?

recent cut

Dean Moor

entrance

entrance

1

50

100 metres

67 The only two 'pastoral enclosures' to be excavated according to modern standards were the subject of 'rescue' digs – Shaugh Moor site 15, now among china clay workings, and Dean Moor, on the edge of the Avon Dam. *After Wainwright et al. and Fox).*

cately bound up with Bronze Age ceremonial. The concept of the 'ritual landscape', a zone of special significance where it was appropriate to build ceremonial monuments, was devised by prehistorians to deal with the situation in Wessex, but it may well apply here too; witness the complexes of stone rows and other monuments at Merrivale, at Drizzlecombe in the Plym valley, and at Shovel Down, near Kestor (fig. 60).[6] The stones which make up the long stone row in the Erme valley may be small, and nowadays half-buried in peat, but the cairn which they lead up to has been sited very carefully at the focal point of the head of the valley, so that row and cairn together make the kind of impressive 'statement' that a modern land artist would be proud of.

The work of John Barnatt, another of my research students doing fieldwork for a doctoral thesis while I was excavating on Dartmoor, is also illuminating on this point. John was able to show[16] that most British stone circles are not true circles, and that this is almost certainly because they were probably laid out by eye. But there are some rings of stone which are truly circular, and must have been laid out with a peg and rope. Many of these are located in south-west England. Dartmoor has five circles which come into this category, all of them on the North Moor – Langstone Moor, Corn Ridge, Whitemoor, and the two at Grey Wethers. As John Barnatt points out, the regular spacing around the North Moor of these circles, which are linked by their careful design, may imply that they were constructed at much the same time, each one serving as a ceremonial centre for a specific tract of upland. These do not look like the activities of scattered bands of shepherds. The density and character of Dartmoor's ceremonial monuments suggest strongly that Dartmoor had an integral place, perhaps a central place, in the world view of the people of the district. For those who came here with their flocks and herds, it is quite possible that social considerations were paramount.

About 1700/1600BC, around the time when the Shaugh Moor houses were being built, came the reaves. Since we know that some of them at least started life as banks (hedge-banks?) or fences, it might be better to say 'the major system of boundaries now commemorated by the reaves'. In my view, most of these boundaries were laid out at much the same time, since in many parts of the Moor they only make sense in relation to each other; the radiocarbon dates from Holne Moor and Shaugh Moor, as far as they go, support this notion. The landscape was already fairly open by this time; nevertheless, Stephen Beckett's diagrams for Lee Moor and Wotter Common (fig. 68), within the northern part of the Shaugh Moor parallel reave system, showed a rise in the pollen of

grassland species and 'clearance herbs' at about the time when the reave systems were in use, and a fall in alder pollen. Beckett's conclusion was that 'the demise of trees and spread of weeds of pasture indicates a grazing pressure which has only been exceeded in very recent times. Bronze Age arable farming appears to have been on only a minor scale, but again the pollen evidence suggests that as much cultivation may have taken place at this time as at any time since, including the medieval period.'[17]

The size of the parallel reave systems and the blocks of grazing land marked out by the reaves, with water-courses used as boundaries in some places, shows clearly that in broad terms the land was claimed by sizeable communities, as I have called them. The prevailing concept was not of small, bounded farms but of large blocks of enclosed land with boundaries aligned along a predetermined axis, running over hills and across valleys where they had to. Beyond the terminal reaves lay open pasture land, and beyond that, in some places at least, the higher-lying grazing land above and beyond the contour reaves. Within the field systems, smaller social units, 'neighbourhood groups', held designated areas of land, and it is tempting to see units of this kind also represented in the walled 'pastoral' enclosures beyond the reave systems, where small numbers of buildings are associated with the enclosures.

Probably the people had access to woods and fenced coppices; many of the earlier houses were probably of wood, and some of the boundaries started life as fences or (hedge-?) banks. The extent to which the land division of this early phase differed from the one preserved by reaves is still unclear. The character of the reaves shows considerable variation, as does the degree of adherence to the layout axis. It seems that beans as well as cereals were grown;[18] although pollen studies usually underestimate the extent of cereal cultivation, it does seem likely that cultivation was confined to small enclosed areas near the houses. Stone clearance was certainly going on at this time, with stones piled against the faces of some of the reaves (fig. 49). It is an interesting question how far the regular use of stone for boundaries was determined by the availability of stones from field clearance, and how far this too implies that we may be underestimating the extent of cultivation here. The quality of grazing land would have been better than it is today, with a good earthworm population in the pastures. Judging by the rarity of lanes and drove-ways, it seems that livestock were not moved around very much; perhaps they were milked in the open, and kept for long periods away from the enclosed land.

In three areas of Dartmoor (Hameldown, Haytor and Whittor) there are cross-ridge reaves which may

LEE MOOR

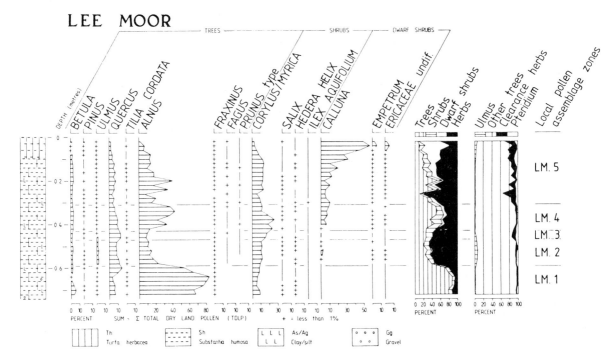

WOTTER COMMON

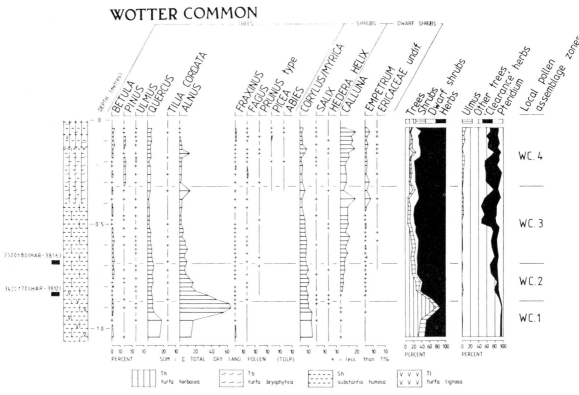

68 Pollen diagrams from south-western Dartmoor, prepared by Stephen Beckett. The chronological order is the stratigraphic order, from bottom to top. The period of the reaves is the beginning of the phase LM5 (in the Lee Moor diagram) and of WC2 (in the Wotter Common diagram). At this time tree pollen falls and pollen from open country species increases. The fall in alder (Alnus) at this time has sometimes been attributed to the needs of tin-smelters, but it might simply be increased demand for fire-wood. Note how heather (Calluna) increases markedly after the period of the reaves, especially on the Lee Moor diagram. *After Beckett*

be earlier in date than the other reaves; on Shovel Down it looks as if at some stage the boundaries were extended further onto the moor. But in general the new boundaries, with their interdependence and characteristic behaviour, look like a sudden, large-scale imposition; there are really no signs of gradual or piecemeal development. So the question is, do they represent the seizure of Dartmoor by invaders, from Cornwall or Dorset for example, or had traditional users of the moorland fringe simply decided to exert closer control over their land? And do the similarities between the reave systems, and the relationships between the boundaries of neighbouring communities, indicate that they were all part of some grand plan, originating from a system of political organisation which had some form of control over the whole area?

These days, prehistorians have rather lost confidence in their ability to recognise 'invasions', and to choose between the several possible interpretations of change in the archaeological record. My own view is that in this case there was probably no 'invasion'. The respect shown by the reave-builders to some of the stone rows, the cairns and the Scorhill stone circle suggests at any rate some continuity of tradition (although one has to remember that outsiders seizing power might seek to legitimate the new regime by creating links with local sacred sites!). Whether the parallel reave systems were devised to meet the immediate need for closer control over land on the fringe of Dartmoor, or whether they simply represent the transfer of a field system type well known in lowland Devon, is unclear. The large size of some parallel systems may simply reflect the opportunities for communities moving into large tracts of open country to implement their land division schemes in an unfettered way.

A lot depends on the view we take of the relationship between upland and lowland Devon in prehistory. Conventionally minded prehistorians tend to assume that Dartmoor must always have been marginal land, so they are very cautious about extrapolating observations made there to other parts of Devon, let alone Britain in general. Usually they do not define what they mean by marginal land; there are several possibilities. We know that the Dartmoor environment, and its climate, has changed a good deal since the Bronze Age, so we cannot assume that areas like Holne Moor were marginal for cereal cultivation. There is no strong reason to suppose that the value of land in prehistoric times was based upon its capacity for growing cereals; if the land-holding body was the large community, the location of its territory would be decided by the availability of a range of economic opportunities, plus presumably relationships with neighbouring communities. In any case, even if Dartmoor was valued less highly than some other

parts of Devon, it does not follow that its land division systems and settlement patterns are bound to be 'atypical' or distorted versions of their counterparts elsewhere. At any rate it looks as if Dartmoor was not marginal in the sense that it waited a long time to be utilised; and it is worth noting that at least two pollen diagrams, one from north Dartmoor and one from Exmoor, suggest that in some parts of Devon plenty of woodland remained to be cleared in the Iron Age.[19]

We do not know very much about the nature of human occupation in the lowlands. Recent aerial survey by Frances Griffith has revealed a Late Neolithic ceremonial enclosure, a sizeable 'henge' dating from perhaps 2500BC, near Bow, some ten kilometres (six miles) NE of Dartmoor.[20] This is the strongest piece of evidence obtained so far for organised prehistoric communities in Mid-Devon. There are prehistoric field systems at Dainton, to the south-east of the Moor, and on rough ground above the sea-cliffs of the south Devon coast.[21] In a few places the character of present-day field boundaries hints at the preservation of bits of an earlier pattern (fig. 69). However, at present it is hard to know how far Bronze Age field systems in the region as a whole were laid out coaxially, in the manner of the parallel reave systems, and thus how far the latter were a special feature of the Dartmoor area.

That the reaves were probably part of a general plan of land division for the area as a whole is shown by boundaries which appear to transcend the needs of local communities. Venford Reave, for example, impressive enough as the southern terminal of the Dartmeet system (figs. 17 and 19), is clearly more than that; the same kind of comment may be applied to Eylesbarrow Reave, and above all to the Great Western Reave. Significantly parts of the latter, and other contour reaves, are unfinished. These indications that local communities apparently did not complete the grand plan may imply that it was too ambitious or encountered resistance in some places. Perhaps local shepherds knew and traditionally respected the boundaries of the upland commons, so that they did not need a continuous barrier here.

A pattern of land division devised by some kind of ruling elite with authority over the whole of Dartmoor would agree well with the picture painted by other prehistorians, who have suggested that Bronze Age elites controlled quite large areas of southern England at this time. Ann Ellison, for example, put forward the idea[22] that the top level of the sociopolitical hierarchy in England south of the Thames involved no more than seven 'major settlements' (including, she thought, one in the Dartmoor area). These settlements were centres of what we would call trade, and their spheres of influence were widespread. It has

been shown that political centres in south-east England were obtaining cargoes of scrap bronze from northern France; one such cargo ended up on the sea-bed just outside Dover Harbour.

Ann Ellison only named four 'major enclosures', not including the one she suggested for Devon, and indeed it is quite difficult to pinpoint any one 'central place' on the Moor which might fit the bill. There is no one ceremonial centre which is obviously more important than any of the others, and the same goes for the settlements. Places like Grimspound and Rider's Rings are large, with impressive walls, but there are four or five other sites which are comparable; they may have been no more than local centres. The largest house in the Dartmeet parallel system happens to be near the centre of the system, and located in one of the most sheltered sites; it could represent the dwelling of a chief or headman of some kind. But it is also possible that the top level of the regional political hierarchy may have been archaeo-logically invisible. Important gatherings could have been held in the open air, like the old tin-miners' 'Parliament' on Crockern Tor.[23] If political status was hereditary, the political 'centres' may have been mobile; at any particular time they may simply have been the places where office-holders happened to live, or to be travelling.

The alternative possibility is that the similarities between parallel systems arose simply because coaxial land division was the local tradition, and that the apparent coherence of the Dartmoor pattern resulted from agreements between neighbouring communi-ties. If these systems are about managing communally held land, they could have been either imposed by some central authority, or developed in the district

69 This pattern of fields lies near Ugborough, not far from the southern edge of Dartmoor; the predominent axial layout is that of the Bittaford parallel reave system. The upper end of which is about a mile further north, below Western Beacon (to the right of the photograph). The possibility that field patterns like this in parts of lowland Devon are based on prehistoric field systems should always be borne in mind, especially if hedge-removal or barn-building gives archaeologists a chance to investigate. Compare figs. 14 and 31. *Photo: A. Fleming*

within communities in regular touch with one another, perhaps in response to pressure for greater production from some kind of elite. At the moment, we badly need new sources of information to try to examine these various possibilities.[24]

Another question is how far the increased control of land reflected by the parallel reave systems also found its expression in the open pastures. It may be that the relatively large enclosures, with thicker walls, associated with relatively large houses, which contrast markedly with the 'shielings', show that some groups of people were now keen to live in the hills all the year round. There are a few settlements, like the one at Merrivale near the stone rows, where large houses appear beside small ones, and not very far away from the Shaugh Moor 15 enclosure is an enclosure which looks as if its builders robbed a smaller, less sub-stantial one with smaller 'hut-circles'. The main period of activity on Site 15 itself certainly occurred at the time of the reaves.

But everywhere else there is a dating problem; we simply don't know which of the settlements in the southern valleys were contemporary with the land boundaries which run along the neighbouring water-sheds. In one or two places, notably in the Plym valley area, walled settlements are incorporated into the line of the reaves, or attached to reaves (fig. 5), relationships which suggest quite strongly that they were inhabited while the boundaries were in use.[25] These enclosures are rather varied in character; perhaps the most striking one is the one on Lee Moor where John Collis and I made our original observation of reaves, the one which we called the Cholwichtown Main enclosure. This is a large, roughly rectilinear enclosure with a thick wall (fig. 3) surrounding 15-16 rather small hut-circles. It is quite similar to Grimspound, and the resemblance is increased by the entrance, physically quite like the (reconstructed!) one at Grimspound, which also faces uphill, towards the higher moors.

On this basis Grimspound too would have been roughly contemporary with the reaves, and possibly some of the larger, more impressive enclosures. This would strengthen the idea that mature and politically significant adults, not simply a few shepherds, had serious commitments on the unenclosed pasture land. However, there is one snag here. The huts at Grimspound and at the Cholwichtown Main enclosure are small, 'shieling' type structures.[26] In any case there are unresolved arguments about whether Grimspound can be said to have been a 'fortified' site or not. A long time ago a bronze rapier dating from about this period was discovered at Fice's Well, near Princetown.[27] It may have been a 'ceremonial' weapon, never drawn in anger, but it must have been an effective reminder of one direct source of power. It is only about 150km (95 miles) from here to Tormarton in Gloucestershire, where not long ago were found the bones of two young men with assorted spear-wounds which made it quite clear how they had met their deaths,[28] and another case has been recorded at Dorchester, in Oxfordshire. It is quite likely that raiding or some form of warfare went with the kind of tensions between groups which are expressed by the construction of fixed boundaries such as the reaves. These tensions could have been one reason for putting substantial walls around settlements (Shaugh Moor 15 had a 'pre-enclosure' phase which may have lasted for some time) and for the presence of the more impressive enclosures in places like the Plym valley. The presence of small huts at Grimspound and elsewhere would then not be anomalous. They might have been the 'bachelor huts' of a group of young warriors; that is, unless there were once much larger, timber buildings here which would only show up on excavation. Archaeological arguments can get quite complicated!

The pollen record, the reaves and perhaps also the character and density of the walled settlements in the pasture zone can be taken to suggest that much of

Dartmoor was more intensively settled and 'exploited' than at any time before or since. It is not clear why. It may well be that areas traditionally visited for the summer grazing season were now permanently settled. Almost certainly both climate and vegetation were more favourable than they are today; other upland regions of Britain saw considerable activity at about this time. On Dartmoor the results are particularly impressive because the boundaries were eventually constructed in stone by sizeable communities with very definite ideas about land division, and because the subsequent land-use history of the region has helped to preserve their handiwork.

This was a time when the use of bronze was becoming more widespread in Britain. The results of analyses of tools and weapons carried out by Peter Northover have suggested that south-west England was a minor source of metal ores at various times during the Bronze Age;[29] tin and copper would both have been available, of course, on Dartmoor. At a time when the reaves were probably in use, a distinctive kind of bronze palstave, along with other tools and weapons, was being produced somewhere in the Moretonhampstead area, and perhaps there was an important political centre in this region.[30]

I find it hard to believe, however, that control of tin and copper resources was the main motivation for constructing the Dartmoor land boundary systems; similar systems in other parts of the country have nothing to do with the extraction of metal. According to one commentator,[31] the density of ancient settlements in places like the upper Plym valley seems too high to reconcile with 'the presumed pastoral and arable ways of life that have been attributed to this period'. But there is no particular reason to believe that these settlements were all inhabited at the same time, that all the buildings were intended for living in, or that they were all occupied by nuclear families. Working out the number of people who could be supported in the upper Plym valley by farming, and showing that this carrying capacity had been exceeded in the Bronze Age are both impossible tasks in our present state of knowledge. But in any case it would be unsafe to assume that the people living in the upper Plym valley derived their food supply solely from the land around their settlements; there was enclosed land further down the valley, and upland pasture on the South Moor. The fall in alder pollen at about the time when the reaves were constructed (fig. 68) has been put down to the fuel needs of tin-smelters, or the effects of tin-streaming on waterside trees, but it could simply be the result of a quest for firewood. I believe that statements about metal extraction should be based on more direct evidence than this.[32]

The impressive Dartmoor boundary systems

suggest that the people of the Bronze Age were confident that they could make a living here, probably on the basis of existing knowledge. Previous generations had lived here and had valued the Moor enough to leave their carefully constructed cere-monial monuments all over the landscape. Not all the hut-circles in the reave systems were occupied at the same time, but the population and their livestock were evidently numerous enough for the making of fixed land boundaries to seem worthwhile. The replacement of wooden buildings by stone-footed houses on Holne Moor shows that the first generations, at any rate, saw a future here. They had access to enclosed pastures and the rougher commons of the South Moor, they grew some cereals and beans, they could get wood from local coppices and perhaps from hedges too (fig. 70). Their houses were dispersed, but the small hamlets in which they lived would have been the right size for pooling labour and sharing resources without too many arguments; the individual family farm, as we know it, was probably rare or unknown. What people felt about large-scale land division is a moot point; had they agreed upon it, or was it an imposition? I will have to deal with that question later.

Judging by the spread of radiocarbon dates, and the limited amount of evidence so far for change and development within buildings and in field systems, this settled, well-organised way of life involving sizeable populations may have lasted no more than about 300-400 years; at present, although our knowledge is limited, this seems a better estimate than 600-700. The pollen record suggests that blanket bog was thickening and spreading, and that grazing quality was declining (although in some places the right grazing intensity might actually have improved the quality of the herbage for a time). Scattered patches of heath and bog were spreading and joining up; Dartmoor was coming into being. At some stage in the earlier part of the first millennium BC a wetter climate probably accelerated the process.

70 A modern hedge-bank at Cochwillan (north Wales) showing how a respectable hedge can grow on what is to all intents and purposes a reave, a low, broad wall with a solid stone core, not an earth one as in the modern 'Devon hedge'. Inspection shows that there is enough humic material in the interstices of the stones to keep the roots moist. *Photo: A. Fleming*

It is hard for us to know how quickly this affected the way of life of people living here and using the uplands; common sense suggests that the retreat may have been gradual. The late occupation of Shaugh Moor site 15, and perhaps the small hut built in the ruins of the house of site F on Holne Moor, help to suggest that the Dartmoor pastures still had their uses in the first millennium BC. If herdsmen and shepherds re-occupied abandoned buildings, and if they used wooden vessels, baskets and leather containers rather than pottery, their activities would be very difficult for archaeologists to detect. Perhaps this kind of land-use explains the notable absence of 'the Romans' from the Dartmoor archaeological record. At any rate this seems to have been in the pattern in the early Middle Ages, when the evidence suggests that people from all over Devon had the right to use common pastures here, and that some quite distant communities actually did so.

Eventually, medieval farms and fields spread on to the edge of the Moor, into areas perhaps unoccupied, though not unused, since the Bronze Age. It is pretty clear that in most places the farmers of the Middle Ages were living on marginal land; on the whole, they were enclosing land piecemeal, not subdividing it. The pattern is very different; we cannot project medieval life-ways back into the Bronze Age, when the ecological situation was different and there was really no such place as 'Dartmoor' as we know it today. We cannot get back to prehistory simply by projecting the medieval situation backwards in time; a leap of the imagination is required to envisage scenery and social patterns which do not exist here today. But that is part of the fascination of prehistory.

8: Reaves and the wider world

The realisation that there are very large prehistoric field systems and an elaborate network of contemporary land boundaries on Dartmoor created something of a sensation among archaeologists – among the other sensations of the seventies, that is. I was not the only archaeologist at that time to find that major discoveries were still to be made in the field of British prehistory. Since the expansion of university departments and archaeology units, which took place at around this time, the pace of discovery has quickened, and so has the generation of theories. Prehistory never stands still, it is always in the process of being rewritten.

When a striking new discovery has been made, questions are immediately asked about its implications. With the reaves, there were perhaps two or three major questions to be answered. Would individual reaves, and parallel reave systems, turn up in other upland areas of Britain? What was the relationship between parallel reave systems and other prehistoric field systems already known, such as the so-called 'Celtic' field systems of Wessex? How far would the well-preserved pattern of land boundaries on Dartmoor help up to understand the nature of ancient land division in areas where the evidence was much more fragmentary? Could the Dartmoor pattern, and its implications for social and territorial organisation, be extrapolated to other times and places – or were the reaves, admittedly spectacular in their fashion, simply an isolated curiosity?

In a way, reaves turned up at just the right time. Colin Renfrew was putting out a strong message about the creativity of the prehistoric peoples of Europe, insisting that they were not simply the passive recipients of wisdom from the East Mediterranean, as prehistorians had tended to assume.[1] On the Wessex chalklands, Collin Bowen, Peter Fowler and Richard Bradley among others[2] were trying to come to terms with 'the organised landscape' (fig. 71) as they called it; they started to attack the idea that small fields implied small-scale organisation. At Fengate, just outside Peterborough in eastern England, a regular pattern of ditches seen as cropmarks on air photos, at first assumed to be Romano-British, turned out to be

a well-organised Late Neolithic and Bronze Age field system.[3] Richard Bradley, trying to synthesise the field system evidence in 1978,[4] suggested that it was useful to distinguish between *aggregate* field systems, in which fields were added to one another on a piecemeal basis, and *cohesive* systems, though I later managed to persuade him that *coaxial* might be a better term to use for systems laid out systematically according to one major axis.

Prehistorians started to wonder whether they had been systematically underestimating the openness of the prehistoric landscape, the extent of well-defined property rights in land, levels of population, and the productivity of prehistoric agriculture; after all, Strabo tells us that south-east England was exporting grain in the later Iron Age. In his much-loved classic, *The Making of the English Landscape*,[5] W.G. Hoskins had told us that 'the great majority of English settlers faced a virgin country'; the title of his chapter one, 'The landscape before the English settlement' was well-chosen, because Hoskins encouraged us to think of prehistoric and Roman times as an overture to the main work to be performed. But perhaps Hoskins was wrong? Archaeologists were asking themselves whether there were 'organised landscapes' waiting to be discovered in other areas.

There certainly were. Mark Brisbane and Stephen Clews, who both worked on the Reave Project in its earlier years, soon drew my attention to two parallel reave systems side by side on East Moor, on the eastern side of Bodmin Moor, in Cornwall (fig. 73b).[6] They have droveways and terminal reaves, one of which incorporates quite a large burial cairn, and beyond them lies a 'reserved area' of open pasture with a stone circle in the middle. Further west, in Penwith, in a complex palimpsest of field-walls, the work of Peter Herring and Jacqui Nowakowski[7] has shown that the oldest fields are not the tiny irregular fields designated as 'Celtic' by W.G. Hoskins; the

71 A coaxial field system in Dorset, laid out according to an axis which has run right across a pronounced valley. *After R.C.H.M*

KINGCOMBE

stream

——— 'CELTIC' FIELDS   ● ROUND BARROW   NORTH _to top of plan_

Scale – Metres

100   0   100   200   300   400   500   600   700   800 _metres_

72 A reave near Reeth, Swaledale, North Yorkshire.
Reaves like this are laid out to form coaxial land division
systems on present-day moorland. *Photo: A. Fleming*

earliest boundaries seem to have been arranged
coaxially, and one or two individual boundaries
suggest that in places the scale of land division
certainly transcended that of the individual farm.

The picture in the uplands of northern England is
patchy. In parts of the Peak District, north-east
Yorkshire, Teesdale and the Cheviots[8] it is now
possible to identify organised field *systems*, as opposed
to the areas of clearance cairns and fragmentary
walling recognised before; they are quite small, but it
is possible that they were once larger systems demarcated by hedges or fences, the parts which survive
being the stretches where clearance stones were
dumped or people started to build walls. However, on
the eastern side of Upper Wharfedale, around
Conistone and Grassington,[9] there are some very
extensive low walls running across the contour,
following the same axis.

In Swaledale (North Yorkshire), work which I have
been doing more recently with Tim Laurie[10] has
shown that there are coaxial field systems, mostly
around the village of Reeth. They lie on the moors,
above and beyond the present-day fields, and the
boundaries are physically very like the reaves of
Dartmoor (fig. 72). The most extensive system is the
one which we call the Marrick system; mostly around
350m (1100ft) above sea level, it lies on a undulating
plateau between the Swale and the Marske Beck, its
boundaries orientated roughly north–south. Parts of
the system are subdivided into small fields and
enclosures, but on the whole there are very few
transverse boundaries and settlement sites, and few of
the settlements which exist can be related to the
boundaries. However, the system is about three
kilometres (two miles) from one end to the other, and
was probably at least two kilometres (one mile) in
breadth, so it is quite a good example of large-scale
land division. To the west of Reeth, on the southern
and eastern shoulders of Calver Hill, the land has also
been laid out coaxially, with low stone walls cutting
directly across quite a dissected terrain. In one area
there is an overlap between two systems, each with a
different orientation. The Calverside systems, and the
coaxial land boundaries on the other side of the Swale,
on the Harkerside moors, contain hardly any settlement sites which can be related to them; they may
represent the subdivision of upland pastures. The
idea that most of the people lived where they do now,
on the daleside, is supported by the existence of
'droveways' leading out through the systems to the
upper moors, as well as by our discovery of numerous

settlement sites in the enclosed land. At present we
need more dating evidence for these systems, which
show that coaxial land division principles were known
in northern England.

In Ireland, coaxial land division has also been
recorded, although not for the Bronze Age. In North
Mayo, the walls of field systems dating from the later
neolithic, around 3000/2500BC, have been found
beneath blanket peat up to about 4m (13ft) deep
(fig. 73a).[11] These are among the earliest field
systems known anywhere in Europe, and they offer a
rare chance to study the land use customs of people
who built and used chamber tombs, since they were
probably laid out quite soon after the local court cairns
were constructed, and in the same areas. Seamas
Caulfield, who has been studying these field systems,
has convincingly shown that the axis of his main
system at Behy-Glenulra was responsive to the
terrain, not imposed upon it. But the size of the system
and its overall planning still suggests, not the
accumulated interests of individual farmers, but the
subdivision of a community's land; the same is true for
a system a little further east which has also been the
subject of recent study.

In county Clare, the limestone country known as
the Burren is covered in all manner of field systems of
various dates which have been recently studied by
Emma Plunkett Dillon.[12] These include some quite
large coaxial systems running across what is now
almost bare limestone pavement in places – on Ailwee
Hill, in the Sladoo/Ranagh townlands, and in
Ballyelly townland, just across from the Aran Islands.
The field walls at the northern end of Ailwee Hill are
particularly dramatic, with wall after wall following
the same axis across this bleak plateau, and dipping
over the edge to lose themselves in hazel scrub. The
evidence suggests that these field systems are linked
with ring-forts, and were probably laid out sometime
in the first millennium AD.

Most of the coaxial field systems which I have
mentioned above are demarcated by walls, visible at
ground level today. However, coaxial field systems
involving ditches have shown up from the air; as well
as the Fengate example which I have already
mentioned, some very extensive ditched coaxial
systems were picked up on the Bunter sandstone and
Magnesian limestone of South Yorkshire and North
Nottinghamshire by Derrick Riley.[13] It looks at
present as if these field systems were laid out in the
Iron Age and were used in some places at least in
Romano-British times, but archaeologists who work
on them have to deal with ditches which have been recut several times, sometimes destroying evidence of
earlier phases and re-depositing artefacts so that
dating becomes quite a difficult procedure.

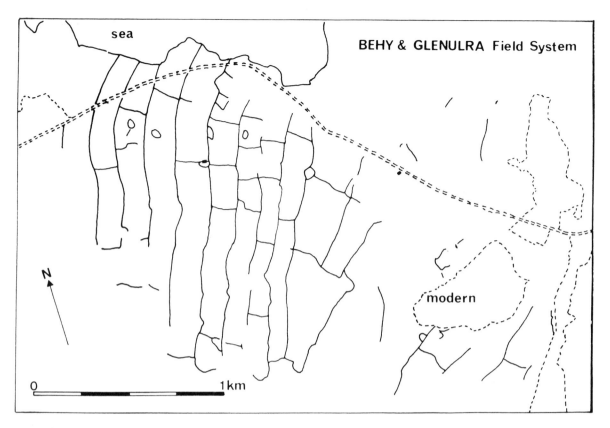

BEHY & GLENULRA Field System

sea

N

modern

0   1km

73 Coaxially-organised landscapes: (a) walls of *c.* 2500 BC revealed by turf-cutting at Behy-Glenulra, county Mayo; (b) reaves (probably Bronze Age) on East Moor, Bodmin Moor, with a stone circle in a reserved area of grazing land beyond them. *After Caulfield, Brisbane and Clews: fig 73b drawn by P. Jones*

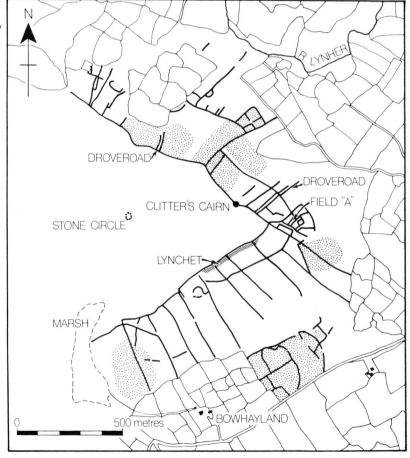

N

R LYNHER

DROVEROAD

DROVEROAD

FIELD "A"

CLITTER'S CAIRN

STONE CIRCLE

LYNCHET

MARSH

BOWHAYLAND

0   500 metres

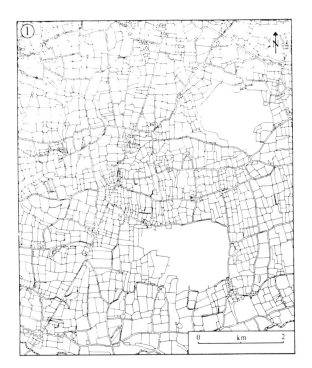

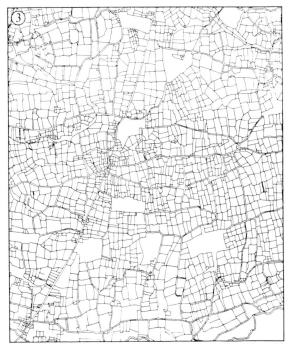

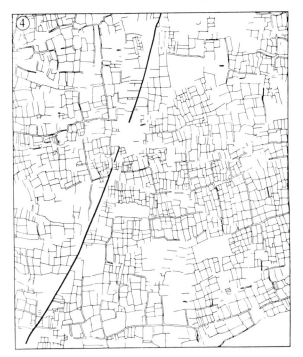

74 Plan of the giant Scole-Dickleburgh coaxial field system, in East Anglia, showing stages in the removal from the map of relatively recent boundaries, to produce the best approximation to the ancient pattern. Note how the fields have been 'slighted' by the Roman road. *After Williamson*

Just before I started to write this chapter I went to a conference on early Irish field systems, and was fascinated to note that very small fragments of ditched coaxial field systems quite similar to those found in the English north-east Midlands had been picked up on air photos of parts of south-east Ireland.

The most dramatic discoveries of coaxial field systems, however, have been made by Tom Williamson in East Anglia.[14] In the early eighties he noticed that in the Waveney valley, in the borderlands between Norfolk and Suffolk, there are large areas where the present-day field pattern, marked out by hedges which are not themselves particularly old, follows a single dominant axis which looks quite striking on a modern map. Tom decided to clarify the picture by taking one of these areas, around Scole and Dickleburgh (fig. 74), and removing from the map all the boundaries which he could demonstrate were relatively recent in date; for example, the ones which encroached upon the commons. He produced several maps, each one stripping away a demonstrably recent episode of land enclosure or subdivision, and thus going back further in time. As he gradually removed the most recent boundaries, stage by stage, not only did the coaxial pattern become clearer, it became obvious that the whole system must have been in place already when a Roman road was laid out here, so must date from at least the late Iron Age. On the whole, Tom is reluctant to believe that his field systems go back as far as the Bronze Age, because of the general scarcity of Bronze Age material in the area. On the other hand, some of them could have been laid out in the Romano-British period; one system appears to have used as the determinant of its axis the line of a Roman road, which happens to have a very distinctive swerve in its course; and there is some evidence that another system may have been laid out in the post-Roman period.

Tom first showed me the evidence on the ground in March 1985, under a lowering sky, with flurries of snow, and hungry-looking hares creeping wearily over the earth. It was strange after Dartmoor to wander around in this gently undulating East Anglian landscape, with its mixture of agribusiness and remote smallholdings, its thunderous trunk roads and its broad and muddy lanes. The roads we followed had some notably right-angled bends, and Tom pointed out that they were conforming to the grid-like pattern of ancient fields. Some of these formed coaxial layouts a good deal bigger than the Rippon Tor parallel reave system, which I had thought was the largest prehistoric field system in the country. Nor are the East Anglian systems unique; Steven Bassett's work at Goltho in Lincolnshire has pinpointed a rather similar layout, again apparently pre-dating a Roman road.[15]

Coaxial systems in the British Isles pose some fascinating questions. Many of them are undated, and the dates which *have* been obtained from some of them vary widely, from around 2500BC to around AD500. Some later medieval layouts are coaxial in character as well. There is a very fine example in the parish of Middleton, near Pickering in North Yorkshire, where walls which are apparently following 'long ploughing curves' are preserving an axis up to about three kilometres (two miles) in length.[16] Some field systems on the edge of the Fens near King's Lynn in west Norfolk, apparently laid out in the twelfth and thirteenth centuries mainly for pasture, were coaxial in character, following an axis in places over four kilometres (2½ miles) in length.[17]

Bringing together these similar field systems, which are apparently widely distributed in space and time, raises some all too familiar archaeological questions. Should they be considered as a group at all? Might they not represent a simple solution to certain problems of land management or property division which was hit upon at various times and places, so that we have several cases of 'independent invention'? On the other hand, can we believe that this very distinctive type of field system, involving quite complicated layout procedures, was invented and re-invented several times within a relatively small geographical area? The alternative may be to consider that coaxial land division was primarily a *concept*, not simply a functional solution to a problem, and that the recognition of its significance was perpetuated in oral tradition, so that it was available for use at other times and places. But doesn't this idea also carry a credibility problem, with its appeal to a mythology inaccessible to the archaeologist, and to a kind of timeless, mystical world of folklore which we would do well to avoid?

Not necessarily. Oral tradition is rather devalued nowadays because it tends to be equated with folklore; its accuracy and durability, in other words, are questionable and regarded as largely outside the scope of scientific enquiry. But we should remember that the role of oral tradition in Britain has been comprehensively downgraded over the past few centuries. It has been overtaken by the written word, religious ideology, science and political propaganda, in a class society stratified to a considerable extent by educational factors. The ideological kaleidoscope resulting from the power struggles and class conflicts of recent times does not provide a suitable guide to the strength, durability, and complexity of oral tradition at a time when it would have been a major cultural resource and maintained as such, available to be re-worked and brought back into a society's ideological and cultural repertoire when required. The survival into recent times of certain quaint country customs seems remarkable when set against the social, economic and ideological changes which have taken place, and we rightly suspect considerable distortion and change of function; but such phenomena also show the underlying strength of these traditions.

Some of today's prehistorians like to talk about 'social reproduction' and the effort which must have been made to secure the continuity of particular patterns of status, power, wealth and authority from generation to generation. This may have been even more important in the remote past. If our evidence on life expectancy is to be trusted, for many people life before puberty was longer than adult life. In these circumstances traditional knowledge would have played a really important role in the perpetuation of the social structure. The importance of maintaining such knowledge would have been considerable. Those wishing for change would have had to manipulate or confront this body of received tradition in various ways; perhaps it was easier to bypass it by establishing other sources of prestige. I believe that when communities became sedentary within defined areas, the landscape with its monuments and natural features would have acquired a rich emotional content, which formed a central core of local traditional knowledge.

The introduction of a highly distinctive form of land division can be seen as a break with tradition,

COAXIAL FIELD
SYSTEMS

0   100   200 km

●Swaledale

●Grassington

S.Yorks/●
N.Notts

●Goltho

Fengate ●

●Norfolk–
/Suffolk

Little Waltham●

●Segsbury

●Beacon Hill

●Black Patch

Dorset 45 ●

East Moor● ●Dartmoor

Penwith/●

Behy-Glenulra

●Burren

75 Map of some recently investigated coaxial field systems in the British Isles. Although many are not well dated,
it is clear that they do not belong to a single chronological horizon; but it is also hard to imagine them being 'independently
invented' several times over.

whose effects must have been traumatic within a community; as such, it requires an explanation. But once it has become established, such a form of land division in turn becomes a part of traditional knowledge; since it is part of the landscape, it is just as much a 'monument' as a chamber tomb or a burial mound. Surrounded by myth and legend, it may become a concept which lies dormant in oral tradition, sanctified and waiting to emerge elsewhere, in other contexts, like 'Victorian values' in the Britain of the 1980s. Thus if coaxial land division occurs at various times in various places, we do not have to assume that it must have been independently developed on each occasion. When they are trying to explain change, archaeologists tend to invoke either 'diffusion' or 'independent invention'. We may be able to kick this bad habit, if we envisage communities which were perhaps fairly immobile, but certainly not intellectually isolated, and an orally transmitted body of traditional knowledge much more stable and serious than mere 'folklore'.

We have had one or two interesting surprises recently. For example, Roger Mercer[18] has been excavating at the Neolithic 'causewayed enclosure', on Hambledon Hill, near Blandford Forum in Dorset, which was constructed well over a thousand years before the Dartmoor reaves. He has interpreted it as a 'mortuary enclosure', a 'vast, reeking open cemetery, its silence broken only by the din of crows and ravens'. It was surrounded by a bank and a discontinuous ditch, with the dug sections separated by 'causeways'. After rituals associated with human bones, the ditch segments were eventually allowed to silt up, which must have taken a considerable period of time. Then comes the interesting bit. According to the excavator:

the entire ditch circuit appears to have been recut, when the profile of the ditch must have been represented by a mere undulation in the surface. It is quite apparent that so denuded was the state of the enclosure at Hambledon at this juncture that while we have come to accept that Neolithic farmers were skilled soil scientists we perhaps have to recognise them as accomplished field archaeologists as well!

Mercer goes on to suggest that this precise re-creation of the earlier ditch, segment by segment, must have something to do with oral tradition. On various other ceremonial sites, where the evidence suggests recurrent embellishment of the structure or a succession of ritual 'performances', it is vital that we take the role of oral tradition seriously as a mechanism linking different episodes in the sequence, even if we cannot reconstruct the content of the message.

However coaxial field systems may be linked in space and time, the question remains: what are they all about? For the coaxial systems of Dartmoor, I have argued that there was no such thing as the 'farm' as a small-scale unit of heritable private property; instead, there were 'neighbourhood groups', in my terminology, possibly based on extended families, living in particular districts within field systems and themselves owing greater loyalties to the larger 'communities' which may have been the sovereign land-holding bodies. If this model is accepted, our interest must focus not upon the individual householder as economic decision-maker, but upon larger social units and the forces which held them together. How did economic and social processes work among the several families living on these tracts of land? Is it perhaps the case that subdividing the land on coaxial principles is something to do with managing land held collectively, by a sizeable community? Could it be that the story of land-use in later prehistory is rather like that of the last few hundred years in England, with the extension of private land claims at the expense of common rights?

It is not difficult to show how communal landholding, joint investment in the exploitation of a terrain's resources and in strategies of production, would have been to everyone's advantage in the early stages of farming. It would have been absurd, for example, to subdivide land used for hunting and grazing, wasting effort on trying to maintain boundaries which individual families could hardly have policed in any case. Collectivities can make economies of scale, employing a communal shepherd for example, and when they need fencing, to keep animals out of fields or coppices, they can build a common fence. Small groups can share resources, setting up work-gangs which make efficient use of the labour of individual families and help out those at a disadvantage. Decision-making may be a bit more time-consuming than it would be for the individual, but the rewards of participation would certainly outweigh any disadvantages. I see early farming groups as robust collectivities, linked by many necessary mutual obligations as far as land use was concerned.

How far these groups were 'egalitarian' in other respects is open to question. Prehistorians usually assume that kinship was the most important organizing principle at this time, which allows for the possibility that seniority of birth could have been used to create and preserve differential status for individuals and families in some kind of clan society. It also makes it likely that many families were linked by networks of kinship obligations extending over wide geographical areas; put these networks and the seniority principle together and you have the material for the development of a hierarchical, essentially tribal society, which could be part-organised, part-dominated by one family grouping. It has been argued that in those parts of north-west Europe where chamber tombs and related monuments were being built, in the fourth millennium BC, there was an ancestor-cult, which established the sacredness of authority based on the kinship principle, and perhaps also rights to local land for all members of a particular clan.

But a system based on hereditary privilege is not immunized against struggles for power and status, as the difficulties of medieval kings in Europe were later to demonstrate. In south-western Britain, at least, the construction of false tomb entrances and the concealment of the real ones, coupled with good evidence for warfare,[19] argues that if 'egalitarian' systems of access to land did operate at a local level, in the wider world there were considerable tensions – struggles into which many people would have been drawn by obligations to their kinsfolk, and by loyalties already in being, ready to be whipped up and intensified by those with an interest in doing so. Prehistorians have argued that bride wealth payments, and exchanges of various commodities, such as stone axe-heads, could soon have developed differential 'wealth' as a more flexible source of power than heredity. The discovery of rare materials and the development of copper and then bronze metallurgy allowed the growth of 'prestige goods networks', as they have been called. It has been suggested by Colin Richards and Nick Thorpe[20] that in some parts of Britain soon after about 3000BC there were 'aristocratic' and 'commoner' lineages; in other words, 'ranked' societies had become stratified, and the commoner lineages may well have owed tribute or labour to the ruling elites.

It is usually suggested that the incentives and pressures promoted by these developments lifted the farming economy well above subsistence level, at which point the increased production may itself have provided the means whereby social and economic competition could have intensified. There is of course some debate about how all this can be related to supplies of land or labour (unfortunately it is hard to avoid using the terminology of western capitalism!). At first, from the viewpoint of those who needed to increase production, it may well have been labour which was in short supply; but if the labour supply was continuously increased, especially within fixed territories in a fully settled district, eventually land would be under greater pressure. Those who used it might well encounter the problem known as the Commons Dilemma; each commoner takes no more than his share, but the resource as a whole is diminished; pastures are over-grazed, soil fertility is depleted, fish stocks decline.

According to Cass and Edney,[21] who discussed the problem in 1978, there are two strategies which may be adopted by those facing the Commons Dilemma. First, the state of the resources must be made more visible to the commoners; in the case of today's fisheries, this might mean commissioning an expert study. Second, the resource pool should be divided into individual territories, thus promoting greater responsibility in the use of resources, and a greater degree of control. Cass and Edney demonstrated the success of these two strategies by getting their students to play a game which simulated the Dilemma and their suggested solutions to the problem. These solutions are known to have been implemented on real commons. One way of increasing knowledge of the resource, by concentrating it, was to put all livestock into the care of a communal shepherd. One practice which avoided 'territories' as such was to 'stint' the common, limiting the number of animals which a given individual could keep there – sometimes to the number which could be kept through the winter.

Land boundaries, including networks dense enough to be called 'field systems', are the more permanent versions of the 'territorial' solution. A community's decision to lay out a large field system would not have been taken lightly, since both construction and subsequent maintenance would have involved a considerable investment of labour. But it may be that as the population grew, the trouble caused by disputes over resources was costly enough to make this investment an attractive proposition. And once the decision had been taken, each commoner would have to participate, making his or her contribution to the new system. In the Dartmeet parallel reave system, we can apparently identify the land habitually used by each neighbourhood group; but in most parts of the system the insistence on a common axis for the land of the community as a whole suggests that the independence of the neighbourhood group was being deliberately made subordinate to the will of the community or those who took decisions on its behalf. At a higher level, it can be argued that the 'regional' character of some of the Dartmoor boundaries, and their unfinished state in some places, represent similar tensions between communities and a more regionally based system of control.

The question of decision-making is an interesting one. It is all very well talking about commoners and collective decisions; but there comes a point where a public monument, say, or an irrigation system is so impressive that most observers instinctively see it as the result of an essentially autocratic decision, taken at the top level of a hierarchical power structure of some sort, and quite possibly imposed upon the lower orders. But how do we know that a more collective decision-making structure was not responsible? What are the limits to a community's powers of self-organisation? At the recent World Archaeological Congress, held in Southampton in September 1986, the debate was posed in terms of 'top-down' versus 'bottom-up' enterprises.[22] The argument is complicated by the fact that in historic times communities have delegated their authority to individuals, who have taken on organisation roles, people like the traditional 'kings' of western Ireland. The role of a 'king' in north-west Mayo, presumably not very far from the Neolithic field systems investigated by Seamas Caulfield, was described as follows in the 1830s:[23]

There was a headman, or king, appointed in each village, who is deputed to cast lots every third year, and to arrange with the community what work is to be done during the year in fencing, or probably reclaiming a new piece . . . or for setting . . . the number of heads of cattle of each kind, and for each man, that is to be put on the farm for the ensuing year, according to its stock of grass pasture; – the appointment of a herdsman also for the whole village cattle, if each person does not take the office on himself by rotation, – a thing not unfrequent. The king takes care generally to have the rent collected, applots the proportion of taxes with the other elders of the village . . . . He is generally the advisor or consultor of the villagers, their spokesman on any matters connected with the village. He finds his way to the 'kingly station' by imperceptible degrees, and by increasing mutual assent, as the old king dies off.

The power of such a 'king' was limited in recent Irish history, but one cannot rule out the possibility that in prehistoric times such a figure, invested with supernatural authority, could have obtained assent for a decision to lay out a major field system which would help a community to manage its land better. This would give us an 'organiser-king' rather than an exploitative one.

On the other hand, the above quotation reminds us that the nineteenth century communities of northern and western parts of the British Isles were not truly free or independent; they were liable for rents and taxes and were answerable to landlords, who in many cases lived elsewhere. Their ways of organising the use of their land are instructive, but we must remember that they lived within a stratified, state society. There is an interesting parallel with the situation in the Middle Ages in many parts of England. The open field system involved complex subdivisions of land, the strips and furlongs which are still visible in some places in the form of ridge and furrow. Open field farming involved complicated and detailed regulations,[24] evolving from the custom and practice within village communities. Yet most of these communities were not autonomous; they existed within the framework of a society stratified economically and socially.

So, although communal land use must be taken seriously as the prevalent organisational form for prehistoric farming, it can be argued that the greatest degree of self-organisation, in matters of land use, would have been achieved within stratified societies, as commoners coped with the demands of an exploitative elite. Some prehistorians have suggested that a truly stratified society developed in Britain in the later Neolithic, around 3000-2500BC, and this does apparently coincide with the origins of field systems as we know them at present. However, historical geographers have reminded archaeologists that the outward form of a field system does not correlate very well with the social organisation which helped to bring it into being;[25] in the Middle Ages, carefully subdivided field systems are associated with relatively autonomous peasant communities as well as with more hierarchical, coercive forms of social organisation. As I pointed out above, coaxial field systems represent a concept, perhaps as powerful a concept as the open field system of the Middle Ages. Probably this concept of land division spread from place to place and re-emerged from time to time, translated and re-translated into the idiom of different communities.

In the ideal world, understanding of the social dynamics should involve more than simply working outwards from field systems and settlement patterns, even when they are as apparently eloquent as the Dartmoor reave systems; prehistorians should take several categories of evidence, and check them against each other, a methodology described by Ian Hodder as contextual archaeology.

On Dartmoor, carrying out contextual archaeology poses formidable problems. The organised landscape provides a wonderful choice of sites to investigate. But other aspects of the archaeology make life more difficult. Human and animal bone does not survive the acid soils, and bronze is vulnerable too. Our knowledge of material culture is scanty, although the finding of wood in a peat-filled ditch at Shaugh Moor is encouraging. Our knowledge of Bronze Age burials on Dartmoor is very poor. Nor is it not clear that burials contemporary with the reaves can be located. We do not really know what was going on in the lowland areas of Devon when the reaves were constructed, and what was the relationship between uplands and lowlands. These problems are not unique to Devon; variations of them are faced by prehistorians everywhere. Investigating prehistory is an ambitious, difficult enterprise!

So my investigation of the Dartmoor reaves can be said to have raised more questions than it has answered; some of these may be unanswerable. In a sense, the project's success has revealed its own inadequacy. After the excavation and survey has been written up, I hope to return to the Moor, to ask the next generation of questions. At present, prehistorians' ideas about the unwritten past and how it might have been seem too sophisticated for existing methodologies.

Pursuing an investigation of this kind, even with the limited resources available, involved me in an epic journey, not special in itself but illustrating very well the range of thought and activity involved in the practice of prehistory. Over the past few years I have found myself wondering what exactly mole tunnels look like, and reading a D.Phil thesis done by a Nigerian research student at Oxford in an effort to find out, not to mention initiating a literature search on the same subject which involved a satellite link-up with a large American computer. I have discussed which parts of a field farm animals defecate in, and thought about what it was like to work as an antiquary in Devon in the early nineteenth century. I have tried to find out how commoners take decisions; perhaps it would be worth finding out from the present-day Dartmoor commoners, some of whom gave me permission to work on the Moor. I have asked myself what I think about neo-Marxist theories of emergent social stratification, and wondered how it is possible to prove the former existence of hedges.

For prehistorians, the world is shrinking. Instead of simply reconstructing local sequences, they are concerned to find out how similar archaeological problems have been tackled in other parts of the world, how far the processes which they are thinking about have occurred elsewhere. Thus European wetland archaeologists may find themselves visiting Florida; in the right company, one may find oneself standing beside the waste tips of Neolithic axe-quarries at the Pike of Stickle, in the Lake District of north-west England, and discussing how stone for similar axe-heads was quarried in New Guinea. I have not pursued ancient field systems very far, but the quest has led me to peat-bogs and limestone pavements in western Ireland, bleak heaths in the Netherlands, and into the woods of Gotland, in the Baltic Sea. But appropriately enough it was at the World Archaeological Conference held at Southampton in 1986, that I first fully understood the worldwide dimensions of questions surrounding land management and the related issues of social organisation and the way landscape is perceived. For the first time in my life I found myself discussing these questions with scholars from Japan and India, from Hawaii and Sri Lanka. Great expanses of time and space seemed to be diminishing; suddenly, the ideal of the unity of mankind seemed more than a mendacious cliché or a dreamer's self-delusion. I had started my journey on a misty Dartmoor hillside; but who could say where it might end?

Further reading

History of reave study

Fleming, A. 1978a Dartmoor reaves: a nineteenth century fiasco. *Antiquity* 52: 16-19

The rediscovery of reaves

Fleming, A. and Collis, J. 1973 A late prehistoric reave system near Cholwich Town, Dartmoor. *Proceedings of the Devon Archaeological Society* 31: 1-21

Gawne, E. and Somers Cocks, J. 1968 Parallel reaves on Dartmoor. *Transactions of the Devonshire Association* 100: 277-91

The reave pattern and its interpretation

Fleming, A. 1978b The prehistoric landscape of Dartmoor. Part 1: South Dartmoor. *Proceedings of the Prehistoric Society* 44: 97-123

Fleming, A. 1983 The prehistoric landscape of Dartmoor. Part 2: North and East Dartmoor. *Proceedings of the Prehistoric Society* 49: 195-241

Fleming, A. 1984 The prehistoric landscape of Dartmoor: wider implications. *Landscape History* 6: 5-19

Dartmoor prehistory

Barber, J. 1970 Early men. pp. 55-75 in Gill, C. (ed) *Dartmoor: a new study*. Newton Abbot: David and Charles. (This book is a useful source for many aspects of Dartmoor's history)

Greeves, T. 1985 *The archaeology of Dartmoor from the air*. Exeter: Devon Books

Spooner, G.M. and Russell, F.S. 1953 *Worth's Dartmoor*. Newton Abbot: David and Charles. (Out of date, but contains much factual information)

Maxfield, V. (ed) 1979 Prehistoric Dartmoor in its context. *Proceedings of the Devon Archaeological Society* 37. (This volume contains several useful essays on different aspects of Dartmoor prehistory)

Todd, M. 1987 *The South-West to AD1000*. London: Longman. (The most recent general account of the prehistory of the region)

Environmental history and prehistoric economies

Caseldine, C.J. and Maguire, D. 1981 A review of the prehistoric and historic environment on Dartmoor. *Proceedings of the Devon Archaeological Society* 39: 1-16

Fleming, A. 1979 The Dartmoor reaves: boundary patterns and behaviour patterns in the second millennium BC. pp. 115-31 in Maxfield, V. (ed) Prehistoric Dartmoor in its context. *Proceedings of the Devon Archaeological Society* 37

Coaxial field systems and community land management

Fleming, A. 1987 Coaxial field systems: some questions of time and space. *Antiquity* 61: 188-203

Fleming, A. 1985 Land tenure, productivity and field systems, pp. 129-46 in Barker, G. and Gamble, C. (eds) *Beyond domestication in prehistoric Europe*. London: Academic Press

Fleming, A. 1988 The genesis of coaxial field systems, in Torrence, R. and van der Leeuw, S. (eds) *What's new? A closer look at the process of innovation*. London: Unwin Hyman

Appendix:
Places to visit

Dartmoor is arguably the best region in north-west Europe for visiting well-preserved 'prehistoric landscapes', as opposed to isolated 'sites'. There are many ceremonial monuments, field systems, land boundaries and settlement sites which are visible on the surface and easily identifiable, and the relationship between monuments of different periods can be readily studied. Although technically they are on privately-owned land, access to most of them is unrestricted. The same goes for the many medieval and post-medieval settlements, field systems, relics of tin extraction, rabbit-warrening, etc. on Dartmoor, which are of considerable interest. Here too it is a question of preserved landscapes rather than individual sites. Many of the later sites are in the same areas of the Moor as the prehistoric ones; it is not very difficult to observe the relationships between the different sites and thus come to understand the basic principles of landscape archaeology.

A visitor should purchase the excellent Ordnance Survey Outdoor Leisure map of Dartmoor, which covers the entire Moor at a scale of 1:25000; its southern half marks reaves (as 'boundary works'). This map marks many archaeological sites, and it is easy to work out which can be visited conveniently by car and short walk, and how to plan longer walks with archaeology in mind. In spring and summer there are guided walks, run by the National Park Authority, many of which involve visits to archaeological sites. I strongly recommend the purchase of Tom Greeves' *The Archaeology of Dartmoor from the Air* (Devon Books, 1985) as a rapid way of understanding what sites look like and how archaeologists work out what they mean.

Incongruously in a National Park, there are military ranges on the northern part of Dartmoor, to which access is restricted; intending visitors to these areas should check on firing times. However, the problem is not a very serious one, since most archaeological sites are outside the range areas. Quite a few sites are best visited in the first half of the year, because bracken starts to obscure them, depending on location and seasonal weather factors, at various times between late April and late June; by Christmas, the problem has largely disappeared. As a generalisation, the bracken is worst at lower altitudes and on the eastern side of the Moor.

Visiting sites by car

The sites which are deservedly well visited already are the following (the SX prefix is omitted in the 4-figure grid references given):

Grimspound (7080). Large walled enclosure with small hut-circles. A short walk to the south gives access to some fine Bronze Age burial cairns on Hameldown ridge, and Hameldown Reave North, a 'cross-ridge' reave with an important place in the early history of reave study.

Merrivale (5574). Ceremonial monuments, including stone rows; large and small hut-circles. A very fragmentary stretch of the Great Western Reave runs past the eastern ends of the stone rows; this reave appears never to have run through the group of hut-circles, suggesting that the settlement here may have been in occupation when the boundary was constructed.

Shovel Down/Kestor (6585, 6586, 6686) The Kestor parallel reave system (fig. 11) includes the Round Pound, an excavated site of Iron Age date, and some prominent reaves, with two good examples of prehistoric lanes or 'droveways'. Further west is the Shovel Down ceremonial monument complex of stone rows etc (with a reave running N–S through the rows, fig. 60); close by the rows, further west, is a small 'early' settlement, with irregular fields and buildings. Further west still the landscape is subdivided by reaves, in what appears to be a late extension, beyond the terminal reave of the Kestor system.

I would add to these:

Holne Moor (6671, 6770, 6771, 6870, 6871). Southern part of the Dartmeet parallel reave system. Easy access from the car parks at Venford reservoir and Combestone Tor (fig. 34). The zone near the reservoir is more confusing because of the presence of extensive medieval field boundaries here; further west, in the Combestone Tor area, it is easier to see unaltered reaves. South of Venford Reave, near Horn's Cross (probably twelfth century in origin) there are burial cairns, including a ring-cairn; beside the O Brook is a group of 'shielings' of probable prehistoric date (fig. 66).

Yar Tor/Corndon Down/Vag Hill (6772, 6773, 6872, 6873, 6874, 6875). The central part of the Dartmeet parallel reave system. From Corndon Tor, the general layout of the system in relation to terrain can be best appreciated, in reasonably clear conditions. In the saddle between Yar Tor and Corndon, some good reaves and a stone row can be seen, and further north is the zone where the reaves all swerve to be sure of hitting the northern terminal reave at right angles (fig. 35). Quite a number of the reaves were converted into hedge-banks in the Middle Ages, especially on Vag Hill (6772) and above Cator and Shallowford.

Walkhampton Common (centred on 5671). The 1:25000 map shows the position of Walkhampton Common Reave (particularly impressive in the evening light, see fig. 9) and the southern end of the Great Western Reave; both, in part, run quite close to the B3212 Princetown-Yelverton road (fig. 24) and there are car parks near Sharpitor. The map shows the postion of local settlement sites, some showing interesting relationships with the reaves.

Archaeological walks

There are many possibilities. These are some of my favourites:

The Plym valley. As can be seen from the map, this easily-reached valley contains many enclosed settlements of 'pastoral' type and one of Dartmoor's finest complexes of cermonial monuments, at Drizzlecombe (fig. 60). Tracing the course of Eylesbarrow Reave, on the Plym/Meavy watershed, is a stimulating exercise, though perhaps not for beginners. The reave starts on Wigford Down, but I advise beginning at the NE corner of Brisworthy Plantation (558658) and following the reave to its end, at Eylesbarrow (599686). Willings Walls Reave, on the easern side of the valley, is not very long, but one can continue onto Lee Moor (fig. 5), follow Cholwichtown Reave and Penn Moor Reave, and see some interesting incorporated enclosures.

The Erme valley. This is much quieter than the Plym valley. It should be possible to take in Dartmoor's most atmospheric stone row on Stalldown

(6362) as well as its longest (the Erme row; southern end at 635644). From the magnificently-located northern end of the Erme row one can head east, following the course of the disused Redlake tramway south to see the imposing Three Barrows (watershed) Reave (fig. 20), its relationship to the Three Barrows, and its puzzling northern end.

The Great Western Reave. It should be possible to walk this more or less from end to end (fig. 24); although there are three places where it passes through enclosed land, these can all be circum-navigated. For a short visit, the sight of the reave straggling up the NW flank of Roos Tor (543766) is impressive, and there are numerous hut-circles and a couple of attached enclosures here too, in a wonderfully scenic part of Dartmoor. From here, if firing on the range permits, there is a fine walk to the Langstone Moor stone circle (557782) and Whittor, with its peculiar (?Neolithic) enclosure and an encounter with the Great Western Reave, plus other boundaries and hut-circles.

Hameldown. This is a linear walk which is very hard to turn into a circular walk! On the Hameldown ridge itself are some large and impressive Bronze Age cairns, with Hameldown Reave North running as a cross-ridge boundary near the northern end. To the north are Grimspound and the Shapley Common parallel reave system, some of which is not very conspicuous, being shrouded in heather. To the south one eventually reaches Dunstone Down, meeting-place of the two great reave systems, Dartmeet and Rippon Tor. Although it is hard work sorting out relationships on Dunstone Down itself (there are many medieval boundaries here) it is not difficult to compare the orientation of the reaves near Wind Tor (708757), which belong to the Rippon Tor system, and those on Rowden Ball (699760) which are at the northern end of the Dartmeet system.

Grey Wethers stone circles (639831). It is possible to reach these circles by parking at Fernworthy Forest and walking from there, but this is boring. In my opinion it is best to start out from the Warren House Inn (674809), visiting the cairn on Water Hill (672813), and the 'shielings' at Caroline (667814), then heading westwards to the northern end of a not very prominent stone row at 655815. This first part of the walk takes one through the Stannon block system (fig. 21). Then one can visit a ring-cairn, marked 'pound' on the map, at 642827, and a possible henge monument (embanked ceremonial enclosure) of irregular form at 640829 (also marked as a 'pound' on the map) before arriving at the Grey Wethers. On the way back, the western slopes of White Ridge have various reaves and settlement sites, and one can also drop in at the 'beehive hut' (640814) a tinners' shelter which Conan Doyle, following local antiquarian opinion, described in *The Hound of the Baskervilles* as a prehistoric house whose roof had survived.

Venford Reave (centre 6671). It is probably best to start from the Holne end, the wall corner at 689698 and follow the reave in a north-westerly direction to Venford reservoir, observing reaves of the Dartmeet parallel system on the right. Then the reave can be followed across Holne Moor (fig. 34) with the reaves on the right and various ceremonial monuments on the left. Then, after the O Brook 'shielings' (fig. 66) one has to follow the upper wall of the fields above Hexworthy, still with reaves on the right; there is also a place where the reave has been spectacularly robbed (fig. 18). The reave picks up again at 638720, just N of a leat, and then there is an attached enclosure before one descends to the Swincombe and searches for the reave on the other side. It is hard to avoid retracing one's steps on the western part of this walk, but it would be possible to return through Hexworthy and then take a more northerly route back across Holne Moor, seeing many enclosures and hut circles on the way.

References

References are given in full except where they have already been listed in the 'Further Reading' section (in which case they are quoted simply as Fleming 1984, for example) or have been listed earlier in this section (in which case the text will say 'see 1.1', for example, referring to chapter 1, reference 1 – in this case, *The Hound of the Baskervilles*).

1:Discovery (pp. 1-11)

1 Conan Doyle, A. 1902. *The Hound of the Baskervilles*. London: Murray.
2 (a) Baring-Gould, S. 1900. *A Book of Dartmoor*. London: Methuen; (b) Baring-Gould, S. 1899. *A Book of Devon*. London: Methuen.
3 Spooner and Russell 1953.
4 Radford, C.A.R. 1952. Prehistoric settlement on Dartmoor and the Cornish moors. *Proceedings of the Prehistoric Society* 18: 55-84.
5 (a) Fox, A. 1954. Celtic fields and farms on Dartmoor, in the light of recent excavations at Kestor. *Proceedings of the Prehistoric Society* 20: 87-100; (b) Fox, A. 1957. Excavations on Dean Moor, in the Avon valley, 1954-56. *Transactions of the Devonshire Association* 89: 18-77; (c) Fox, A. 1954. Excavations at Kestor, an early Iron Age settlement near Chagford, Devon. *Transactions of the Devonshire Association* 86: 21-62.
6 Curwen, E.C. 1927. Prehistoric agriculture in Britain. *Antiquity* 1: 261-89.
7 see 1. 5a, p. 89.
8 Gawne and Somers Cocks 1968.
9 see 1. 4, p. 72; 1. 5a, pp. 100-2.
10 Fleming and Collis 1973.
11 (a) Simmons, I. 1962. An outline of the vegetation history of Dartmoor. *Transactions of the Devonshire Association* 94: 555-74; (b) Simmons, I. 1963. The blanket bog of Dartmoor. *Transactions of the Devonshire Association* 95: 180-96; (c) Simmons, I. 1964. Pollen diagrams from Dartmoor. *New Phytologist* 63: 165-80; (d) Simmons, I. 1964. An ecological history of Dartmoor, pp. 191-215 in Simmons, I. (ed) *Dartmoor Essays*. Exeter: Devonshire Association. (e) Simmons, I. 1969. Environment and early man on Dartmoor, Devon, England. *Proceedings of the Prehistoric Society* 35: 203-19.
12 Crossing, W. 1909. *Crossing's Guide to Dartmoor*. Plymouth: Western Morning News.
13 (a) Bowen, H.C. 1975. Pattern and interpretation; a view of the Wessex landscape from neolithic to Roman times, pp. 44-56 in Fowler, P.J. (ed) *Recent work in rural archaeology*. Bradford on Avon: Moonraker Press; (b) Bowen H.C. 1972. Air photography: some implications in the south of England, pp. 38-49 in Fowler, E. (ed) *Field survey in British archaeology*. London: Council for British Archaeology; (c) Fowler, P.J. 1971. Early prehistoric agriculture in western Europe: some archaeological evidence, pp. 153-82 in Simpson, D.D.A. (ed) *Economy and settlement in Neolithic and Early Bronze Age Britain and Europe*. Leicester: University Press.
14 Mortimer, J.R. 1905. *Forty Years' Researches in British and Saxon burial mounds of East Yorkshire*. London: A. Brown & Sons Ltd.
15 (a) Clarke, D.L. 1968. *Analytical Archaeology*. London: Methuen, fig. 114; (b) Stanford, S.C. 1972. The function and population of hillforts in the central Marches, pp. 307-19 in Lynch, F. and Burgess, C. (eds) *Prehistoric Man in Wales and the West*. Bath: Adams and Dart. (figs 2 and 3); (c) Renfrew, C. 1973. *Before Civilisation: the radiocarbon revolution and prehistoric Europe*. London: Cape, figs 29 and 30; Renfrew, C. 1973. Monuments, mobilization and social organization in Neolithic Wessex, in Renfrew, C. (ed) *The explanation of culture change: models in prehistory*. London: Duckworth, pp. 539-558.

2:A curious case of lost knowledge (pp. 12-24)

1 Daniel, G. 1950. *A Hundred Years of Archaeology*. London: Duckworth.
2 Pengelly, W. 1868. The literature of Kent's Cavern, Torquay, prior to 1859. *Transactions of the Devonshire Association* 2: 469-522.
3 (a) Blewitt, O. 1895. *The Panorama of Torquay*. London: Simpkin and Marshall; (b) Lee, S. (ed) 1895. *Dictionary of National Biography*, pp. 201-2.
4 see 2. 3; also *Transactions of the Devonshire Association* 62 (1930), p. 32. Shillabeer's plan of Grimspound is in the West Country Studies Library, Exeter.
5 *Besley's Exeter News*, December 8th and December 14th, 1825.
6 Jones, J.P. c.1830 folio 103, Hundred of Teignbridge, in *The Historical and Monumental Antiquities of Devonshire*, Ms. top. Devon. 1 (Bodleian Library, Oxford).
7 see 2. 5.
8 Jones, J.P. 1823. *Observations on the scenery and antiquities in the neighbourhood of Moretonhampstead and on the forest of Dartmoor*. Exeter: R. Bond, p. 60.

9 see 2. 6, folio 104.

10 see 2.6, folios 103 and 104.

11 Rowe, S. 1848. *A Perambulation of Dartmoor*. Exeter: J.G. Commin.

12 Ordnance Survey 1:25000 First Series (provisional edition), sheet SX 57.

13 Wilkinson, Sir J.G. 1862. British remains on Dartmoor. *Journal of the British Archaeological Association* 18: 22-53, 111-33.

14 listed in Spooner and Russell 1953, p. 132.

15 Burnard, R. 1890. *Dartmoor Pictorial Records* (vol. 1). Plymouth: W. Brendon & Son, p. xi.

16 Burnard, R. 1889. The great central trackway – Dartmoor. *Transactions of the Devonshire Association* 21: 431-6.

17 Rowe, S. 1896. *A Perambulation of Dartmoor*. (3rd edition, revised by J.B. Rowe). London: Gibbings & Co., p. 64.

18 see 1. 2a, p. 47.

19 see 1. 12, p. 32-3.

20 see 1. 4, p. 72 and 1. 5a, pp. 100-2.

21 Gawne and Somers Cocks 1968.

22 Atkinson, R.J.C. 1952. The date of Stonehenge. *Proceedings of the Prehistoric Society* 18: 236-7.

23 Renfrew, A.C. 1968. Wessex without Mycenae. *Annual of the British School at Athens* 63: 277-85, p. 284.

3:The search for a pattern (pp. 25-39)

1 see 2. 11, p. 124.

2 see 1. 12. p. 91.

3 Prowse, A. 1890. Notes on the neighbourhood of Taw Marsh, north Dartmoor. *Transactions of the Devonshire Association* 22: 185-99.

4 see 1. 12, p. 122; Burnard, R. 1891. President's address. *Transactions of the Plymouth Institution* 11: 139-53 (p. 150); Bray, Mrs 1836. A description of the part of Devonshire bordering on the Tamar and the Tavy. London: Murray, p. 136.

5 Hoskins, W.G. 1955. *The Making of the English Landscape*. London: Hodder and Stoughton, p. 36.

6 Fox, A. 1958. A monastic homestead on Dean Moor, South Devon. *Medieval Archaeology* 2: 141-57, p. 150; 1. 12, p. 378.

4:The pattern revealed (pp. 40-56)

1 Spooner and Russell 1953, fig. 74.

2 Fleming 1978b.

3 Britnell, W. 1982. The excavation of two round barrows at Trelystan, Powys. *Proceedings of the Prehistoric Society*, 48: 133-201.

4 Somers Cocks, J.V. 1970. Saxon and early medieval times. In Gill, C. (ed) *Dartmoor: a new study*. Newton Abbot: David and Charles. pp. 76-99; H.S.A. Fox, pers. comm.

5 Pryor, F. 1980. *Excavation at Fengate, Peterborough, England: the third report*. Northampton: Northamptonshire Archaeological Society, p. 183; Coles, J.M. The Somerset Levels: a concave landscape, in Bowen, H.C. and Fowler, P.J. (eds.) *Early Land*

Allotment. Oxford: British Archaeological Reports, British Series no. 48: 147-8.

6 see 1.5c.

7 Collis, J. 1972. Cranbrook Castle, Moretonhampstead, Devon. A new survey. *Proceedings of the Devon Archaeological Society* 30: 216-221.

8 Fleming 1983.

9 see 1. 12, p. 296.

5:Anatomy of a field system (pp. 57-70)

1 1. 12, p. 358; 1. 5a, p. 101-2.

2 Yar Tor and Sherberton Common stone rows, Spooner and Russell 1953, pp. 228 and 226.

3 1. 12, p. 360.

4 Müller-Wille, M. 1965. *Eisenzseitliche Fluren in den festländischen Nordseegebieten*. Münster: Geographischen Kommission, fig. 19.

5 Seebohm, F. 1911. *Tribal custom in Anglo-Saxon law*. London: Longmans Green, pp. 36, 37. See also Seebohm, F. 1904. *The tribal system in Wales*. London: Longmans Green.

6 Hannan, D. 1972. Kinship, neighbourhood and social change in Irish rural communities. *Economic and Social Review* 3: 163-88, p. 186.

7 Rees, A.D. 1968. *Life in a Welsh countryside*. Cardiff: University of Wales Press, p. 94.

8 Page, W. (ed) 1906. *Victoria County History of Devonshire*. vol 1. London: Archibald Constable & Co., p. 490.

9 Hassan, F.A. 1981. *Demographic archaeology*. London: Academic Press, p. 57.

10 see 5. 6, p. 187.

6:Excavation (pp. 71-93)

1 Ralph, N. 1982. *Assessment of ancient land use in abandoned settlements and its influence upon soil properties on Holne Moor, Dartmoor, England*. Unpublished Ph.D. thesis, University of Sheffield.

2 see 1. 11e.

3 e.g. Anati, E. 1964. *Camonica Valley*. London: Cape, pp. 115, 117.

4 Fleming 1979, p. 124.

5 Smith, K. et al. 1981. The Shaugh Moor Project: Third report – settlement and environmental investigations. *Proceedings of the Prehistoric Society* 47: 205-73, pp. 209-14.

6 see 6. 5., plate 14.

7:Reaves and the prehistory of Dartmoor (pp. 94-111)

1 Caseldine and Maguire 1981; Maguire and Caseldine 1985. The former distribution of forest and moorland on northern Dartmoor. *Area* 17.3: 193-203.

2 Jacobi, R. in Maxfield 1979.

3 Simmons, I.G. 1969. Evidence for vegetation changes associated with mesolithic man in Britain, in Ucko, P.J. and Dimbleby, G.W. (eds)*The domestication and exploitation of plants and animals*. London: Duckworth. pp. 111-19; Simmons, I.G., Rand, J.I. and Crabtree, K.

1983. A further pollen analytical study of the Blacklane peat section of Dartmoor, England. *New Phytologist* 94: 655-67.

4 see 1. 11e, pp. 207-9.

5 Emmett in Maxfield 1979.

6 fig. 60 is based on Spooner and Russell 1953, figs. 73, 74 and 75.

7 Bate, C.S. 1872. Ancient tumuli on Dartmoor. *Transactions of the Devonshire Association* 5: 549-57.

8 Wainwright, G.J., Fleming, A. and Smith, K. 1979. The Shaugh Moor Project – first report. *Proceedings of the Prehistoric Society* 45: 1-33, pp. 26-27.

9 Grinsell, L.V. Dartmoor barrows. *Proceedings of the Devon Archaeological Society* 36: 85-180.

10 Eogan, G. 1964. The excavation of a stone alignment and circle at Cholwichtown, Lee Moor, Devonshire. *Proceedings of the Prehistoric Society* 30: 25-38; the report contains an account of pollen analysis carried out by I. Simmons.

11 (a) Beckett, S.C. 1981. Pollen analysis of the peat deposits. In 6. 5, pp. 245-66; (b) Balaam, N.D. 1982. Soil pollen analyses. In Balaam, N. D. et al. The Shaugh Moor Project: Fourth report – environment, context and conclusion. *Proceedings of the Prehistoric Society* 48: 203-78, pp. 204-15.

12 Miller, R. 1967. Land use by summer shielings. *Scottish Studies* 11: 193-221; Love, J.A. 1981. Shielings of the Isle of Rum. *Scottish Studies* 25: 39-63.

13 see 1.5b.

14 Wainwright, G.J. and Smith, K. 1980. The Shaugh Moor Project: second report – the enclosure. *Proceedings of the Prehistoric Society* 46: 65-122.

15 Worth, R.H. et al. 1897. Fourth report of the Dartmoor Exploration Committee. *Transactions of the Devonshire Association* 29: 145-65.

16 Barnatt, J. and Moir, G. 1984. Stone circles and megalithic mathematics. *Proceedings of the Prehistoric Society* 50: 197-216.

17 see 7.11a, p. 262.

18 M. Jones, pers. comm.; see also Maguire, D., Ralph, N. and Fleming, A. 1983. Early land use on Dartmoor – palaeobotanical and pedological investigations on Holne Moor. In Jones, M. (ed) *Integrating the Subsistence Economy*. Oxford: British Archaeological Reports, International Series no. 181: 57-105.

19 see 1. 11c, p. 170; 1. 11e, p. 211; Merryfield, D. and Moore, P.D. 1974. Prehistoric human activity and blanket peat initiation on Exmoor. *Nature* 250, no. 5465: 439-41.

20 Griffith, F.M. 1985. Some newly discovered ritual monuments in mid Devon. *Proceedings of the Prehistoric Society* 51: 310-15.

21 Silvester, R.J. 1980. The prehistoric open settlement at Dainton, South Devon. *Proceedings of the Devon Archaeological Society* 38: 17-48. An example of ancient fields on rough pasture on the coast may be seen at Deckler's Cliff (SX 7536), about 2km NW of Prawle Point.

22 Ellison, A. 1980. Settlements and regional exchange. In Barrett, J. and Bradley, R. (eds) *The British Later Bronze Age*. Oxford: British Archaeological Reports, British Series no. 83: 127-40.

23 Spooner and Russell 1953, pp. 282, 398.

24 see also Fleming 1984.

25 Fleming and Collis 1973.

26 Spooner and Russell 1953, fig. 37 for plan of Grimspound; Fleming and Collis 1973, fig. 3. for Cholwichtown main enclosure.

27 Pearce, S.M. 1983. *The Bronze Age metalwork of south western Britain*. Oxford: British Archaeological Reports, British Series no. 120, p. 448.

28 Knight, R.W., Brown, C. and Grinsell, L.V. 1972. Prehistoric skeletons from Tormarton. *Transactions of the Bristol and Gloucestershire Archaeological Society* 91: 14-17.

29 Northover, J.P. 1982. The exploration of long-distance movement of bronze in Bronze and Iron Age Europe. *University of London Institute of Archaeology Bulletin* 19: 45-72.

30 Pearce, S.M. in Maxfield 1979, pp. 136-45.

31 Price, D.G. 1979. The moorland Plym – a reassessment. *Transactions of the Devonshire Association* 111: 125-37; Price, D.G. 1981. A settlement site on Harford Moor. *Transactions of the Devonshire Association* 113: 53-57; Price, D.G. 1985. Changing perceptions of prehistoric tinning on Dartmoor. *Transactions of the Devonshire Association* 117: 129-38.

32 Fleming, a. 1987. Prehistoric tin extraction on Dartmoor: a cautionary note. *Transactions of the Devonshire Association* 119: 117-22.

8: Reaves and the wider world (pp. 112-123)

1 Renfrew, C. 1973. *Before Civilisation: the radiocarbon revolution and prehistoric Europe*. London: Cape.

2 e.g. (a) Fowler, P.J. 1971. Early prehistoric agriculture in western Europe: some archaeological evidence. In Simpson, D.D.A. (ed) *Economy and settlement in neolithic and early Bronze Age Britain and Europe*. Leicester: Leicester University Press, pp. 153-82. (b) Bowen, H.C. 1978. 'Celtic' fields and 'ranch' boundaries in Wessex. In Limbrey, S. and Evans, J.G. (eds) *The effect of man on the landscape: the Lowland zone*. London: Council for British Archaeology Research Report no. 21, pp. 115-22. (c) Bradley, R. 1978. Prehistoric field systems in Britain and north-west Europe – a review of some recent work. *World Archaeology* 9: 265-80. See also Palmer, R. 1984. *Danebury: an Iron Age hillfort in Hampshire*. London: RCHM (England).

3 Pryor, F. 1982. *Fengate*. Aylesbury: Shire Books (which contains further references, including the four reports on the site).

4 see 8. 2c.

5 Hoskins, W.G. 1955. *The Making of the English Landscape*. London: Hodder and Stoughton.

6 Brisbane, M. and Clews, S. 1979. The East Moor field systems, Altarnun and North Hill, Bodmin Moor. *Cornish Archaeology* 18: 33-56.

7 P. Herring and J. Nowakowski, pers. comm.

8 Spratt, D.A. 1982. *Prehistoric and Roman archaeology of*

north-east Yorkshire. Oxford: British Archaeological Reports, British series no. 104 fig. 4; Coggins, D. 1985. Settlement and farming in Upper Teesdale. In Spratt, D. and Burgess, C. *Upland settlement in Britain; the second millennium BC and after.* Oxford: British Archaeological Reports, British Series no. 143: 163-76., fig. 9.3.

9   Raistrick, A. 1938. Prehistoric cultivations at Grassington, west Yorkshire. *Yorkshire Archaeological Journal* 33: 166-74; King, A. 1985. Prehistoric settlement and land use in Craven, North Yorkshire. In Spratt, D. and Burgess, C. (eds) *Upland settlement in Britain: the second millennium BC and after.* Oxford: British Archaeological Reports, British series no. 143, pp 117-34.

10 Laurie, T. 1985. Early land division and settlement in Swaledale and on the eastern approaches to the Stainmore Pass over the North Pennines. In Spratt, D. and Burgess, C. (eds) *Upland settlement in Britain.* Oxford: British Archaeological Reports, British Series no. 143, pp. 135-62.

11 Caulfield, S. 1983. The neolithic settlement of north Connaught. In Reeves-Smyth, T. and Hamond, F. (eds) *Landscape archaeology in Ireland.* Oxford: British Archaeological Reports, British Series no. 116, pp. 195-216.

12 Plunkett Dillon, E. 1985. *The field boundaries of the Burren, co. Clare.* Unpublished Ph.D thesis, Trinity College Dublin.

13 Riley, D.N. 1980. *Early landscape from the air.* Sheffield: University of Sheffield Department of Archaeology and Prehistory.

14 Williamson, T. 1987. Early coaxial field systems on the East Anglian boulder clays. *Proceedings of the Prehistoric Society* 53: 419-31.

15 Bassett, S. 1985. Beyond the edge of excavation: the topographical context of Goltho, in Mayr-Harting, H. and Moore, R.I. (eds) *Studies in medieval history presented to R.C.H. Davies.* London: Hambledon, pp. 21-39.

16 Hall, D. 1982. *Medieval fields.* Aylesbury: Shire Books, fig. 31.

17 Silvester, R. pers. comm. (the parishes referred to are Wiggenhall St. Mary Magdalen and Wiggenhall St. Mary the Virgin, Norfolk).

18 Mercer, R. 1980. *Hambledon Hill: a neolithic landscape.* Edinburgh: Edinburgh University Press, p. 36.

19 Grimes, W.F. 1960. *Excavations on defence sites, 1939-45.* London: H.M.S.O. Darvill, T.C. 1982. *The megalithic chamber tombs of the Cotswold-Severn region.* Highworth: Vorda. see also 8. 18; Mercer, R. 1981. *Excavations at Carn Brea, Illogan, Cornwall.* Exeter: University of Exeter. Dixon, P. 1971. *Crickley Hill, Gloucestershire.* Cheltenham: Gloucestershire College of Art and Design.

20 Thorpe, I.J. and Richards, C.C. 1984. The decline of ritual authority and the introduction of Beakers into Britain. In Bradley, R, and Gardiner, J. (eds) *Neolithic Studies.* Oxford: British Archaeological Reports, British Series no. 133, pp. 67-84.

21 Cass, R.C. and Edney, J.J. 1978. The commons dilemma: a simulation testing the effects of resource visibility and territorial division. *Human Ecology* 6: 371-84.

22 Torrence, R. and van der Leeuw, S. (eds), forthcoming. *What's new? A closer look at the process of innovation.* Unwin Hyman.

23 Knight, P. 1836. *Erris in the 'Irish Highlands' and the 'Atlantic Railway'.* Dublin.

24 Ault, W.O. 1972. *Open-field farming in medieval England.* London: Allen and Unwin.

25 Baker, A.R.H. and Butlin, R.A. 1973. *Studies of field systems in the British Isles.* Cambridge: Cambridge University Press, p. 628.

Index